Web Portfolio Design and Applications

John DiMarco
St. John's University, USA, and
New York Institute of Technology, USA

IDEA GROUP PUBLISHING

Hershey • London • Melbourne • Singapore

Acquisitions Editor:	Michelle Potter
Development Editor:	Kristin Roth
Senior Managing Editor:	Amanda Appicello
Managing Editor:	Jennifer Neidig
Copy Editor:	Jennifer Young
Typesetter:	Sharon Berger
Cover Design:	Lisa Tosheff
Printed at:	Integrated Book Technology

Published in the United States of America by
  Idea Group Publishing (an imprint of Idea Group Inc.)
  701 E. Chocolate Avenue
  Hershey PA 17033
  Tel: 717-533-8845
  Fax: 717-533-8661
  E-mail: cust@idea-group.com
  Web site: http://www.idea-group.com

and in the United Kingdom by
  Idea Group Publishing (an imprint of Idea Group Inc.)
  3 Henrietta Street
  Covent Garden
  London WC2E 8LU
  Tel: 44 20 7240 0856
  Fax: 44 20 7379 0609
  Web site: http://www.eurospanonline.com

Library of Congress Cataloging-in-Publication Data

Web portfolio design and applications / John DiMarco, editor.
    p. cm.
  Summary: "This book defines and gives an overview of the web portfolio and how it is being used in academic programs and professional scenarios"--Provided by publisher.
  Includes bibliographical references and index.
  ISBN 1-59140-854-7 (hardcover) -- ISBN 1-59140-855-5 (softcover) -- ISBN 1-59140-856-3 (ebook)
  1. Portfolios in education. 2. Internet in education. 3. World Wide Web. I. DiMarco, John, 1969-
  LB1029.P67W43 2006
  374.126--dc22
                        2005023880

British Cataloguing in Publication Data
A Cataloguing in Publication record for this book is available from the British Library.

Web Portfolio Design and Applications

Table of Contents

Preface

Rationale

Back in 2002, I spoke at an educational technology conference sponsored by *Syllabus* magazine. My topic was Web portfolios for students and instructors. I proposed the topic out of a desire to feed my own curiosity regarding the research front. At the time, I was teaching a wide variety of digital art and design courses. One of my core principles when teaching in the digital medium is to have learning objectives that direct students toward creating tangible projects and ultimately harvesting portfolio-level work. It made sense for my students and for me to have evidence that the material presented in the course was put into practice, and students needed a dynamic platform to display their work. To accomplish this, I planned and developed a comprehensive Web portfolio of student work with over 100 student Web portfolios (unfortunately, a year later, the university changed over servers and the online sites were lost). I presented the Web site and explained the process to an audience of 150 technology educators. I opened the cluster session with two questions.

When I asked the first, "How many people in this room are provided free Web space from their institution?" almost everyone in the room raised their hand. Then I asked, "How many people are actually taking advantage of it and using it?" Ten hands rose.

I was shocked. These are technology people! Then I realized that they were not behind the curve, they were just reaching the point where they wanted to begin embracing Web portfolio development. That's when I knew that the information I was about to provide would have residual value for them and their students. After further research, I realized that Web portfolio development was in its infancy and I needed to devote research efforts into helping more people embrace the Web portfolio. There are some initiatives in place at the college level to implement Web portfolios. One such example is LaGuardia Community College. The school has mandated the development and output of electronic portfolios for all graduating students. The initiative brought in technology and specialists to provide the instructional and infrastructure support that such a project requires. Regardless of mandates, it is the responsibility of the professional educator to integrate Web portfolios into their pedagogy and teaching and learning initiatives. Ultimately, the instructor must pass on the skills and experience in Web portfolio design and development to their students.

The Web Portfolio as an Information Product for Communication

The desire to help people succeed with communication was a major influence in my decision to dig into Web portfolios as a research initiative. The Web portfolio is ultimately a platform for communication and the concepts, images, and messages within the Web portfolio are centered on persuasion, a major area in communication studies. The Web portfolio takes on the form of an information product for communication. To develop the information product properly, you must first analyze, retrieve, categorize, and manage your professional data so that it is refined into information. The refined information is put into a communication context, the Web portfolio. The communication generated from the Web portfolio is shaped by content, design, visual quality, usability, and overall experience visiting the site. The communication should be persuasive with the goal of getting the visitor to act favorably towards the author, whether consciously or subconsciously. I want this book to serve the reader as a tool for helping establish the foundation skills and act as a motivational force.

In addition, this book intends to give a well-rounded view of the Web portfolio and how it is being used in academic programs and professional scenarios. The skills and experience acquired while creating a Web portfolio must be passed on to others as they begin to explore Web portfolio development.

The Focus and Benefits

In this text, we focus on several areas inside the realm of the Web portfolio:

- The virtues of the Web portfolio;
- The professional software tools needed to create a Web portfolio;
- The important processes that are needed to execute Web portfolio development and production;
- Beginner and advanced techniques using multimedia and Web authoring tools; and
- What electronic/Web portfolios may evolve into as what I call "the postmodern professional appearance" of the information society.

We will examine brainstorming, design, and development. The process outlined in the text takes you through the creation of a Web portfolio. I use examples from my own Web portfolio and others to illustrate key points about design and development. The tools and techniques used in this book can be applied to developing a Web portfolio for a person or an entity in any industry or position. My infinite hope is that this book becomes a results-driven resource for the teaching and learning of Web portfolio development and that the book becomes a cookbook for getting a Web portfolio created. This will hopefully result in students and instructors creating Web portfolios. Putting together a Web portfolio does require some work, but the work is not without benefits. The learning process that occurs during the Web portfolio design process will give you skills and experiences with technology, self analysis, and Web design. When it comes to making the commitment to creating a Web portfolio, both students and instructors will see tremendous payoffs. For the instructor, the Web portfolio is not a course Web site. It has the same purpose as a student portfolio, to persuade. There are other common benefits shared by students and instructors who create Web portfolios. The Web portfolio gives the author nine worldwide mediums to freely disseminate professional information. A Web portfolio offers the creator a cost effective promotional tool. The Web portfolio also serves as a dynamic hub for communication, between students, faculty, employers, and academia. The power of multimedia applications on the Web such as Macromedia Flash allows a rich multimedia environment for presentations and collaboration. The Web portfolio gives the author an integral advantage in real-world self-promotion. Creating a Web portfolio shows a tangible technology achievement. The Web portfolio and subsequent redesigns throughout your career will yield lifelong learning in Web technology and self promotion. Specifically for instructors, the Web portfolio can act as a testing ground for experimenting with Web technology for pedagogy, exhibition, program, promotion, collaboration, online learning, and archiving.

Here is a brief overview of each chapter.

- **Chapter I — Introduction to the Web Portfolio**

  This chapter puts the Web portfolio into perspective and describes several thoughts supporting the Web portfolio as a communication tool for lifelong learning that presents a professional appearance. The chapter explains how the Web portfolio development process is a skill-building experience that has dynamic benefits.

- **Chapter II — Conceptualization**

  This chapter guides you in developing concepts, images, and messages needed for the Web portfolio. Content collection and evaluation is discussed as the Web portfolio is put into the context of a content management tool. The chapter gives examples on how to develop the scope documents needed to organize the Web portfolio. The concept statement, content list, and content outline are explained and exampled. This chapter represents the first step in the Web portfolio design and development process.

- **Chapter III — Information Design**

  This chapter shows you the process of information design for Web portfolios. You get a chance to display navigation and usability in a functional flowchart that is based on the concept and content scope documents that you worked on in Chapter II. The chapter concludes with creation of a flowchart. This chapter represents the second step in the Web portfolio design process.

- **Chapter IV — Visual Design**

  This chapter explores the visual aspects of creating attractive well-designed Web pages. Focus is on basic design principles and establishing ideas on how you want the Web portfolio pages to look. Color, composition, and typography are explained so that novice designers can be guided on how to create strong pages. The chapter concludes with instruction and development of story boards that represent rough site designs. This chapter represents the third step in the Web portfolio design process.

- **Chapter V — Content, Collection, Development and Management**

  This chapter provides techniques and strategies for collecting and creating content from existing assets and project files. The chapter gives advice on scanning and photography as well as how to use the resume in the Web portfolio and how to describe projects you present in the Web portfolio. This chapter represents the fourth step in the Web portfolio design process.

- **Chapter VI — Web Page Design**

  This chapter introduces digital tools in the design of Web page screens and graphics. Discussion includes design of buttons, navigation, and pop-up windows. Coverage includes slicing, optimizing, and exporting Web pages. An easy to use workflow is presented that allows rapid development of Web pages using visual tools instead of handwritten code. This chapter represents the fifth step in the Web portfolio design process.

- **Chapter VII — Web Authoring**

  This chapter introduces Web page authoring tools and provides tutorials and workflows for using Macromedia Dreamweaver. Major Web functionality issues are covered and appropriate techniques are explained. The chapter goal is to get the Web portfolio to a stage of functionality. This chapter moves you toward a working Web portfolio.

- **Chapter VIII — Motion, Graphics and Multimedia Production**

  This chapter provides discussion and instruction on using Macromedia Flash for multimedia production and Adobe Audition for audio editing. The tutorials shown guide you in developing essential multimedia components that can be integrated into the Web portfolio seamlessly. Coverage includes creating text animation and using audio tracks in Web pages with Macromedia Flash.

- **Chapter IX — Uploading and Testing Your Web Portfolio Site**

  This chapter provides the last technical step to getting the Web portfolio up on the Internet. Coverage spans the Internet and FTP and discusses how to use Macromedia Dreamweaver for uploading, downloading, and managing site files. The theories of Molich and Nielsen are presented in the context of Web portfolio usability. The chapter ends with discussion on redesign and the commitment to continual improvement and content flow in the Web portfolio.

- **Chapter X — Launch and Promotion**

  Getting the Web portfolio launched and marketed is the topic of this chapter. The Web portfolio marketing process involves traditional and electronic media to be effective. The chapter provides some marketing ideas that can be used in a comprehensive launch plan or individually for small scale promotions.

- **Chapter XI — Server-Side Technologies**

  This chapter provides the last technical data on server-side technologies and discusses dynamic integration into the Web portfolio. Coverage includes ASP, ASP.net, Coldfusion, PHP, and CGI/Perl. The chapter is intended to give an overview of the technologies and some technical information on versions and updates. I try to provide the latest data, but data is obsolete quickly after deployment when it comes to application technology.

- **Chapter XII — Cases and Interviews**

  This chapter discusses cases and shares interviews that describe Web portfolio challenges and successes. The focus is on exploring different approaches to Web portfolio development in order to illustrate that there is no one defined way to make a Web portfolio. Creating Web portfolios and Web portfolio programs is a subjective process that centers on the needs and goals of the authors. This chapter provides interviews with educators and applies possible characteristic criteria to Web portfolios across disciplines.

- **Chapter XIII — Web Portfolios in the Information Society and Future**

  This chapter focuses on theoretical examination of the Web portfolio in the knowledge worker age and the information society. Theorists' views are synthesized into my theory on the future of the Web portfolio. As technology flattens the world and masses of people continue to get digital for multitude of reasons, the Web portfolio will become a vehicle for responsive communication and connection to the world of work for hire. This chapter concludes the book and I hope it provides food for thought as you continue your expedition toward making Web portfolios a staple part of your public existence. As well, I hope to encourage further research on Web portfolios from scholars across disciplines.

Conclusion

During my literature review over the past two years, I noticed that there are no comprehensive textbooks that describe the Web portfolio from a process centered approach and a theoretical approach. Most books describe the Web portfolio in the context of the K-12 teacher and give descriptive instruction on artifact evaluation and standards based development. This makes sense due to the standardization of the Web portfolio into the curriculum of education departments worldwide. I refer to and quote education based portfolio development texts throughout this book. The clarity of explanation that the education field has developed in the promotion of Web portfolios is exceptional. I could not provide only the views of educators because I wanted the focus of this book to give a wide angle view of Web portfolios. So, I begin the book by describing the Web portfolio and the critical skills and benefits you get when making one. Then, I discuss concepts and content. Next, I provide a quick study of the important design principles needed to create a Web portfolio that has visual presence and shows your work in the best composition possible. Then, focusing on Macromedia tools, I give you professional level tutorials to help you begin the software engagement that you will need to be confident and active in Web portfolio design and development. I provide some thoughts on uploading and launching and lastly there are a wealth of cases and interviews to build your exposure to options for instituting a Web portfolio program in your institution. By taking a pan disciplinary approach to the Web portfolio and its components, I hope to enable you to build your own thoughts and realize your own success with Web portfolios within your institution, your pedagogy, your career, and your life.

I encourage scholars and students to work toward advanced research in Web portfolio development that goes beyond technical situations and software applications to dissect the interactions and behaviors that play a role in Web portfolio development, ownership, and presentations.

Please enjoy this book and the journey into the world of Web portfolios.

Acknowledgments

It takes many people to produce a book. I would like to gratefully acknowledge the people who contributed to this project. My appreciation extends to many different groups who were instrumental in helping me to stay the course and overcome the mental, physical, and organizational challenges that exist within any extensive project.

I want to thank the extraordinary staff at Idea Group, Inc. for supporting this project from conception to completion. Dr. Mehdi Khosrow-Pour, Renée Davies, Jan Travers, Amanda Appicello, Jennifer Neidig, and Kristin Roth provided me with the guidance to transform my concepts, processes, and research into this book. Throughout the development process, the team at Idea Group worked with me to find and communicate my vision for the Web portfolio and its future in society.

Next, I want to thank my colleagues at Canon, USA, Paul Balsamo and Mitch Bardwell, who graciously supported my scholarly endeavors for the past two years. I am especially thankful for the thoughtfulness shown to me by Paul Balsamo. Paul's propensity towards being a mentor, teacher, and a friend cannot be denied, and those qualities have made many of my interactions with him valuable learning experiences. Other people in my professional life who helped me with this book and career and need to be thanked are my sincere friends John Fekner and Rick Mills. I also need to thank Dr. Frank Brady for his mentoring and help. Lastly, in the professional category, I am appreciative to the Information Studies Doctoral Program faculty members at Long Island University who were my professors this year. Dr. Hildreth, Dr. Chu, Dr. Spaulding, and Dr. Smiraglia taught me research methods and exposed me to theories that I applied in writing this text.

I want to gratefully acknowledge my family and friends who are truly the most important part of my life. To Steve and Debbie, and Joey and Laura, thanks for being the greatest friends Kim and I could have. Mr. Lawrence, Paulie, Ginger, Brianna, Tori, and Justin have become my immediate family and I am grateful that I have them in my life. I also want to thank the Borowski family and Mrs. Florence Borowski for making me part of the whole family and for giving me the competitive and social outlets I need to have fun and enjoy life. Stolat!

On the Arizona side of my heart, sincere thanks to my family; I miss and love you all very much! Thanks to my parents, John and Frances DiMarco, for giving me the opportunities to explore life and the strength to embrace challenges. Thanks to my lovely sister Roseann and her family, my dear niece Gina and her new husband Richard, Corinne, and their boys Tristan and Ricky. And, thanks to my sister Margaret and the Marino family: Jerry, Alexis, and Joey – for always being there for us.

I must thank the people who contributed to the writing of this book. David Power contributed to the research and writing of the chapter on server-side technologies. Thanks, Dave, for the help with the book and for becoming a good friend. You have made my experiences at Canon and on the golf course special with your humor, kindness, and insight. Finally on the topic of help with the book, I must acknowledge Kimberly DiMarco, my wife, who contributed to the chapter on cases and interviews and provided editing and organizational help throughout the manuscript development.

The most important person to me in this world is my wife Kimberly. She truly is my partner, my love, and my life. So, sweetie, thank you for enduring and contributing to this project. Thanks for giving me the support to go for it. And, thanks for working hard to take care of Molly, Emma, and me.

This book is dedicated to the memory of Karen Lawrence. We all miss you and love you.

John DiMarco

Chapter I

Introduction to the
Web Portfolio

Introduction

This chapter introduces the concept of the portfolio and defines the electronic portfolio and Web portfolio. In print, electronic form, and through the Web, the portfolio has become a standard tool for success in many disciplines. In the future, the Web portfolio will be part of the success of people in all disciplines, not just those who traditionally utilize portfolios, such as artists and teachers. The chapter frames the Web portfolio as a tool for persuasion and lifelong learning. I introduce many different concepts, cases, and relevant information from literature and Web reviews. I want to stimulate your ideas about the Web portfolio so I provide some interesting uses of the Web portfolio within academic settings.

The objectives of the chapter are to define the electronic portfolio and its most utilized format, the Web portfolio. Discussion will focus on how the Web portfolio benefits those who explore its creation. Finally, I explain what to expect from the rest of this text.

Background

Goldsby and Fazal (2001) cited that student created portfolios are commonly "used in teacher preparation programs to demonstrate teaching skills and expertise. This practice was introduced as test scores alone lack the comprehensive scope needed for effective assessment and evaluation, portfolios can be implemented to interpret/make decisions regarding learning of teaching competencies" (pp. 607-608). The case for the student portfolio in any discipline can be made on the same basis; electronic portfolios provide a new level of assessment that cannot be measured by traditional methods such as standardized tests, applications, and resumes. Electronic portfolios and Web portfolios provide assessment of competency within a discipline.

The old models of professional and personal identity, skills assessment, and promotion are fading in what Dr. Stephen Covey (2004) describes as the age of the knowledge worker. In the knowledge worker age, the focus is on intellectual capital and exhibiting the skills of someone who is technologically savvy, but sensitive to the vision and voice of traditional values that enable people to thrive, such as mentoring. The Web portfolio feeds the emergence of intellectual capital by providing a platform for the knowledge worker to exhibit their personal and professional qualities. Mentoring will be increased as the Web portfolio becomes a standard learning tool within mainstream education at all levels. Teachers will need to teach students how to make Web portfolios. In turn, these students will later become mentors to others in their lives who are creating Web portfolios. Electronic portfolios and Web portfolios feed the process of lifelong learning.

Educators on all levels need to embrace the Web portfolio as a tool, regardless of their discipline. As a tool, it should be mastered by teachers and taught to students within the appropriate contexts of their disciplines. If a student creates an art portfolio, it has a structure and presentation style that will focus on the artwork and the skills of the artist. If the portfolio is for a student in the discipline of English, the portfolio should focus on the writings and literature aptitude of the creator. In his personal case study on Web-based portfolios for technology education, Professor Mark E. Sanders (2000) states that:

"The information age is not just a cliché-we're living it! Global networked information systems such as the World Wide Web are changing nearly every aspect of our lives. These technologies should be prominent within our curriculum. Often, they are not. Web-based portfolios offer a meaningful way for technology students to gain a thorough understanding of these critical new technologies beyond mere Web research. Web-based portfolios provide benefits that can never be realized with conventional portfolios" (p.11).

To follow up Professor Sander's statement, it is critical for all instructors and students to embrace Web portfolio exploration, creation, and development not only in technology and education driven disciplines, but also in all disciplines. The Web portfolio is growing well beyond the boundaries of education and technology fields and is finding its way outside of educational institutions and into human resources and other corporate directions. This idea is supported by Moonen and Tulner (2004) who reported:

> But also beyond regular education, interest in electronic portfolio is growing. EIfEL that commencing in May 2004, EIfEL (European Institute for E-Learning) is going to provide all of its Members with an electronic portfolio, the most innovative and fastest growing technology in the field of education, training and human resource development. While most current ePortfolio initiatives happen in primary, secondary, and higher education, the full potential of ePortfolios will be demonstrated through lifelong learning. 'The ePortfolio will be central to support EIfEL's members' continuing professional development, and the provision of certificates of competence to education, training, learning and human resource development professionals. Those certificates will cover all the activities involved in individual, organizational and community learning, as defined in the forward looking learning standards of competence developed by EIfEL. (p. 7)

This quote and the commitment to Web portfolios from the European Institute for E-Learning is a prime example of the initiation of Web portfolios outside of academia and into the information society and prophesies the eventual trickling of Web portfolios into mainstream society. With this in mind, the Web portfolio should be viewed as a new medium for human persuasion, promotion, assessment, and communication. The e-portfolio is finding application in business. Carliner (2005) suggests that portfolios are to be used for job seeking or developmental purposes. This is extremely important in creative fields, technical fields, and education. These fields have designated electronic portfolios as mandatory tools for learning, assessment, and presentation. A portfolio carries or contains something of value. The metaphor is the professional value of the person or organization. Portfolios historically have carried meanings rooted to finance or art. Clients of financial firms hold portfolios of securities. Artists have sheet bound and loose content portfolios which play a duel role as containers and presentation platforms for their artwork. Now, in the information society, new portfolios have spawned called e-portfolios or electronic portfolios. E-portfolio or electronic portfolio encompasses several application specific portfolios called Web portfolio, teacher portfolio, and digital portfolio (all are considered e-portfolios). Individuals, teachers, academics, and businesses can effectively utilize e-portfolios. The definitions vary by scholar and context, but the purpose for all electronic portfolios is the same, to persuade the user.

Web Literature and Review

This book project has evolved over years of research, development, and practice. The references section includes monographs as well as Web resources that will give a view of the wide range of data referred to during the development of this text. In this section, I would like to discuss some Web data I found that is particularly relevant to helping you understand the Web portfolio process. The Web portfolio process is a subjective process with varying objective guidelines which are particular to discipline, that drive the creative activity of developing a Web portfolio.

One thing that all academic research and publishing projects have in common is that the information that they are based drives and supports the project is emergent. The data surrounding electronic and Web portfolios is evolving at rapid speeds which cause researchers to search for patterns over time. One pattern is evident, more and more institutions and people are embracing electronic portfolio on the World Wide Web. A search for Web portfolios on Google turned up some interesting cases that focused on academia and commerce. This growth is found not only in academia as you might expect, but also in business, especially human resource development. There are numerous companies selling Web portfolios to executives, job seekers, and academics. The trend will obviously continue as the world becomes flatter and masses of people worldwide "become digital". Human resource departments are geared to rely more and more on Web portfolios to provide a clearer picture of an applicant or a vendor. The Web portfolio will provide a professional appearance for job seekers and companies looking to engage in business.

As I sorted through hundreds of portfolios, my general observations included many poorly designed Web portfolios that were content abundant. I also found that the processes in place for asset collection were dominant in most Web portfolio sites in both academic and business categories. I found many sites providing recommendations on what a Web portfolio should be. Reflection on accomplishments was also a central theme common to Web portfolio development recommendations. Design of Web portfolio sites was only discussed at academic or business Web resource sites that catered to target markets or audiences of students who were artists, designers, and photographers. That is what I find interesting; the artists who have design training are getting the design directions while the people who are not formally trained in art and design are getting most of their help in content collection. In response to that problem statement, I try to cover all of these bases in this book to help with the major stages of Web portfolio development and to provide a broad overview of many approaches and techniques associated with successfully creating a Web portfolio that fits your specific needs and goals. Let us look at some different approaches to Web portfolio programs and activities found on the Web.

Google's 4,550,000 hits revealed to me that the Web portfolio is becoming an enigma that has evolved into a trend which will gain momentum and become common practice in academia, professional, and personal environments. Web portfolios are integrated in society on infant levels in many disciplines; however activities on the Web reveal a wealth a valuable resources and programs that need to be discussed in this text. Here are few interesting ideas and approaches that illustrate why Web portfolios are important as vehicles for lifelong learning, assessment, and marketability and how they are challenging students and faculty to respond to the demands of societal Web portfolio integration.

Lifelong Learning

On its Web site, I found that Wofford College in South Carolina has developed a sound student Web portfolio program centered on developing a timeline of activities that align with the students' academic life span at the college. The development process outlined on the Wofford Web site gives students guided approaches to content development for academic, personal, and professional categories that span over freshman, sophomore, junior, and senior years. The

Web portfolio is presented metaphorically as two components: a file cabinet and a briefcase, the file cabinet being a place for storage of work and the briefcase being a place for presentation of work. The program neatly breaks down a timeline of activities for the students to help them keep on track with the Web portfolio development process through their college career. In addition, the process makes the student practice Web portfolio development activities from their freshmen year, it does not assume that Web portfolio skills are need only in junior and senior years. I found this approach very thoughtful in helping students succeed because it takes the somewhat takes the responsibility out the students hands and transfers it to the university in making the student portfolio an institutional learning objective with measurable outcomes.

Assessment

The portfolio has become a premier tool for assessment. Outcomes assessments provide tangible evidence of student growth and learning. Many universities have adopted Web portfolio programs for the purpose of assessment. Although the benefits of Web portfolios reach far beyond assessment, this use is a good one because it forces people to embrace the use of Web portfolios.

One such example is found at the University of Wisconsin Eau Claire. Found on a page governed by academic affairs and the provost, the university has in effect a policy document that outlines and is titled "Plan for Assessment of Student Academic Achievement, Baccalaureate Portfolio Project". This project requires students to publish a Web portfolio consisting of 12 of their best papers for projects completed during their coursework at the college. The school must have realized that creating Web portfolios might be a tough sell to students. Although the Web portfolios will benefit the students greatly in the future, they may be perceived as extra work. So the clever program administrator added this statement to the academic policy: "Except for completing a brief cover sheet for each submission, and then uploading the paper to your Web portfolio, you do nothing in addition to your regular course work." I was amused by that statement and a bit concerned. The importance of content in the Web portfolio must go beyond a dozen artifacts. However, the university in the Web page states that the Web portfolio is beneficial. The premise of the benefits are based on the fact that more and more employers and graduate schools expect graduates to present more than transcripts and letters of recommendation; they often want to see specific examples of what you have learned and learned how to do. They add that "keeping a portfolio also allows you to monitor your progress and development at UW-Eau Claire. You will be able to look back over your academic work and literally see your growth and learning".

The benefits of the Web portfolio need to be promoted before making students feel at ease. A portfolio must be looked at as something of value for the student not just another assignment to be completed for a course grade. However, the university senate created an action in 2001 that has required students to participate in some sort of assessment which may include "interviews, focus groups, surveys, or portfolios". The University of Wisconsin provides a good example of how Web portfolios have been mandated in education. Eventually, Web portfolios will be mandated as tools for success in society. The level of assessment will go beyond academia and deep into all professions.

Marketability

The arts have embraced portfolios forever. The ability to show a collection of work is critical in selling artwork to others. In today's highly specialized, highly competitive professional marketplace, more artists are embracing digital portfolios in addition to high resolution print portfolios. One such field is architecture. At the University of California Berkeley, the architecture department provides a specialized portfolio class in which students learn about creating digital portfolios and all of their different media components which include print, video, and Web. The course description has a paragraph that does more than define the coursework; it also defines the inevitable place of the Web portfolio in commerce or professionals, not just those within the arts. This statement gives the indication of the portfolio in general migrating solely from the hands of artists into the hands of all specialized and non specialized professionals. The use of Web portfolios will eventually trickle down to nonprofessional levels.

The UC Berkeley architecture portfolio course description reads: "While the printed portfolio conveys high-resolution graphical information, today's designer needs more than paper and vellum to sell their ideas." CAD models, digital photographs, video animations, GIS databases, and other multimedia files are now readily exchanged over the Web. To be competitive, architecture students must adapt their printed portfolios to incorporate these new media. This Arch 198 group-study explores the integration of print, video, and Web media into a coherent and marketable whole."

This description can be adapted to fit any professional discipline. The central idea which is critical here is that students must begin to explore the "integration of print, video, and Web into a coherent and marketable whole". The integration of assets into a coherent professional narrative is a critical process that must be taught and practiced. The importance of the success of the Web portfolio is evident when the ultimate deliverable is truly marketability. The Web portfolio gives you marketability.

Enhancing Professional Techniques

We see the use of Web portfolios in every aspect of education. At the 2004 California State University Technology and Persons with Disabilities Conference, Birnbaum and Kritikos (2004) described how Web portfolios are used in special education in several capacities. First, they are used by special needs students and secondly they are used by special education teachers. In the case of special education, the Web portfolio becomes a place for artifact collection and management. This is consistent with the idea that the Web portfolio acts as a portable storage and presentation platform regardless of industry specialization. This is supported by Birnbaum and Kritikos (2004):

> *With few exceptions, students with disabilities can learn to develop Web portfolios as a means of reviewing and understanding their work. The Web portfolio is an excellent means of teaching computer skills to these students. Also, it helps keep track of student progress in an orderly manner. Web portfolios can be used in IEP meetings so the teacher can demonstrate student progress in all areas. These portfolios become legal documents that can be used should due process or court action become necessary. The use of Web portfolios also is acceptable to most states' boards of education. In fact, several states encourage their use. (p.1)*

The application of Web portfolios in special education provides strong evidence the Web portfolio is a tool for developing tangible working knowledge and skills. It has now been added to the toolset of the special educator and is not only a viable platform for displaying teachers' credentials but also has become a technology tool that is valuable in a variety of critical individualized education plan situations. The ability to publish information for presentation and assessment that the Web portfolio provides is adding to the overall growth of technology and professional techniques in the special education field.

Faculty and Student Concerns

In 2000, at The **Council for Programs in Technical and Scientific Communication** (CPTSC) annual conference, Geoffrey Sauer of the University of Washington described his university's problems getting students engaged in Web portfolio development. Sauer (2000) stated: "Interviews revealed that many Web-savvy students felt alienated from campus Internet publishing options — which serve students while they remain students, but eliminate accounts (and remove alumni Web sites) soon after graduation. CMU students in professional programs are exceptionally career-oriented, and interviews revealed that they instead planned to postpone Web site production until they had graduated, when they could create (more) permanent Web sites — which often did not happen" (p.1).

This statement is indicative of one of the typical obstacles standing between students and Web portfolios. Many on the university level do not understand how the Web portfolio says a tool for communication when the student graduates. The communication occurs between the student, his or her faculty mentors, his or her colleagues, and most importantly communication with potential employers. With this in mind, Sauer (2000) presented data from his experiences at advising students in Carnegie Mellon's MAPW (Masters in Professional Writing) and CPAD (Masters in Communication Planning and Design) he found that there are several revisions that needed to be made to the processes behind the creation of student Web portfolios.

Sauer (2000) suggests that specific communication elements be initiated in Web portfolios. They include making Web portfolios act as "succinct overviews" which are guided guide the user using narrative devices. The idea of narrative devices becomes clearer when students understand that the Web portfolio is a place to tell their story to the Web community. The narrative must take on a professional tone that is persuasive and sells.

Sauer (2000) also warns of instances that cause problems such as students who receive e-mail questions about programs. He recommends that some formal education for students about how to field questions about the program might be a useful addition to programs which Web portfolios. This is a very valid concern that must be looked at within all academic Web portfolio programs. Although the notion of educating all students with Web portfolios on how to handle other students inquiries would be highly difficult and unfeasible simply due to the mass quantity of portfolios, students can be taught in Web portfolio classes to forward inquiries to other students to the appropriate college office Web contact address. Another problem that Sauer highlights which surrounds Web portfolios is the actual time and effort that needs to be devoted to Web portfolios. It is critical to understand how the Web portfolio will impact the workload of the student and the professor. Sauer states: "The cost of such as system is almost entirely in labor. Hardware and software to run a high-quality Web site are quite inexpensive. But it is helpful to consider how to balance student and faculty efforts into such a system" (Sauer, 2000, p. 1). Sauer brings up an extremely important concern surrounding successful and failed Web portfolio programs within academia. The concerns of many faculty members surrounding their absence from Web portfolio engagement is that it is "too much work and I do not have time." This is evident when checking some New York colleges and finding less than 50 percent of faculty had a Web portfolio or even a Web page. With other scholarship issues looming, courses loads, and publications needing to be written, many scholars leave the Web portfolio for the bottom of the heap. Even in cases where the students of the discipline need an electronic portfolio for graduation, faculty members are still not involved in creating their own Web portfolio. Streamlining and simplifying the Web portfolio process will help build faculty involvement in Web portfolio development.

Who Needs a Web Portfolio?

Everyone who is active in the information society, especially those who need to find work for hire, should have a working Web portfolio. Web portfolios are for everyone, and, in the future, everyone will want or need one. Regardless of skill set and specialty, the Web portfolio will come to contribute to defining a person's public and professional appearance. This appearance will be directly involved in communication and commerce. The Web portfolio will be a conduit and persuasion tool for getting work for hire and therefore will be common among knowledge workers and businesses of all types. An individual or business that needs to present experience level, skill set, accomplishments, project aptitude, and technology expertise needs a Web portfolio. A Web portfolio is a Web site, true, but it is also a targeted marketing project. This gives the project a different scope and goals.

The Web portfolio is a marketing site that promotes an individual or business to potential and existing clients, and the rest of the wired world. For an individual, the personal Web portfolio provides a personal marketing tool to help secure a job, promotion, chronicle achievements, disseminate information, or to assist in gaining freelance work. A personal Web portfolio may include a variety of content specifically based on the background and goals of the person.

More support on the development of personal Web portfolios comes from Kimball (2003), who titles his definition of the personal Web portfolio the "professional marketing Web portfolio". Kimball (2003) suggests that within the job market, Web portfolios can do at least three things which include "demonstrating to employers that you have the qualities and skills they want", demonstrating that you have "technical skills that will be useful" (pp.152-153), and he adds the Web portfolio "emphasizes your communication skills". He adds:

> *after all, the Web is primarily a communication medium — and many employers cite communication skills as one of the most sought after qualities in a new employee" (p. 153). Finally, Kimball considers the fact that there are no predefined standards for professional marketing Web portfolio, he concludes that the author should "use all your professional skills and instincts to speculate on what qualities and materials of professional audience might like to see in a Web portfolio, then build a Web portfolio that fits those expectations.* (Kimball, 2003, p.153)

Professionals in any field can have a Web portfolio. However, it is quite important for educators to have Web portfolios. Web portfolios are so important that state university systems and school districts across the world are researching, developing, and teaching Web portfolio courses. Web portfolios have become viable assessment tools in elementary and higher education administration (Kilbane & Milman, 2003). Academia has been investigating and massaging Web portfolios for the past decade or so. Limited research along with a number of successful, semi successful, and unsuccessful programs and initiatives have been part of the Web portfolios history.

Defining the Electronic Portfolio and the Web Portfolio

I will provide my synthesized definition of the electronic portfolio and Web portfolio initially to provide a background for the rest of this text. My definition is specific to meeting the needs of all disciplines, even those that sit outside the academic realm. In addition, the definition I provide is consistent with my thoughts on the future of the Web portfolio within society and more importantly, how electronic portfolios will fit within the information society of the future. This definition is based on field experience and meta analysis of past and current trends in electronic portfolio development. Literature review will provide additional definitions that establish a framework for electronic portfolios. You will find a multitude of variations on how an electronic and Web portfolio is defined, most of which has content as a central piece of the definition.

To define the Web portfolio, we must first define the e-portfolio, also known as the electronic portfolio. The electronic portfolio is a collection of artifacts, project samples, cases, and focused content presenting the messages and professional and public appearance of an individual or a company through electronic media (Web, DVD, CD-ROM). The e-portfolio provides evidence of skills, experience, and learning. I define the Web portfolio as: an electronic portfolio that is an Internet delivered, interactive, mass communication used to persuade users. The Web is the container for displaying work of all types. Much like the artist's vinyl portfolio book is used to display paintings and drawings, the Web portfolio shows off work in any discipline. The Web portfolio carries messages from the company or individual to the cyber public and natural public. When Web portfolios are created they are promoted by the creator, either company or individual, by all the common methods of advertising and market-ing, the most basic being word of mouth. Web portfolios get seen in most cases because people are told to go to them on the Internet. A Web portfolio address atop a resume or a corporate letterhead invites the reader the further their investment in communicating with the sender. When the reader visits, he or she will be exposed to messages and appearance. The messages are focused on a favorable reaction. Favorable reaction might be a job, a purchase order, a gallery venue commitment, or simply a compliment on a site well done. The Web portfolio is a multimedia vehicle that allows a company or individual to show their work without spatial and geographical boundaries. The goal of the Web portfolio is to seek a positive action from users, possibly resulting in work for hire.

The Web Portfolio as the Preferred Electronic Portfolio

E-portfolios are new media products and are delivered using a variety of electronic media. Current e-portfolio delivery methods are Internet, DVD, and CD-ROM. However, DVDs and CD-ROMs are not available to the world as is the Web portfolio. The delivery platform of the Web portfolio, the Internet, has the most effective potential for developing and delivering the finest portfolio experience to the most people. Being networked to through the Internet allows the Web portfolio to become a cyber appearance that helps bring people to a higher level of "digital comfort". Digital comfort comes with knowing that you are part of the opportunities available in the digital world and information society. The Web portfolio is always ready to promote you.

The Web portfolio is the most widely used new media format for electronic portfolios. This is due to cost, scalability, and reach. A Web portfolio is a collection of work that is presented in the form of a Web site. This text focuses on the Web portfolio as the preferred method for e-portfolio delivery.

Variable Definitions of the Electronic Portfolio

Scholarly definitions of the electronic portfolio vary from discipline to discipline. Taking the research methodology of using a meta-analysis of research articles and monographs, I realized when attempting to synthesize my own definitions of the electronic portfolio and the Web portfolio that a true definition would be hard to establish.

Gary Greenberg, the executive director for IT teaching and research initiatives and director of the Collaboratory Project at Northwestern University provides a definition that extends beyond traditional definitions. This definition is one that

I feel begins to explain the essence of what we want the electronic portfolio to become. Greenberg (2004) writes:

> *Ideally, all work in an electronic portfolio not only is digital but also is available on the Internet. Yet even though materials may be visible on the Web, the e-portfolio is not simply a personal home page with links to examples of work. In addition, unlike a typical application program, such as word processing, an e-portfolio is a network application that provides the author with administrative functions for managing and organizing work (files) created with different applications and for controlling who can see the work and who can discuss the work (access). And unlike a course management system, in which instructors manage assignments and materials within the framework of a specific course, e-portfolios are controlled by the author (student), who manages his or her work across multiple courses throughout an academic career.* (pp. 28-29)

This definition presents several items for closer analysis. First, Greenberg makes a distinction that the electronic portfolio is not only digital but also available on the Internet. Development of the electronic portfolio and delivery are typically centered on using the Web. With using the Internet for delivery, electronic portfolios become less effective and more prone to failure. The next point that Greenberg makes surrounds the electronic portfolio as a not just a home page. He is correct in that statement. Any portfolio, in general terms needs to be filled with work samples and evidence of growth and learning throughout someone's career. How can that amount of information be delivered effectively in only one page? It cannot. An electronic portfolio must be a narrative that gives a perspective to the user. The perspective of the viewer is shaped by the content and structure of the Web portfolio. Greenberg continues to describe the e-portfolio as having a network function. The Web portfolio specifically is a content container that allows dynamic storage capabilities as well as obvious delivery features. The content management concept that the Web portfolio provides is going to be essential to bringing Web portfolios to everyone across jobs and disciplines. The creator of a Web portfolio will gain technical skills by acting as an administrator for his or her own Web site which will be their electronic portfolio.

Finally, Greenberg affirms that the electronic portfolio is not a course management system such as Blackboard or WebCT. To add to this, the electronic portfolio allows a student to manage his or her work throughout an academic and a professional career. The use of the electronic portfolio has greater potential for adding value to someone's professional life after he or she graduate more so than as students. The grass roots of how to create an electronic portfolio is fostered within a learning environment. Or, the skills are gained through self learning. The electronic portfolio provides opportunity for both. The electronic portfolio is a tool for lifelong learning and will be part of learning and growing throughout college and professional life. Having to gather materials and create Web pages provides the author of the electronic portfolio a learning experience that will carry over into his or her professional skill set. As network computers and the Internet become standards in every aspect of our lives, the skills and abilities needed to present creative and intellectual capital will become paramount to one's success in a technological marketplace.

Greenberg (2004) defines three types of electronic portfolios. The definitions of the three are based on the assumed goals of the author. He believes this arrangement can be helpful in developing content management structure in a simplified manner. The structure of each is based on when the work is organized relative to when the work is created. Greenberg believes these results in three types of e-portfolios (p. 29):

1. The **showcase e-portfolio:** organization occurs after the work has been created.

2. The **structured e-portfolio:** a predefined organization exists for work that is yet to be created.

3. The **learning e-portfolio:** organization of the work evolves as the work is created.

I find that the three types of portfolios that Greenberg defines are effective in establishing types of portfolios based on content. This point can be argued by saying that a more appropriate structure would focus the electronic portfolio specifically to the audience established by the author. The electronic portfolio must be user and audience centered. I think Greenberg's e-portfolio types need to be looked at as fitting into an author-based definition of electronic portfolio types. Looking at author types, we look at a broader approach to classifying electronic portfolios. Specifically referring to the Web-based electronic portfolio, I feel that three types of portfolios can be defined:

1. The **personal Web portfolio** for students or individuals
2. The **teacher Web portfolio**
3. The **business Web portfolio**

An individual owns each of these portfolio types. Throughout the life span of the Web portfolio, the author will go through periods of development that align with the three types of electronic portfolios described by Greenberg. The process begins with learning, then structure, then showcase and then it repeats. The types of portfolios defined by Greenberg are stages of the electronic and Web portfolio process. The learning stage exists as work is created, the structure stage exists after work is created and content management and organization is needed to put information into a hierarchal and narrative form. Showcase happens after everything in the process of conceptualization, design, and development is complete. The whole process of electronic portfolio development relies on work development. The Web portfolio becomes a catalyst for creative thinking and technical skills that truly exemplifies how someone or an organization learns to structures and showcases their work.

Types of Web Portfolios

I have categorized different applications of Web portfolios that explored in this text. They include personal Web portfolios which can be used by students, job seekers, and professionals in any field. Also discussed are teacher Web portfolios which are used by K-12 teachers, faculty, and staff in educational institutions. The uses of Web portfolios in education are widely researched. I overview techniques and approaches for educators to use when developing an electronic teacher portfolio that can be enhanced by specific curriculum and development techniques offered in education based e-portfolio texts. Finally, business Web portfolios are examined from the view point of persuasive communication and information design and management for a freelancer. Organizational portfolios are a larger topic that is not densely covered in this text. However, the principles and processes behind the creation of the Web portfolio can be applied to many business applications.

Print Portfolios, Digital Portfolios, Electronic Portfolios, and Web Portfolios Compared

The objectives of the print portfolio, digital portfolio, electronic portfolio, and the Web portfolio are to present experience level, skill set, accomplishments, project aptitude, and media expertise with the goal of initiating positive action from the user, viewer, and client. All portfolios help validate someone's professional appearance. Key ingredients to successful portfolios in any medium are organization, clarity, and consistency. Editorial style and text layout should conform to a standardized structure. The portfolio must communicate effectively; therefore we cannot stray from the principles of good editorial and visual design. Content quality, organization, and design are critical to the overall success of the portfolio, regardless of medium. Most importantly, the portfolio provides a personalized channel of presentation for the owner to communicate strengths that may persuade the viewer to act positively towards the author. The result can be a career promotion, a sale of professional work, an invitation to exhibit, or the acquisition of a job. Let us closer examine the different types of presentation portfolios used to gain credibility and acquire work for hire.

The print portfolio gets delivered on paper. The goal of the print portfolio as with all portfolios is to sell. Artists have long revered the use of portfolios for showing off and marketing their works. Ideally, the presentation of the portfolio yields an opportunity to sell work or get work for hire. Print portfolios yielded by graphic designers, brag books offered by sales people, and dossiers presented by executives are all built to sell. These items are forms of personal marketing. The advantage of the print portfolio is that it is easily controlled; no technical errors or performance issues here. Also, print allows the highest level of data quality. Output can be large and full color, not conforming to a browser window or a viewers computer speed.

The digital portfolio gets delivered digitally. Synonymous with electronic portfolio and now more and more delivered as a Web portfolio, digital portfolios deliver work interactively through the digital medium of a computer or DVD player. The digital portfolio can be delivered via any digital medium including CD-ROM, DVD, or the Internet. The problem with CD-ROM and DVD based portfolios is that they need distribution channels to be seen and they can be flawed in performance due to a multitude of platforms and applications running in the world. Also, removable media portfolios are expensive to produce because they need to be recreated when things change. When recreation occurs, new media must be burned, thus incurring added costs to the portfolio process.

The worst problem a digital portfolio can have is failure to initialize and operate. The second worst problem is performance that is slow and visually poor. The non-networked portfolios are susceptible to various failures. This fact causes me to embrace Web portfolios over CD and DVD portfolios when applicable. Video, film, and high end gaming/multimedia portfolios need to be delivered completely using DVD media. However the Web can be used to show off snippets of film and movies and can establish dynamic relationships with the audience beyond that of piece of removable media. A Web portfolio for a programmer, designer, writer, teacher, musician, or theorist shares the objective of all portfolios in selling someone or something to somebody and creating an appearance. All portfolios should be built to market and sell the value of the content and the virtues of the creator.

The Web portfolio is a great media to deliver a portfolio due to its dynamic nature and extensive reach. As you grow, your Web portfolio will grow. This dynamic nature puts the Web portfolio ahead of the other mediums in price, flexibility, scalability, reach, and overall author return on investment.

Personal Web Portfolios for Students and Individuals

A personal Web portfolio serves as a self-selected, self developed multimedia presentation of work that offers multiple views of a person's learning and development. Driven by creative expression and college learning experiences, Web portfolios provide tangible evidence of growth and accomplishment. Web portfolios also allow students to present research papers, essays, and academic projects that incorporate text, images, audio, and video. The disciplines of computer science, art, and education have embraced Web portfolio development most frequently. However, students in all disciplines need a Web portfolio when they leave college.

After college, the Web portfolio can become a personal hub for professional communication to potential employers and the public. It can serve as a platform for publishing career accomplishments and presenting skills and experiences through content.

Teacher Web Portfolios

Academic literature today is still lacking in a grounded definition of the electronic portfolio as an information product across disciplines. Disciplines such as education have defined the electronic within their own contexts. They have done this successfully partly based on the fact that discipline is has implemented standards that help guide content. This content is specific to the field and therefore, fits around the standards implemented within pedagogy and practice. The electronic portfolio in education is regarded as an electronic teaching portfolio. The teaching portfolio is one variety of electronic portfolios.

Kilbane and Milman (2003) describe the teaching portfolio as "a special type of presentation portfolio that demonstrates the professional competence of anyone who engages in the active teaching at any academic level" (p. 6).

Kilbane and Milman also reference the fact that the electronic portfolios, especially those on the Web are becoming more and more popular with college instructors. As well, the teaching portfolio is not a tool specifically for instructional work but, is geared towards displaying evidence of professional competence. However in the future, the responsive environment provided by Internet Web applications will allow more interaction and ultimately enhance the value of the Web portfolio as not only a display platform but also a tool for the educator, inside and outside of the classroom.

An educator can use the Web portfolio to present student work, provide a forum for credentials and accomplishments, and to establish a lifelong learning project that will be dynamic throughout their career. This becomes important to the educator when approaching tenure and promotion. The Web portfolio can present many items including a vita, syllabi, student work, lesson plans, and educational philosophy statements. A longer list of artifacts used on the teacher Web portfolio will be listed later in the text.

Web Portfolios for Business

For a business, the Web portfolio demonstrates the company's ability to succeed in providing project results and deliverables. A business Web portfolio may contain sample work, product profiles, client case studies, process samples, or testimonials. In the business Web portfolio, the content is adjusted to fit the marketing communication goals of the business. Most importantly, companies that perform design, development, programming, or creative output should have a Web portfolio to market and promote their corporate philosophy and their professional project work. The Web portfolio can be a separate appended micro-site. The Web portfolio does not replace a corporate site; it enhances it by isolating the most important work and highlighting it.

The business context of the Web portfolio is expanded to include the hybrid individual who needs a Web portfolio to act as an instrument for both business and personal use — the freelancer. The freelancer may or may not be a corporation or a regular employee of an organization. The freelancer is someone who needs work for hire. They fit into the personal Web portfolio author category and the business Web portfolio category. A freelancer is someone who needs credibility and promotion throughout his or her life cycles to continue surviving, whether financially or professionally. The Web portfolio is critical to the personal business practices of the freelancer. The Web portfolio evens the playing field for the freelancer. It provides a mass media vehicle at a cheap price. This allows the freelancer to compete with the larger company from a digital marketing perspective. The Web portfolio takes on a larger perspective for the freelancer because it can provide a narrative connection that is lost by large, sterile corporate sites that seem to have insincere looks and feels. Most large corporate sites are suited for e-commerce, technical support, or pure information delivery. The freelancer's Web portfolio site concentrates on promotion and identity, not for use as a commercial application such as with most corporate sites.

The Web Portfolio Fosters Valuable Learning Experiences

The Web portfolio conceptualization, design, and development processes call upon hard and soft skills that are required to accomplish each task. Hierarchal task analysis of Web portfolio creation involves providing sequential information from the ground up. Although creating the Web portfolio requires a systematic approach to concept development all the way through to final output, Bloom's Taxonomy of Cognitive Domain illustrates the same learning outcomes that fit into the Web portfolio process through its course.

Bloom identified six levels within the cognitive domain, from the simple recall or recognition of facts, as the lowest level, through increasingly more complex and abstract mental levels, to the highest order which is classified as evaluation. A description of the six levels — knowledge, comprehension, application, analysis, synthesis, and evaluation — and how they represent intellectual activity and learning during the Web portfolio process are listed (Bloom, 1956, p. 1).

According to Bloom, knowledge is defined as remembering of previously learned material. This may involve the recall of a wide range of material, from specific facts to complete theories, but all that is required is the bringing to mind of the appropriate information. The appropriate information for the Web portfolio constitutes anything deemed as valuable in the quest for work for hire and promoting ones appearance. Bloom stated that knowledge represents the lowest level of learning outcomes in the cognitive domain. At this level, the Web portfolio creator must remember what they have done and accomplished in the past. Then, without hesitation, they must write down a list of the things that they will eventually need to start to hunt and gather. A collection of artifacts must be named in some way and listed loosely, without classification.

Comprehension is defined as the ability to grasp the meaning of material. This may be shown by translating material from one form to another (printed materials to Web portfolio pages), by interpreting material (explaining qualifications through a Web portfolio), and by estimating future trends (developing the Web portfolio as a perceived status symbol and professional credential). These learning outcomes go one step beyond the simple remembering of material. The Web portfolio creator must begin to review and classify the materials found in the knowledge stage to begin to understand if and how they may be used to persuade some and to translate into a positive appearance to all publics.

Application refers to the ability to use learned material in new and concrete situations. This may include the application of such things as rules, methods, concepts, principles, laws, and theories. The application of what someone has learned and has experienced will be intertwined into their Web portfolio. Application of skill sets and expertise will be evident in the design and content of someone's Web portfolio. Poems posted will illustrate the application of writing. Critical analysis, essays, and published research papers posted to the Web portfolio will exhibit ideas backed by theoretical perspective and discourse. This area requires a higher level of understanding than those under comprehension because it involves the learner to demonstrate their abilities through content on the Web portfolio. And, to add to learning outcomes of the application level, Web portfolio design and the technical skills used are learned and relearned throughout the Web portfolio cycle. Skills and problem solving are put in application again and again as the Web portfolio design and redesign process becomes iterative through practice, but fresh in its harvest of new learning for future edits. Foundation skills in developing the Web portfolio become intuitive and new learning occurs due to the introduction of new findings, new techniques, new requirements, new software, new delivery methods, new media, and new focus on what is perceived as important and persuasive to the public.

Analysis refers to the ability to break down the Web portfolio into its component parts so that its organizational structure may be understood. This includes the identification of the Web portfolio categories, analysis of the relationships between Web portfolio categories, and recognition of the organizational principles involved in presenting the Web portfolio as a hierarchical structure that allows nonlinear navigation for unrestricted usability. Learning outcomes here represent a higher intellectual level than comprehension and application because they require an understanding of both the content and the structural form of the Web portfolio and how it has been conjoined into an electronic narrative that informs, entertains, and persuades all at the same time. Analysis of the audience and how they will perceive the Web portfolio also takes place and has high value as a learning outcome. Analysis, the learning and practice of it during the creation of the Web portfolio will guide appropriate content discrimination while maintaining a healthy level of experimentations without compromising the effectiveness of the Web portfolio on gaining work for hire and illuminating a positive electronic appearance. Appraisal of integrity, continuity, and appropriateness for the Web portfolios of others will also be guided by the ability to compare, contrast, and criticize their work and narrative against your own. The analysis of others Web portfolio can be beneficial and feed a curiosity about credibility and interests, or maybe simply just to gain inspiration for the next Web portfolio redesign.

Synthesis refers to the ability to put the parts of the Web portfolio together to form a new whole. This may involve the production of wholly new creative content, a detailed site plan that encompasses goals for gaining work for hire and establishing an identity which require thinking about and recording a set of abstract relations that act as a scheme for classifying information portrayed in the Web portfolio. Specific learning outcomes in this area stress creative behaviors, with major emphasis on the formulation of new patterns or structures for presenting the personal narrative using the Web portfolio. Synthesis learning occurs in the Web portfolio development process as the knowledge, comprehension, application, and analysis of content is synthesized into a working, live Web portfolio available to all on the Internet. The parts are connected to form a communication that has many messages and plenty of content to illustrate and reinforce those messages. The messages in the Web portfolio that are meant to persuade the user into acting favorably. If the parts are not synthesized effectively, the wrong messages are communicated. An example of this might be the user assumes the Web portfolio author has bad technical skills because the Web portfolio does not perform properly from the user's point of view. Bad performance sends a nonverbal or non content message that may influence the user in a negative fashion. Thus, retarding the possibility of a work for hire opportunity and contributing to the tarnishing of a positive public appearance. The Web portfolio must be managed in order to keep it running efficiently. When efficiency halts, user perception and confidence become damaged.

Evaluation is concerned with the ability to judge the value of Web portfolio assets (artwork, reports, letters, journals, photos) for the given purpose and audience. The purpose of the Web portfolio is to persuade the user. The audience is made of a population of users who have interest in the Web portfolio for entertainment, information, or commerce reasons. Maybe the user wants to hire the creator of the Web portfolio for a work assignment. Judgments made on content inclusion, message, and overall design are to be based on definite criteria that needs to be addressed when creating a Web portfolio. These may be internal criteria which include personal artifacts thought of as important and valuable. And it will include external criteria which focus on relevance to the purpose of getting work for hire and promoting a positive professional appearance to the world and the local communities that we occupy. A concrete example of this would be the Web portfolio of a kindergarten school teacher. He or she must determine the appropriate content of her Web portfolio, without sacrificing personal identity and without compromising her professional appearance or position as an educator within a community. Learning outcomes in this area are highest in the cognitive hierarchy because they contain elements of all the other categories, plus conscious value judgments about the Web portfolio based on clearly defined criterion dictated by personal values, societal norms, and professional standards. The Web portfolio creator/owner must be able to predict the perceptions that the Web portfolio will illicit. And, he or she must be prepared to defend or argue the intellectual and professional value of the Web portfolio, the credibility of the work sources, and subject matter of the content. The Web portfolio author must continually evaluate the standards of the times, ethically, legally, and professionally in order to appraise the compliance of the Web portfolio. The Web portfolio is dynamic in content and must be updated regularly to be a current representation of the lifelong learning and professional growth of the author.

Throughout the Web portfolio life cycle, evaluation and enhancement are constants which the author struggles with personally, professionally, intellectually, and physically. These constants are focal points which engage the Web portfolio creator/author in new learning activities within the six levels of the cognitive domain as theorized by Bloom in 1956.

Skills Fostered by the Web Portfolio Process

The very idea of creating a Web portfolio makes people cringe. This is especially evident in those who do not embrace technology and the Internet. But the Web portfolio and the creation process that is needed to effectively create one is a lifelong learning, skill building process in which the creator comes away with more than technical skills, but also personal reflections that can be shared and may evolve into a greater idea. The ability to take a personal inventory of creative content and software and design skills is invaluable in the lifelong learning process. You can take a step back and think about the things you know and compare them to the things you want to know in order to design and post a Web portfolio. The skills needed and acquired by creating a Web portfolio are extensive. When you really get down to examining the Web portfolio and its benefits in a critical fashion, you realize that the Web portfolio development process helps develop the central skills needed by the new millennium knowledge worker; that is to say anyone who hopes to succeed in the new millennium by securing and retaining meaningful work-for-hire situations.

Creating a Web portfolio is most definitely, an intense learning experience. The experience brings the creator through emotional highs and lows with each new success and failure. Along the way, the Web portfolio learning experience will enable you gain a massive amount of information. Then you take the information and process it. Finally, the Web portfolio has been transformed into a technology project that requires an extensive learning (compared to simply sending an e-mail) of software and digital processes. But, this learning and the time it takes is well spent. You, as the learner, walk away with the ability to create a Web site. The same conceptual and technical processes learned through Web portfolio development are the same as those used in creating any Web site, regardless of goals or audience. In the larger sense, learning how to create a Web portfolio gives you digital skills that will reap rewards for you throughout your life.

The list of skills needed and learned during involvement in the Web portfolio can be quantified in technical terms. To identify specific discipline skills need to develop content all would require a dedicated research effort looking at the Web portfolio content collection and development practices of students and instructors within in that particular discipline. That is not the purpose of this text. However, there are some important skills and personal attributes that become critical to the Web portfolio development process, both in development and during learning and growth cycles. They include conceptual and logical skills such as brainstorming, information seeking, knowledge organization, classification, sketching, flowcharting, writing, visual design, and artistic engineering. The technology skills include basic computer skills for managing files and folders, graphic application skills to create and prepare text, graphics, and multimedia artifacts, Internet development to test and post Web pages, and critical evaluation and usability identification skills to determine the quality and effectiveness of the Web portfolio.

The Web Portfolio as an Appearance

The Web portfolio is an extension of the public, professional appearance of an individual or a business. I'm going to describe a brief analogy to explain the underlying purpose of the Web portfolio. Later on in the text we will get process specific. The new media portfolio, the financial portfolio, and the artist's portfolio are the same in the fact that they are content containers. However, they differ drastically in their purpose and application. Simply described, financial portfolios are used to make money for people in the financial markets. The content is stocks, bond, funds, and other financial instruments. This is a private portfolio, seen only by the user, advisor, and creditors. The artist's portfolio has content that includes photographs, drawing, paintings, and other artist representations. The artist's portfolio is used in interpersonal situations where the artist and the viewer are both present, sharing the experience. Contrary to restricted situations, the Web portfolio is a mass communication experience. Just as in the case of the moving image mass communication mediums such as film and television, the Web portfolio has the potential to be anonymously viewed by anyone with Internet access. Web portfolios are a media that illustrates a construct that connects with the ideas put forth by Marshall McLuhan when he declared the existence of the "global village" created by electronic media. In 1997, in his book *On McLuhan: Forward Through the Review Mirror*, McLuhan stated that "In the electric age, we wear all mankind as our skin" (p. 47). This was extended by his concept that technology is an extension of man. He puts the idea into literal terms by explaining in his book *The Medium is the Massage* that the wheel is an extension of the foot, and electronic circuitry is an extension of the central nervous system. So following Professor McLuhan's theory, I propose to say that the Web portfolio is an extension of the appearance. Specifically, the Web portfolio is an extension of the public and professional appearance of the creator within cyber space and transferring into everyday public life. So when developing the Web portfolio, we must take care to insure that it properly represents our intended appearance. The appearance is constituted by content, design, functionality, and the overall persuasive impression that the Web portfolio makes on the viewer. Let's say a job candidate goes in for an interview and shows his Web portfolio to the potential employer. When the site loads, rather than present his latest project accomplishment at his programming position with ABC company, hardcore heavy metal begins to play and a photo montage of the job applicant slamming a beer and banging his head at a concert loads on the homepage. This is not a very constructive Web portfolio page. It has nothing to do with personal likes or dislikes, it is about persuasion. If that was a Web site for a heavy metal band or a personal site for a band member, that would be great, but for a Web portfolio, you need to focus on the specific goals you have for the viewer. The Web portfolio creates an appearance that you as the creator must control.

The Benefits of Web Portfolios

The creation of a Web portfolio offers the following benefits to individuals:

- Creation of a Web portfolio makes you a learner
- Creation of a Web portfolio provides opportunities for you to learn about technology

- A Web portfolio will improve your impact when trying to persuade an audience
- A Web portfolio is an effective tool for demonstrating your competence
- A Web portfolio can help you get a job
- A Web portfolio is portable storage and presentation capability
- A Web portfolio promotes a sense of accomplishment and satisfaction
- A Web portfolio is evidence of personal growth
- Skills learned while creating a Web portfolio can be applied in other projects (Kilbane & Milman, 2003, pp. 22-28)

The creation of a Web portfolio offers the following benefits to businesses and freelancers:

- Creation of a Web portfolio makes the company identify its accomplishments
- Creation of a Web portfolio provides opportunities for the company to learn about technology
- A Web portfolio will improve the company's impact when trying to sell
- A Web portfolio is an effective tool for demonstrating organizational competence
- A Web portfolio can help get clients, projects, and sales
- A Web portfolio is a portable storage and presentation capability
- A Web portfolio promotes a sense of accomplishment and satisfaction in the organization
- A Web portfolio is evidence of company growth
- The Web portfolio is a dynamic asset to the organization

What You Should Get Out of This Book

Your learning is my objective. Learning about Web portfolios and applying techniques and processes to develop a Web portfolio are important objectives for you to achieve. The following are the learning objectives I want you to achieve during your experiences with this book.

- Understanding what a Web portfolio is and is not
- Commit to building your design and technology skill by creating a Web portfolio
- Define and execute the conceptualization process used in Web portfolio design
- Define and execute information design for Web portfolio development
- Define and execute visual design for Web portfolio development
- Define and execute asset collection and graphic art creation for Web portfolio development
- Define and execute Web page design for Web portfolio development
- Define and execute Web authoring for Web portfolio development
- Define and develop motion graphics for Web portfolio development
- Develop an applied understanding for uploading, testing, and re-uploading
- Demonstrate an applied understanding of how to create a Web portfolio for you or your business by completing the Web portfolio creation and development process
- Understand the social and technological theories and impacts that Web portfolios are having and will continue to have as they ascend in importance due to the demands of society and industry for the knowledge worker of the information society

Philosophy and Aims

This book contains theoretical and technical chapters which offer a comprehensive view and valuable resource in your journey towards developing a Web portfolio or electronic portfolio program at your institution. Regardless if you are student, a faculty member, a freelancer, or a business owner, you will get value from the ideas presented in this text. The focus of this book is to assist you in exploring different aspects of Web portfolios. To do this, I realize that I must give you my viewpoint and the viewpoints of others who have been researching electronic portfolios and Web portfolios since the early 1990s. Giving you background and theory is important to helping you grasp the subject of portfolio development as a whole. In addition, I try to present ideas that are seen across disciplines. Most published material that I came across was specific to a discipline. Education, art, and information technology seem to lead the pack. With backgrounds in all three of these areas, I decided to take a pan disciplinary approach and not rely on one interpretation of what a Web portfolio should be. With this interdisciplinary approach in mind, I present a well rounded cache of viewpoints and theories that put the Web portfolio into an applicable perspective to achieve goals. I also give viewpoint as to what the future of the electronic portfolio and Web portfolio will be as the information society continues to flourish. I give these points of view with hope that you will establish your own definition of an electronic portfolio that fits into your disciplinary context. As well, my goal for this text is to provide somewhat of a technical guidebook to help you build your Web portfolio using industry standard tools.

I have helped hundreds of students and individuals develop Web portfolios across disciplines. In my experience, I have seen the technical obstacles that stand in the way of developing a great and effective Web portfolio and I have realized solutions. These solutions are presented in this text.

This book is written in modular steps. I did this because the process presented in this book can guide you towards creating a real Web portfolio. However, each module is filled with sub-processes that provide completely new learning and skills on their own. Each chapter holds a piece of the Web portfolio development process but also provides information on a reusable skill that can be utilized in future projects. I tried to give you the nuts and bolts for each step in the Web portfolio development process. The best way for you to learn about Web portfolio design is to work through creating a real Web portfolio. As we do this, moving through the book, we're going to use www.portfolio.cc, a fully functional Web portfolio that serves me as an educator and as a communication design consultant as a working prototype. The portfolio was built with academic content and business content. This site will be out in the real world as a commercial project. It can be viewed as a business Web portfolio or an educator's Web portfolio. This fits my specific goal of using the site as a portal for my professional and academic endeavors. When you complete your Web portfolio, I give you instructions on how to upload it and provide suggestions for low cost and free Web portfolio hosting. My site is used for examples presented throughout the book and I strongly state that my Web portfolio is only one example and it is specific to me. You should use the technical samples as reference as you develop your own style, visual and technical designs.

Tools

This book is not a software manual. It is volume that provides theories, processes, and a tutorial view of industry standard Web applications. Some of the processes are worked out on paper or in a word processing program. Some processes require using graphical or Web design software. For many of these, I provide step by step tutorials so that you can try to execute the techniques on your own. Obviously, you can't learn every conceivable application in one book. The tools mentioned in this book can be amended to suit your particular skill level or the platform and tool set used in your company. The intent is to help you understand the applications betters so that you can do further exploratory learning. For a more detailed and expanded coverage of the applications in this book, consult the reference section and suggested readings provided in the appendix. The applications exemplified in this text are industry standards for high end Web design and development. Pure HTML coding will be kept to a minimum. We will explore the applications to expand your tool set and challenge your abilities. Here are the applications that will be presented in this text:

- **Macromedia Dreamweaver MX 2004** for Web authoring and site management (FTP)
- **Macromedia Fireworks MX 2004** for Web graphics creation and slicing
- **Macromedia Flash MX 2004** for motion graphics
- **Macromedia Freehand MX 2004** for logo type and illustrations
- **Adobe Photoshop** for Web graphics creation
- **Adobe Audition** for audio editing and output

Layout Elements in This Book

Following are the specific layout styles that you will see throughout the text:

Menu commands will be in bold and will follow this form **Menu > Sub-Menu > Sub-Menu.**

This book uses Windows PC commands as a default.

Here are the common substitutes:

PC	**MAC**
Right+click	CTRL+click
CTRL+click	Apple+click
CTRL+Z (undo)	Apple+Z
CTRL+Enter	Apple+Enter

Review and Conclusion

Hopefully, this first chapter has laid the foundation for your understanding what a Web portfolio is and what it does. The Web portfolio is an electronic portfolio which is specifications and context are variably defined from discipline to discipline. Most definitions share the fact that the Web portfolio is a collection of artifacts that exhibit lifelong learning. In addition, I add that the Web portfolio is an appearance that exists professionally and publicly. The Web portfolio fosters learning and growth and is a platform for exhibition of skills and experience, regardless of discipline. A person or business can have a Web portfolio. A Web portfolio is not simply a Web site, it has a specific purpose. It is to persuade the user to act or think favorably about the portfolio and the author.

The Web portfolio process is a learning experience in itself, requiring the author to reflect and gather important artifacts from their previous learning experiences. These materials are dispersed in different media and format and must be uniformly processed and published in a Web site. Knowledge organization, information architecture, software skills, and visual design are learned and used repeatedly throughout the Web portfolio development process.

The next chapter will help you brainstorm and develop the concepts and messages needed to convey your best professional appearance. This stage is critical to getting the process started and developing a strong idea that is backed by a creative theme and intelligent messages. Conceptualization is the first step in the Web portfolio development process.

Chapter II

Conceptualization

Introduction

This chapter provides instruction, examples, and steps on how to begin the creative production process. Focus will be on user centered design, conceptualization, and creation of documents that define the scope of your personal Web portfolio project. Topics include understanding the user, brainstorming to determine audience, messages, and supporting images needed as well as development of scope documents for the Web portfolio. The scope documents are the concept statement, content list, and content outline. These documents help you, the author, to gather your thoughts and begin to record the ideas in hardcopy form. The ideas you put down on paper will go through revision and possibly redefinition during the conceptualization process. Don't worry, this is natural. This initial struggle with ideas is important to establishing solid content and design. Without conceptualization, communication is lost in the translation from the author to the media. This can be deadly in the case of the Web portfolio. Because the goal of the Web portfolio is to persuade, it is vital that all important messages are to the forefront. Without them, it is difficult to establish a personal credibility, identity, and communication channel with the user.

Defining the User, Understanding the Audience

This book mostly focuses on communication design. Design solves a problem. You are solving a problem when you create a Web portfolio. The problem is rooted in persuasive communication. Persuasive communication involves delivering a message with the goal of changing someone's perception. You want your portfolio to change someone's perception favorably. That someone is known as the user. You want the user to have a positive experience when they visit your Web portfolio. This means that your Web portfolio is entertaining, easy to navigate, performs well, and is chock full of vital content. Spending time on conceptualization will help you provide a great experience for the user. In addition, spending time on testing and maintenance helps insure the user remembers you and your site.

The most important rules in designing any interactive project are to design for the user and design for communication. The Web portfolio design process should focus on yielding a user-centered design. Providing a user-centered design means that the needs, expectations, requirements, and navigation abilities of the user are met indefinitely throughout the Web site experience (Lynch & Horton, 1999). We want the users' needs to be met, but what are their needs? Users want to feel in control. They want to have an error free experience in which they can absorb the content and submerge themselves in the experience. The content drives the experience and the users' curiosity to engage the Web portfolio, probing for more evidence and more identity. Navigation plays a major role in the value of the experience. If the experience is a negative one, the perceptions of the author will be negative also. This hypothesis is disturbing because it means that our Web portfolio has an influence on the public who views it. The public opinion of our Web portfolio will trickle into our social interactions and professional situations. An example of this might be a poorly designed teacher portfolio that cannot be viewed successfully or does not deliver a positive experience for users is likely to lessen the opinion of the students, parents, and supervisors towards the author. The Web portfolio validates and provides an assessment vehicle which exceeds professional observers and audiences. More and more, you'll see the Web portfolio become the symbol for validation of someone's professional background, ethical standards, and technology skills. There will be pressure to conform in the information society to having an effective and persuasive Web portfolio. As we have mentioned previously in this text, Web portfolio authors must have deep understanding of their particular audience and specific user in order to tailor the contents to persuade. Understanding an audience and a user requires research and critical thinking. The thought process must go beyond "everyone on the net". You simply cannot persuade everyone, but you do need to persuade your target audience. Throughout the life of the Web portfolio, you'll be defining your audience as you change, technology changes, and the audience changes. An example of this changing environment and audience is the advent of a Web browser based cell phones that allow Web sites to be seen through the interface of cellular devices. This new medium of cell phones requires different thought and technical processes for design and as different audience members who may not fit standard profiles of computer-based users. We do not know unless we do the research. My point here is that although this text does not cover design for cell phone interfaces, you should realize that things are constantly changing and you must make your Web portfolio change in stride. Now let us focus some more on the user.

In their Web Style Guide, Lynch and Horton (1999) suggest researching the potential audience to uncover their inherent needs. Let us think about our potential users in the case of the Web portfolio.

Who is your user? Previously we described the Web portfolio as a selling tool. We also focused on the goal of persuading our audience members. Your audience will depend on your individual or company's goal for the portfolio. Who do you or your company need to persuade? That is your audience definition. It could be a potential customer or employer. It might be your tenure committee or student's parents. Maybe the audience includes art galleries or museums. To define the audience, ask the question, "who do I want to persuade with my portfolio?" Think of sample scenarios: my students' parents are looking at my Web portfolio, or potential clients are using my Web portfolio to build an opinion about my company's capabilities. Or, a gallery curator is looking at my Web portfolio to decide if my artwork is worthy of a professional venue. The tenure committee is reviewing my Web portfolio during the application process. Try to narrow down the potential visitors to your site and begin to focus on their needs. And remember, the Web portfolio provides an appearance that trickles into every audience we interact with, so make the experience something that you can be proud of professionally and socially.

Lynch and Horton (1999) serve up some important items to consider when developing user-centered design for the Web. Coupled with our Web portfolio mission, they establish a good set of general Web portfolio usability guidelines which are listed next. Think about Web sites which you recently have visited or examine a few before you read this section. Look to see if the Web sites have characteristics that make them usable and if they are user-centered in design.

Following is a list from Lynch and Horton (1999, pp. 14-18) that I have adapted to fit the Web portfolio application:

- **Provide clear navigation aids for users.** Specifically consistent icons, text, colors, and graphic schemes should provide a transparent and intuitive interface design. Simplicity becomes a priority when designing the Web portfolio. Showing off can be done with the portfolio files them-selves. The interface should not become a monster of complexity — for you or the user. When the navigation and interface overwhelm the content, the user gets confused. They do not know what to look at first or most. The navigation should never distract the user from concentrating on the work, so no blinking navigation and keep the interface motion to a minimum.

- **Eliminate dead end pages that lock in users.** Make sure that links to home, contact, and top level pages are included on every page. If the Web portfolio has dead ends, your presentation is dead! The life and death of the Web portfolio depends on its ability to work when it is supposed to work. The best way to root out dead links and problem pages is to go through the Web portfolio completely, accessing and testing each link and navigation element. You will do that later on in the process, but keep it in mind while you begin the creative process.

- **Provide direct access to the information users want.** Keep the hierarchal structure of your site based on your users' needs. Important items are top level and should be accessible throughout the site, regardless of the page. Don't turn the Web portfolio into a treasure hunt where the user has to search to find the golden content. Let access to the most important and most impressive work be immediate, if not faster. You want to engage the user by giving them what they are looking for.

- **Consider users' bandwidth, and design accordingly.** Users will not tolerate long delays. So keep the Shockwave Flash files lean. Optimize your graphics to be as small as possible, but look as good as they can without crippling user performance and creating a bad user experience. The Web portfolio may be your shot to get someone's attention. You don't want performance to issues to waste the opportunity. Spend time doing things right when developing the Web portfolio. Don't use extra large graphics and expect to scale them down later, the Web pages demand all text, graphics, motion, and animation items be to scale (the final size needed for output)

- **Ask for feedback and encourage dialog from the user.** This allows you to gain inquiries, comments, and interaction with your users. It could help build the communication ties between you and the person you are trying to persuade. Always include feedback forms and e-mail contacts on your site. Proactively work towards developing an ongoing relationship with your audience members. Adding feedback forms and e-mail links are a great way to allow the user to connect with you. Get a multitude of friends and family to visit the Web portfolio before the real "official launch" this way, bugs and problems will raise to the surface before the Web portfolio is unleashed on the critical work for hire audience.

Define Your User and Their Goals

Here is your chance to spend some time thinking about your audience. Define it in terms of who you need to inform, impress, and persuade with your Web portfolio. Does your audience consist of customers, prospects, parents, students, communities, or groups? Think about the answers to these questions and begin to jot down some rough notes. After some loose brainstorming, tighten the focus a bit and answer the following questions to establish some basic definitions for your user and your goals:

My Web portfolio will promote my:

The goals of this Web portfolio are:

My audience consists of:

My ultimate message to the user is:

The following are my responses to this exercise:

My Web portfolio will promote my:

design work, publishing projects, academic history, and abilities as a teacher and designer.

The goals of this portfolio are:

to educate my audience about my accomplishments and abilities and provide and entertaining and fun interactive experience.

My audience consists of:

students, colleagues, prospective clients, current clients, academic publishers, prospective colleges, schools, and universities.

My ultimate message to the user is:

I am an expert in communication design, computer graphics, and multimedia development. I am a dedicated teacher, designer, author, and consultant in communication arts.

With your audience defined and your initial goals for the user established, we are now ready to move forward and discuss the conceptualization process for developing your Web portfolio.

Concept

By now, you probably have some ideas swirling in your head. Let's begin to solidify them by explicitly defining the concept. A concept is a thought, notion, or idea. When you begin to develop your Web portfolio, concept is used to help drive design and ultimately determine appropriate content. Defining the concept of the site is the first step in a series of goal-driven decisions. Conceptualization will culminate with the creation of an outline-listing content.

Your first exercise in conceptualization is already complete. By completing the conceptualization exercise, you have defined an audience, you know what the portfolio is promoting, and you have a notion about your message and know who you want to persuade. Conceptualizing a Web portfolio starts out like thinking about writing something. When we write, the first steps are to define an audience and then define a purpose. We do this so that the writing has direction. The same steps must be taken with Web portfolios. Defining the audience is something we have addressed. Now we must explicitly define a purpose. The purpose lies in the concept.

Let's polish a loose concept to get it the next level. We will write out, in simple, general terms, the important components of our concept. To do this, let's put together a **concept statement**. The concept statement simply explains the **concept**, the proposed **navigation**, and the **expected assets** needed to pursue the project. It acts as a springboard for the brainstorming process and content development. Concepts are supported by content. To be utilized effectively, content must be categorized. That's where headers and sub-headers for navigation come into play. You should think about the main headers and the sub-headers as the signposts that guide your users through the Web portfolio. It is important to drill down to get the proper sequence of information into the right hierarchical order. Otherwise, you risk losing the user somewhere along the way.

Content consists of **graphic** and **multimedia assets** and **text assets**. Graphic and multimedia assets include: static images (photos and clip art), audio, animation, and motion graphics. Text assets include text/word processing items that populate the site, including text-based navigation elements, body copy, and other text-based content pages. Your resume is an example of a text-based asset if it is in the form of Web based html text on a page. If it is in Adobe PDF format, it would be considered a graphic asset because it is formatted into a single file without HTML editing capabilities. A text-based item is also considered a message, something that must be read and understood by the user. A photo is an example of a graphic asset. A text animation is an example of a multimedia asset. Let's start to get our content recognized and organized. The concept statement will help us move forward and get our content in an order. You should list your proposed main and sub navigation titles in the concept statement under Navigation. Then you will list the major text assets and major graphical and multimedia assets that you will have to prepare for the Web portfolio.

The concept statement allows you write out what you expect to publish in your Web portfolio. It is a rough statement of what you will need to get for the project. It provides a scope for you to polish and perfect as the Web portfolio process moves further.

A Word about Navigation Headers:

Develop the main categories and sub categories of the Web portfolio based on your expected content. These are **main** and **sub-navigation headers**. To keep things simple, we identify our main categories of information within the concept statement. These categories will become text or graphical navigation buttons. Each navigation and sub navigation category header will be a page with content.

Here is my concept statement starting with navigation items:

CONCEPT STATEMENT – John DiMarco//Web Portfolio

Concept: develop an interactive Web portfolio that showcases my design and art work, the work of my students and provides a forum for my scholarship and current publishing projects.

Navigation

about—main navigation

      CV — sub nav

      Contact — sub nav

portfolio—main navigation

      print and Web — sub nav

      motion graphics — sub nav

          digital art — sub nav

e-learning — sub nav

design lab — main navigation

          book projects — sub nav

          student gallery — sub nav

          links – sub nav

Items that I will need to gather or write (I may or may not use all of these):

Text Assets

- One paragraph of informational copy for a book page
- Main page has current news/topics
- Bio
- Educational philosophy
- Sample syllabi and class materials
- Published work information (details, testimonials, ISBN)
- Links to sites that I found inspirational or valuable

Graphic and Multimedia Assets

Items that I will need to gather create:

- My professional design and art work
- Student work in print, Web, and illustration
- Splash page -Flash intro with audio
- Home page artwork
- Header artwork (banners)

This exercise is aimed to provide a loose framework of potential items to use in your Web portfolio. Don't worry about getting everything down at this step. This is a starting point for the assembly of the portfolio structure. This may change and we may need to adapt our plan to the dynamics of the project. After this step, you will develop a detailed content list which will list every tangible asset that you must gather, write, or create.

Write Your Concept Statement

(Get as many ideas down as possible — remember the user. Make it easy for them to get to the important pieces of the your Web portfolio.)

Take a piece of paper and write the following words and proceed as shown in the previous concept statement example: **Concept; Navigation and Sub Navigation; Text Assets; Graphics and Multimedia Assets.**

Content Gathering

The assets that you place in your Web portfolio should be in coordination with your category headers (navigation and sub-navigation) and ultimately they should represent your skills and experience in a variety of forms. These skills and experience assets are most persuasive and have the greatest impact on presenting your expertise or the expertise of your company. These include, but are not limited to:

- Project samples
- Student work
- Art and design work
- Photos from professional events and presentations
- Project case studies
- Animations
- Video
- Audio clips
- Illustrations and graphic typography.
- Educational philosophy
- Career and Professional Goals
- Mission statement
- Research reports and papers
- Professional development plan

- References and recommendations
- Lesson plans

This list could span many pages. The content is up to you and your specific goals. It is important that you narrow down your content. You do not want include an overwhelming amount which is too much for you to handle in the development process. Try not to include content simply for having more content. Everything should have value to the viewer. Most importantly, you do not want include too little. It really is about quality over quantity. Yes, you want to show an assortment of materials. But the critical component to success is the quality of those materials. Don't give the user a reason to have a negative opinion about you or your work. You may think the work is great, but if it is borderline, get it to someone else more qualified than you for a second opinion. Seek out assistance from a teacher, counselor, friend, or relative that is qualified to assess your work. It is nice to get compliments, if you do not receive critical feedback you may be presenting something that is poor or may even be offending. I do not want to scare you and I want you to be free and open with your content presentation. But remember, the Web portfolio has professional goals and its content has an impact on how the author is viewed. So to be certain that content is good or should I say appropriate, use your best judgment and if needed the judgment of someone more experienced in your field.

The assets that you use in your site should present your value, communicate a message, and they should make a point. Remember that this is a narrative. A narrative tells a story, the Web portfolio narrative needs to be backed by facts. Keep outside content such as links to external sites updated and make sure that the content presented at the linked site is appropriate. Do not link to images, papers, artwork, music, animations, and other media that is not yours without providing credit to the original author (blind links). Obviously do not post materials that are not yours on your Web portfolio. This is an infringement of copyright law as well as a form of academic plagiarism. Doing this will quickly reduce your credibility and tarnish your appearance.

Another issue that I would like to bring up is the use of clipart. Now, some clipart is okay in certain situations for certain Web portfolio authors. However, in the case of artists and designers it is important that they use clipart sparingly, if at all, and effectively as an iconic element in their designs. The ineffective use of bad clipart by artists and designers hurts their appearance as skilled experienced designers. As well, here is another reason to eliminate the usage of low impact, low quality clipart; it just clutters up the interactive space and takes away from your important content. Make your content have a purpose. Content should help achieve your goals to make your final design more focused, potent, and persuasive. A better choice for images that tell a story is to use stock photos or photographs taken by the author either using a digital camera or a film camera. Before using clipart, think about using an image that is photographic as opposed to an image that is weak. Clipart only works when it is used consistently and sparingly in the design. Most clipart needs to be edited to make it more appealing. This can be a tedious process and digital illustration software such as Adobe Illustrator, CorelDRAW, or Macromedia freehand must be used. This makes using bitmapped photographic images even more appealing. They can be easily edited, cropped, and corrected for the Web using Adobe Photoshop or Macromedia fireworks. For novices to computer graphics, the process is much simpler and can be done more quickly than manipulating vector clipart. As well, the control that you get when you take your own photographs is amazing. It allows you to tackle any creative problem by generating usable, effective content. You should try it for at least some pieces of your Web portfolio.

Text as Content

Your Web portfolio will have two types of text items. Items to be read, printed, and downloaded or body copy, navigation items, and captions.

Items that are to be read, printed, and downloaded should be contained in the same page and not "chunked" into smaller pages. Pages such as your resume, lesson plans, mission statements, and philosophies should be single Web pages that provide scrollable text content. For critical text in the Web portfolio, use small pieces of text. Be sure to scrutinize the clarity and conciseness of the copy you present in the Web site. Body copy, navigation items, and captions should be written is small pieces or "chunks" to insure that users have direct access to specific information (Horton, 2000).

Text also includes links within your Web portfolio. Your links can send the user to another site entirely, or you can have a pop-up window launch and load a micro Web site (microsite) while your Web portfolio stays open in the background. When the launched site window is closed, your Web site will be available as originally launched. Think of the Web sites that are important to your inspirations as a professional. You can present links to research or to your institution. Links can go to organizations and societies of which you are a member. You might link to student Web sites or sites of other colleagues. All text-based content is editable and may need updating when content changes.

It is important to have HTML based text in your Web portfolio. This will allow search engines to find your site easier than if no HTML text existed and all navigation and text components were made of graphics. Plan to have HTML text in your Web site. Using all graphical text will create difficult revisions later on in the life span of the Web portfolio. Things that change often must be HTML text. An example of this would be a résumé presented on a Web portfolio. The resume will change and the author will need to change the text over and over again. Keeping it flexible will be critical to making on-demand updates. Now that you understand the types of content a bit more, let us move forward and start to develop a content list.

Create Your Content List

The content list breaks down assets into a list consisting of all the content pieces. These are things that you expect to put into the Web portfolio based on the concept statement. The pieces must be created, developed, recorded, animated, and then collected for arrangement into a hierarchical structured outline. This structure will be the skeleton of the Web portfolio. The Web portfolio should be content rich. When the content becomes massive, it is hard to manage. The task of keeping track of everything that will go into the portfolio is simplified with asset organization. Confusion and mistakes are lessened by following a structure.

Now it is time to create your detailed content list. In this stage, you write down all of the tangible assets that you will need to gather, write, create, or design. This allows you to begin to see the scope and volume that your content will represent. Also, you can begin to get a sense of impact your Web portfolio will have on the user. The user wants content. You want to engage and persuade the user. Are you giving them content? Will the content persuade them to act accordingly in your desired goals? The content list will provide some justification to these questions.

Making a content list is an important task in the Web portfolio development process. It requires you to brainstorm and list every asset and text piece into an informal list. This list consists of raw materials. Don't be too concerned with the organization of the list right now. Be sure to use the concept statement as a starting point for developing the content list. Later, you will take the content list and assemble it into a comprehensive outline.

You can use a word processing program such as Microsoft Word to type out your list. It will save time and will be editable later on. Once the list is typed, the pieces of information can be arranged to help you better understand the site concepts and components. If the document is electronic the text can be copied and pasted into the right spot. Or you can do it the low tech way. Write it out and type it out later. Whichever method you prefer and is most comfortable for you is best. I'll describe the process using the old fashioned way. Take a sheet of paper and make a line down the center. On the left side, write "Graphical Assets" and "Multimedia Assets", and on the other side write "Text Assets". List every item that you want to put in your Web portfolio on either side. Now keep in mind, this is a brainstorming exercise, so some items that make this list may not make the Web site. This is due to a variety of reasons. Some items you may label as outdated or not worthy. Other items may not be complete and still need additional work before posting to the site. This list helps you think out the content. Next, you will organize the content and weed out damaging items. Remember, this list is being used to get you started. You can always, and should always be posting new content to your Web portfolio. The portfolio is all about content. The more content, the better the user experience.

Create Your Content Outline

Now, you have a rough list of content. You need to refine it. To do this, we create a content outline. The content outline will have category headers that represent main navigation. Under each main navigation header, you will place

Figure 2.1. Sample content list

Graphic and Multimedia Assets	Text Assets
Photo of me	Syllabi in Word
Introduction animation	Personal statement
CV in PDF format	Office hours

the appropriate asset from your content list. In the last exercise we took a general approach to listing information. Now, we will manipulate our information into a more precise structure.

To create the content outline you must first list out your main navigation header categories — refer to the concept statement for your previous ideas (I used about/portfolio/design lab in my concept statement). Under each header category, you will place appropriate sub headers and then list items from your content list. Place the appropriate item under the main or sub-navigation header.

Here is an example of how to start:

> **About** — main navigation
> > Photo of me
> **Curriculum Vitae** — sub-navigation
> > CV in PDF format
> **Contact** — e-mail link

Notice how about, is main navigation. This means that about it at that of the hierarchical structure. Curriculum Vitae and contact are sub navigation. You want use this structure to develop the content list fully so that it reflects all the components of your Web portfolio.

Once you have the headers filled in, put a number next to each header to signify its importance in the hierarchy of your site. For example, if you think that your biography is most important, make it number 1 (my sequence is about-1-, portfolio-2-, design lab-3). If you feel contact is the least important, make it the last number in your sequence, or make it a sub-navigation if it sits below a category in structure. I did this by making "About" a main navigation and contact a sub-navigation component sitting under "About". The Web portfolio is built to be nonlinear in design. This means that the user can pretty much go anywhere in the site from no more than two pages deep. Rather than a linear site that requires the user to go through the site in a predetermined sequence. Your navigation will be nonlinear, but it still needs order to be represented consistently throughout the Web site. The numerical order will help you to establish a perceived order for you to follow and will create a consistent point of view and navigation order. What is of paramount importance is that categories (headers) are clearly defined so they do not have any overlap which could confuse communication (Kristoff & Satran, 1995). This structure allows you create a literal page by page outline of the Web portfolio. I realize this process is difficult. But it is so necessary to gain organization and truly grasp content.

A Note on Headers

Keep the headers in the same order on each page. The numbering will help you remember the order. The user can go to any link they want. The site is non-sequential, but you will use a numbering system to track the pages. The more ordering you do at this stage, the easier it is to make a flowchart in the next phase of development.

Here is a portion of the content outline for John DiMarco's Web Portfolio:

CONTENT LIST BY PAGE SAMPLE

1. **Home Page**
   - Faded graphic
   - Welcome/Splash text
2. **Splash Page**
   - Motion graphics/Communication tools introduction
3. **About** — main navigation
   - Photo of me (content needed)
   - 3.1 **Curriculum Vitae or Resume** – sub navigation
      - CV or Resume in PDF format (content needed)
   - 3.2 **Contact** – e-mail link
4. **Portfolio** – main navigation
   - Graphic for page
   - 4.1 **Print and Web**
      - **List all names of work pieces**

Print eg: DiMarco Associates identity brochure

LIU Art Department Poster

Heartbeat of The city, TV show Media Kit

Thumbnails for the pages

Web eg: Canon and the imaging industry screenshot

Canon IR flash animation screenshot

Thumbnails for the pages

4.2 Motion Graphics

Canon and the imaging industry motion graphics work

Canon IR flash motion graphics work

Thumbnails for the pages

5. Digital art

Digital sign 1

Digital sign 2

Her eyes

Thumbnails for the pages

6. Design Lab

6.1 Book Projects

Book description and jacket cover-links to .pdf flyer and Amazon.com

6.2 Student Gallery

Student illustration (20 works)

Student Page Layout (12 works)

Student Web Design (10 works)

Thumbnails for the pages

6.3 Links

List the links (50)

Link headings:

Publications

Galleries/Museums

Art/Design resources

Vendors/Technical info

Files/Tutorials

Figure 2.2. Sample content outline

ABOUT	PORTFOLIO	DESIGN LAB
<u>curriculum vitae</u>	<u>print and Web</u>	<u>book projects</u>
<u>contact</u>	<u>motion graphics</u>	<u>student gallery</u>
	<u>digital art</u>	<u>links</u>

Make sure that you descriptively name and number each item. Categorization, grouping, and listing are important here. When you complete the content outline, you have a nice checklist for you to keep track of your content items. Keep the content outline handy so that you can refer to it when you are creating your Web portfolio site. Many times I have seen students get confused and literally lost while creating a Web portfolio without using their content outline. What typically happens is they eventually get so frustrated that they must get back to basics and prepare the content outline again. After that, they usually listen to my recommendations to use content outlines liberally. You can never have too many organizational tools when you are creating a Web portfolio.

I provided samples and thorough description of how to develop, on paper, a list of content items which will be used in the Web portfolio. Now you should go through the process of creating a content outline. Refer back to the entries you wrote in on the content list you created earlier. Put the items in a simple order as shown earlier. You may want use a pencil if you are going to use a low-tech method such as paper. You want to make changes easily — and there will be changes. This is a difficult process because you need to get your thoughts together and then simplify them so that they are clear. With a content outline you want to develop a roadmap for guidance as you begin hunting and gathering all of the assets that will be part of the Web portfolio. The ordered list you create will help in the development of a flowchart. With the flowchart, you will execute the critical step of information design. The design of information is what gives the Web portfolio its technical structure and narrative impact. If the information is presented in such a way that it does not provide a basic narrative about the author, the connection with the user will not be as strong and ultimately appearance, persuasion, and effectiveness will suffer.

The Web Portfolio as a Content Management Tool

The Web portfolio serves a dual purpose when it comes to content. As we realize that the Web portfolio acts as a presentation platform in a communication media, we should also understand the value of the Web portfolio as a content management tool. As a content management tool, the Web portfolio provides a place for information storage and retrieval. The storage and retrieval features provided by Web portfolios are valuable because they are portable. This portability allows the author or his or her clients to access this content management system simply by using FTP passwords. File transfer protocol (FTP) allows access to the Web portfolio host fileserver and any allowable files. By accessing the fileserver anywhere, the Web portfolio acts like a portable hard drive. Personal or client content can be stored in hidden folders not accessible to the public. This off-line storage is valuable archive for content. As server space continues to go down in price and up in capacity, the Web portfolio becomes more and more attractive as a content management tool for dynamic storage and retrieval. Obviously, the accessibility to network computers must be available to make this concept real. As we have seen, wireless technology and high-bandwidth access have provided a network solution to consumers in most technology savvy regions in the world. Hopefully, areas of the world that are slow to meet the expectations of the information society will leapfrog towards connection sooner than later. When that happens, the Web portfolio will offer the advantages of using itself as a content management tool to users who may not have local hard disk storage capabilities and stable residences. The Web portfolio allows virtual storage combined with global presentation.

Review and Conclusion

Before we move forward, let's briefly review where you should be at this point. You have learned that a Web portfolio is a communication tool that helps someone create a positive appearance by providing a platform for presentation of skills and experience through text, graphics, and multimedia. The goal of the Web portfolio, as you have learned, is to persuade the audience members who are also known as users. Our goal as Web portfolio authors is to create an experience which fosters action by the user. The action will hopefully result in work for hire. In the information society, the Web portfolio will become more important in success for people of all disciplines, backgrounds, and occupations.

In the Web portfolio process, so far you have defined your user and the goals of the Web portfolio. You have brainstormed to create a concept statement, content list, and content outline. At this point, you should be ready to take this base information and refine it to give it hierarchal structure that can be translated into a Web site. We will now go forward and examine information design.

Chapter III

Information Design

Introduction

This chapter provides explanation and steps on transforming ideas into information architecture. The main emphasis is on developing a framework of content that focuses on priority, simplicity, and organization.

Priority and simplicity are terms that become synonymous with good information design. By priority, I refer to prioritizing the information into a structure that will enable the user to gain access, interaction, entertainment, value, and connection with your Web portfolio. Prioritizing information relies on information design. You have already taken steps to begin the process of information design and organization has occurred. By creating a content outline, you organized the proposed content that will be presented in your Web portfolio. Refinement of the organized content relies upon navigation and usability to be thoughtful to the audience requirements.

Simplicity refers to keeping navigation and usability simple and organized so that no mistakes can be made when traveling throughout the Web portfolio. Confusion in the Web portfolio cannot be tolerated by the user. He or she will not stand for not getting what they want, which is content. If the need for content discovery is not met, the connection and the communication have failed. The scary part is that we may never know if the user has had a bad experience. Later on in this book, we talk more deeply about usability from the viewpoint of Jakob Nielsen, the usability guru of the Web. We will also examine usability testing for our own Web portfolios to see how the user might feel when they hit our URL. One thing that we want to keep in the forefront of our navigation and usability design is that users need to get to where they're going through navigation as simply as possible. This is nonnegotiable. Therefore, creating an easy to navigate, usable site is more difficult and then dumping loads of unorganized materials on the user.

Let us examine the components that help insure usability and good design in the Web portfolio. The guidelines in the next sections can help you develop an organized structure that will help you in the rest of the Web portfolio development steps. Remember, the development of the Web portfolio is an individual, subjective experience that provides a structured narrative in Web form.

Structure

Kristoff and Satran state: "As an information designer, you are a gatekeeper. Even though users make their own choices, it's up to you what choices they have; what they see first, where they can go, and what they don't see at all" (1995, p. 31). The idea of gate keeping presents an interesting metaphor when we talk about Web portfolio design. As the author of the Web portfolio and as an information designer in the process we are gatekeepers to our own cyber appearance, credentials list, and identity. More importantly, however, we are gatekeepers to effective communication with the user. We must understand the responsibility we have to be conduits in getting the user to learn about us and to persuade the user to recognize our skills and abilities. We are gatekeepers to success with the user.

Web Portfolio Information Organization

Organizing information that we put into the Web portfolio gets done on several levels. We completed one of those levels when we conceptualized and created the scope documents. Using the scope documents as a basis for further refinement of the Web portfolio content information, we now must add structure and organization to the accumulated information. The structure and organization in the next steps will be more rigid than the loosely developed concept and content documents created in the previous chapter. In the next phase of Web portfolio development, the technical aspects will require you to organize the content into a visual diagram. You have done much of the technical work of organizing information by creating a content outline; now you will refine the content outline into a flowchart. Before you do that, let us talk a little bit about how the flowchart as a metaphor for a skeleton. The skeleton is a frame. The flowchart is the frame of the Web portfolio site.

Flowcharts as Skeletons

Hierarchical presentation and organization of information are the most important aspects of Web portfolio and all Web design structure. To develop information in organized, hierarchal form we must build a skeleton for the Web portfolio. The flowchart is the skeleton. Just as a programmer uses pseudocode, a filmmaker writes a storyboard and shot list, and a painter makes a rough paper sketch, we too as Web portfolio authors, must map out our project. Information design provides a data structure that is crucial to Web development. Navigation, usability and organization are connected components in creating a successful Web portfolio site structure.

The creation of the flowchart is based on the content outline. However, this is the time when you can evaluate the relationships between the navigation and sub-navigation to determine if the best choice of structure and organization are being used for the site. Remember the process we went through. We listed categories of content. Under these categories were listed subcategories of the types of assets that would reside to represent these categories. When organizing information, you will need to try some different arrangements to see how things fit under categories. As I mentioned earlier in this text, this process of information gathering and categorization is dynamic and requires several passes through examination to validate and refine the structure.

Sometimes it is difficult to figure out how to arrange information. By using categories and subcategories, you can begin to arrange information into a visible structure. By creating a visible structure on paper, you allow the final design to have an effective invisible structure. This invisible structure has to work in a positive way. Kristof and Satran (1995) explained that as an information designer you can impose a point of view that makes the product interesting. The advantage to creating a visual structure document is that we do not sacrifice our goals to persuade the user and impress them by inadvertently structuring the information of our Web portfolio site in an indirect way. The site structure documents such as flowcharts give illustration to the guts of the user options when traveling the site. The flowchart becomes important in getting an overall sense of how this information product will work. The flowchart gives a clear picture of navigation during the planning and development stages.

Navigation

Navigation is steering for the user. Just as a captain guides a ship, the user will navigate your Web portfolio in search of content and a positive experience. Navigation should be simplified to provide seamless usability and serve to communicate a functional hierarchy. It is your job to provide clear, direct navigation to all your Web portfolio offers. The navigation you provide will be in the form of hyperlinks. The structure of the site dictates the navigation elements. Structure and navigation work hand-in-hand in providing pathways for the user to access information in the most direct way. Navigation that has indirect access to assets should be eliminated or never conceptualized. Sometimes novice developers and novice designers waste precious time on making extravagant navigation that does not serve the purpose of helping the user access information. We must take care to fight the urge to make navigation overwhelming to the site and to the content. Navigation needs to be transparent in existence but evident when needed.

Navigation Guidelines

Navigation systems are essential components to visual representation of information on a Web site. Better known as buttons or links, navigation allows the user accessibility to the site content. The design of the navigation requires an understanding of the structure of the site. By creating a comprehensive content outline, you should have a pretty good understanding of the basic site structure. An information flowchart defines a product's structure. Once a flowchart exists, a lot of the navigation design work has already been done (Kristoff & Satran, 1995).

In their book *Interactivity by Design*, Kristoff and Satran (1995) offer three main thoughts to good navigation design.

> *Minimize travel: create the simplest and shortest path between two points, minimize depth: create a hierarchy with the fewest possible levels (extra levels mean extra travel steps), minimize redundancy: avoid creating multiple paths to the same place from the same screen, this causes confusion about which to use.* (Kristoff & Satran, 1995, p.42)

Navigation relies on access. According to Kristoff and Satran (1995), there are two levels of access:

- Access to a new topic (category)
- Access within a topic (sub category)

In this book, I refer to topics as headers or categories — main navigation, specifically. Sub topics are sub navigation and are placed under main navigation items. Keeping the user occupied is easy if you provide them access that is obstacle free.

The clarity of access and navigation is something that tends to get lost in modern Web designs that overdo navigation. Navigation should not be inconspicuous to the user. It should not be so blatant that it distracts the user from the content.

We will now look at the factors which affect usability.

Usability

The user experience for our Web portfolio project relies on persuasive communication and exquisite presentation of our skills and experience. If the Web portfolio has ambiguous, difficult usability issues, the experience and the attempt at persuasion will fail. Usability cannot be achieved simply with repetition. It must be a thoughtful hierarchy. True, we want navigation to be super consistent throughout the Web portfolio site. We do not want to sacrifice cost or time by creating redundant designs that do not serve our needs, simply to think that we have covered the bases when it comes to usability.

There are three important usability issues to focus on when you design your Web portfolio (Kristof & Satran, 1995):

- **Keep the interface and navigation clutter free.** Resist the temptation to put something on your page that has no content or navigation value. Do not be redundant and duplicate the same controls on the same page. This wastes time, effort, and screen real estate. Moreover, cluttered interfaces can be a cause for user confusion.

- **Use shortcuts to get to your most impressive assets.** Do not wait around and expect the user to hunt for your portfolio pieces or your highest regarded work, provide a quick route right to the work. Get creative on the lowest, simplest levels and focus to design access that will move the user towards what is most important. For example, during my last Web portfolio design, I placed publications as the first content that is seen when the main navigation page is loaded. I did this because I recently published an edited book. I felt that my users, who include academic colleagues, potential clients, and students, would want to know about my recent publication. I feel that the accomplishment of producing an edited book was one that I needed to communicate to my audience immediately. As you assemble content, you will notice that some things are more important than others are. Make these items prominent in their access routes. You want to keep that in mind as your information design of evolves. As well, when you have new accomplishments you would like to have them immediately available on the most accessed Web page in your Web portfolio. This page is obviously the main page. However, you can structure the site to work so that after any initial animation or motion graphic, the site will go to any page or location that you decide.

- **Give the user escape routes.** Let the user control the multimedia elements in the site with standardized, intuitive controls. Avoid expectations that the user will migrate to the navigation controls of the assumed Web browser—they won't. Provide close buttons and on/off controls for audio, video, and pop up windows whenever you can. I realize that sometimes attention to this level of detail requires extra time and effort on the project. Many times, these details are left out. We should make an effort to try and cater the experience to the users' tastes. Escape routes should always be on the menu.

Pre-Evaluation of Usablity

We will discuss usability in more detail after we create the Web site. We will test the usability of the site against a set of usability guidelines developed by Nielsen and Norman and adapted by me for use on the Web portfolio. By doing an evaluation of the completed Web portfolio, you can learn which components of your Web portfolio are failing the usability test. Testing the usability of the Web portfolio after it is up sounds backwards, right? Actually, we should be thinking about usability before and after the Web portfolio is designed. Why? Because the process has so many interactive components that are needed for successful user interaction and communication that usability must be addressed throughout. So here is a little piece of usability investigation that you can perform on the information that you have already brainstormed. You will repeat this exercise later on in the text after you have created your Web portfolio and uploaded it to the Internet. But for now, let's examine the information design components that you should question about your Web portfolio site with regards to organization, structure, and your idea of effective usability. Questions surrounding visual aesthetics are stripped out and saved for post Web portfolio evaluation. Think of the following questions in respect to access for the user. We have not gotten to the visual stage yet. Right now concentrate on user access and making it a simple as possible.

Ask yourself what the user would say if asked these questions of the Web portfolio design and usability based on the content outline and flowchart:

- In this Web portfolio, is there a visible, clear navigation path to the body of work?

- Was the navigation presented in easy, understandable terms?
- Did you feel you had control of the interface and portfolio content?
- Was it easy to quit out of the Web portfolio pop up windows?
- Did you require help at any time while using the Web portfolio site?

Thinking about these questions before you fully design the Web portfolio site will help you keep a grip on usability. Did you discover something that doesn't seem right with your anticipated information design? If so, simply make a change before you create the flowchart. After creating the flowchart, ask the questions again to see if the skeleton is solid and provides access to content in the most direct routes available.

Now let's map out how the Web portfolio site will work by creating a visual diagram or flowchart.

Create Your Flowchart

The flowchart is the product of information design. It provides a top down structure for the entire Web site and allows the designer to estimate the approximate number of Web pages that are needed to accommodate the content. The flowchart also allows organization of navigation and external links. This scope paperwork becomes extremely important when designing a site with lots of pages and enhances usability through critical vision focusing on how the site will work. The structure of a Web site is planned on paper first to insure that functionality and user convenience is consistent and correct. The structure planning results in a flowchart. Every box in the flowchart represents a page. Every link in the flowchart is access to a page, URL, or content.

Use the content outline to work from as you develop the flowchart. Each header or category is going to be a top level item in the flowchart. All content will be a sub level item, also known as the subcategory. Here is an easy way to plot out the flowchart: Use boxes for pages (main navigation/major categories), lines for links, and italic text for loose content. Use indentation to branching of topics within subcategories.

Boxes for pages/main navigation represent containers for content. Organize the site structure further by expanding the flowchart with a branch off each box with

Figure 3.1. Sample flowchart (The flowchart allows for a visual inventory of pages within the Web portfolio. Creating a flowchart allows you to show the hierarchal relationships within your site. This flowchart is an abridged version of the flowchart used in my portfolio. Counting up the boxes will provide a tentative page quantity for the site.)

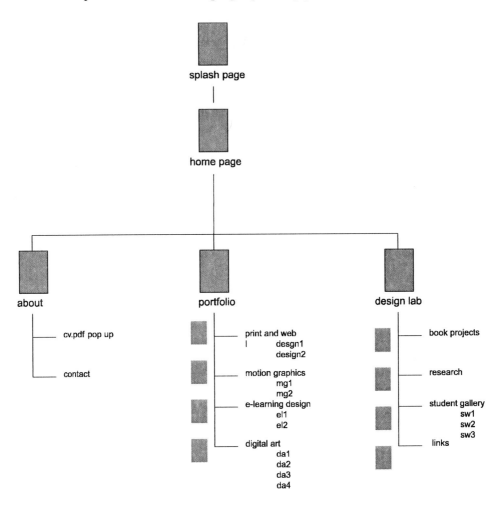

lines listing the content of each page. This will allow you to see a larger view of the entire Web portfolio on paper. It is important that you make the most expanded version of the flowchart that you can. The expanded flowchart will help as you design the Web portfolio and add and delete content.

Count up the boxes and triangles to get a tentative Web page count for the portfolio site. This counts as important. It gives you a basis to understand how large or how small the Web portfolio project will be. Later on, as you develop

Web sites for other purposes, this technique will help you again and again to gain reference to page count. Also, the flowchart is valuable as a visual reference while designing and updating the Web portfolio throughout its life span.

Review and Conclusion

Now that we have the basic scope documents of what the site will be about and how the site will be structured, we will establish how the site will look. In the next chapter we begin the visual design process.

To this point you have worked in a logical, calculated way. This methodology is important because you want to realize a clean, calculated route for our users to learn about our professional capabilities. You have taken care to bring information to the simplest levels of presentation on paper, in outline form and using a flowchart. Now, you must continue to take care to bring information to the simplest levels using visual tools. What you do not want is for navigation to overwhelm content in any way. Computer graphics and multimedia software has revolutionized the way we create content. You must respect the tools, but more importantly respect the design of the Web portfolio so that it does not have a lack of balance when it comes to navigation and ornamental items versus pure content. You want the appearance mixture to favor pure content. You want navigation to act as a conduit, a threshold, and a pathway to content. Navigation can never be a distraction to content.

Up to this point, you have made some important decisions about the Web portfolio. Although computers have not been discussed yet, you have laid the groundwork for taking information and putting it into a hierarchical structure that you can now begin to present visually. If you have been following along in the text, you should now know what the Web portfolio is going to contain, who your target user is, and what your goals are in creating this multimedia product. Now that we have discussed information design, let us explore visual design.

Chapter IV

Visual Design

Introduction

This chapter explores visual design and the methods used to develop Web site storyboards and screen creation. This process is a critical step in the Web portfolio design process because it enables visual persuasion and allows for a cohesive composition throughout the product. Many Web portfolio sites are poorly designed visually. The reasons surrounding this are too many to be discussed fully in this text. However, we will take a proactive approach and explain the qualities that are important in good visual design of Web pages. In addition, we will look at some bad Web portfolio design attributes to get a sense of what is not quite effective when it comes to visual persuasion. The notion of bad design is subjective, but also, design has objective, measurable attributes that lead to visual quality. Many bad designs come from non-art and non-visual disciplines. Technology experts may be poor designers because they focus too much on technology bells and whistles and less on the user. However, design is emergent and eventually everyone can get better with practice and exposure to design.

I hope this chapter will act as a catalyst for people who already have a Web portfolio to assess the quality of their design. I would like the new readers to begin to build good habits in their actions as visual and communication designers. Regardless of discipline, when you create a Web portfolio you become a designer. You are developing an information product that serves to solve a communication problem. Therefore, you are playing the role of information designer, communication designer, and graphic designer. These are roles which you must take seriously because they affect persuasion and appearance. Making your Web portfolio site look good is as important as feeling good about it, because if it looks good and you feel good about it, you'll tell people about it. Remember, the goal of the Web portfolio is to promote you and your accomplishments, so looks count.

The idea that the visual rhetoric of the Web portfolio is vital to its success is supported by Kimball (2003):

> *Just like words, appearance can play and important role in how a piece of work is assessed. This is particularly true in a Web portfolio, because the Web is such a visually intensive medium. The Web gives authors tremendous flexibility to design have the documents look, any appearance of the documents can make a big impact on how readers perceive the content and the author.* (p. 25)

Kimball's point cannot be clearer. Visual design effects user perceptions. He also suggests that the established Web design principles of "subtlety, consistency, easy navigation, legibility, and a clear page design" guide you through your Web portfolio page designs. We reinforce these suggested principles extensively throughout the text. As your experience with Web portfolio design increases, so will your fluency with visual design. Remember that the Web portfolio provides an appearance for you as a professional and a specialist in your field. Ineffective communication caused by poor visual design will result in a lack of credibility.

Now, we need to turn our content outline pages and flowchart into site storyboards and develop a style of our own. This process ties in our brainstorming activities with visual design. We are beginning to establish a look to our Web portfolio.

Style

The visual decisions you make about the look, feel, and experience established within your Web portfolio all contribute to style. Ultimately, the content and framework that supports the assets and text will define the style. Style and its connection to the Web portfolio are important because it contributes to identity. The identity of the Web portfolio is critical to establishing the appearance of the author. We brought the topic of identity up several times in this text but now we are going to expand upon it.

Identity defines the Web portfolio. Different identities are needed for different purposes. For example, a designer needs an identity that projects an image that clicks with to her target audience. If the designer specializes in pharmaceutical marketing design, he or she must project a Web portfolio that has clean typographic stature, vivid photographic elements, and an aura of professionalism that is felt the moment you enter the site. If the designer focuses on the fashion or entertainment industries, he or she must adapt to a style that fits eloquently into popular culture. This may mean designing towards a certain target audience to gain acceptance as a worthy partner in design.

The style needed for educator is quite different from that of the cutting-edge designer. Depending on discipline, educators need to think seriously about their own style and how it will be blended into the Web portfolio. The style issues that challenge educators seem to be to achieve the goals of the institutional audience while feeding their own personal stylistic desires.

I have found that Web portfolios designed by artists seem to be good at meeting individual and institutional style parameters. In my research and unobtrusive observation of many other educator Web portfolios in the technology disciplines, I found that the sites seem to lack personal identity and were boring or unattractive. I have noticed that a higher level of style linked to identity is seen in the Web portfolios of teachers, those specifically in the discipline of education. My observations also revealed many poor designs by teachers in

Figure 4.1. Style sample — John Fekner (A simple interface gateways the user to wealth of audio, video, and still image content. Professor Fekner integrated video into the Web portfolio successfully in the late 1990s. He deeply explored QuickTime movie compression schemes needed for quality output at multiple bandwidths.)

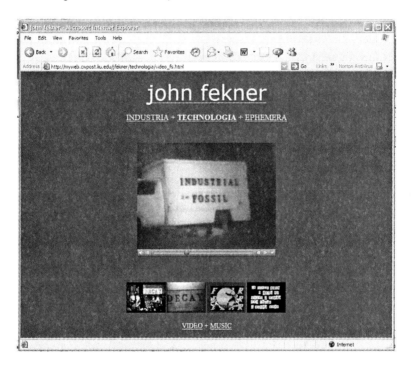

both K-12 and higher education. Again, my interpretation of poor design is completely subjective. However, I do base my ideas on the principles of art and visual design that I received at the Masters level and through years of working in the fields of computer graphics and digital design. The poor designs that I noticed were typically bad in fundamental artistic areas including type, color, proximity, scale, contrast, composition, abuse of clipart, and use of poor interface elements such as blinking text or excruciatingly annoying animations.

Let's look at some good examples of style and design in Web portfolios.

myweb.cwpost.liu.edu/jfekner

In artist John Fekner's artist and educator Web portfolio, titled INDUSTRIA + TECHNOLOGIA + EPHEMERA, the goal was to produce a site that was heavy in multimedia and artistic content. Professor Fekner explained to me that he wanted his Web portfolio to have a style that was parallel to his artistic style. His artistic style is one of mixing media and technology to produce work that revealed his passion and sorrow for things within society that he cannot control. This is evidenced in his body of work in the areas of graffiti art, original music, and public display.

Observation of John Fekner's Web portfolio reveals a media rich experience that evokes emotion and wonderment about how the artist came to create his work. Professor Fekner revealed that generating thought-provoking feelings and providing an emotional experience through media were part of the design plan. The main navigation is original in its vocabulary, which are postmodern terms that have crept into the life of the artist. Examination of the words Industria, Technologica, and Ephemera in the context of Professor Fekner's Web portfolio reveals that each one leads to a separate section of media. Industria, refers to images representing John Fekner's graffiti and public display art. Content includes outdoor stencils that were spray-painted in the New York City area from 1976 through 1985. Still images are set in a simple left side frame set. When clicked, the individual images load in the main section of the Web page. In the Technologica section, videos and music are prominently displayed in simple, easy to navigate text-based menus. The Technologica section provides a robust multimedia experience filled with QuickTime movies of Fekner's new media video art. Also featured are QuickTime sound clips that provide snippets of original music written, performed, and produced by John Fekner. In the Ephemera section, Professor Fekner has sub navigation linking to a resume, poems, and a personal abstract. The body of work presented in this Web portfolio is a great example of how an academic and artist can use technology for the purpose of art and identity.

www.soultooth.com

Looking at designer Tommy Spero's portfolio, www.soultooth.com, you see the identity of the designer shines through. The Web portfolios style is highly effective and meets the goals of the author by explicitly reaching out to a targeted audience of advertising agencies and high-end design shops. The site is unique because it does target the user by specifically presenting categories relating to the user. The main navigation categories include: on-air, online, offline, and contact. From the start, this site is easy to understand and easy to

Figure 4.2.   Style sample — Tommy Spero, SoulTooth Designs (This robust site combines motion graphics and graphic design in an engaging Flash-based format.)

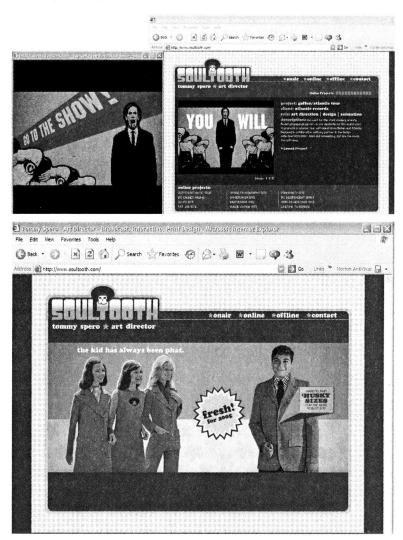

navigate. Usability is high due to an integrated interface that provides a wealth of work that is easily viewed and easily accessed. The interface is elegant while somewhat edgier in its theme and identity elements. The use of color, including brown, pink, and magenta with retro photography on the homepage give this site a memorable look and feel. The site content includes dozens of samples of design work created for broadcast, print, and new media.

Tommy Spero's Web portfolio, soultooth.com was built using Macromedia Flash. The simplicity behind the operational features of the site can be attributed to thoughtfulness during the content development, information architecture, and design stages of the project. The site is a great example of individualized, audience appropriate style with exceptionally usable functionality. The complexity of this site design cannot be seen from screenshots or even from visiting the site. However, soultooth.com is an advanced Web portfolio in the production methods used to create it.

www.portfoliovillage.com/kimdimarco

Special educator and kindergarten teacher Kimberly DiMarco had specific goals when she created her Web portfolio. As a kindergarten teacher, Mrs. DiMarco wanted to have a Web portfolio that was fun and showed a thematic metaphor that included crayons. Creatively, Mrs. DiMarco used in interface in a Web portfolio made of crayons. When rolling over the crayons, a line rolled out with the navigation text. This clever idea is a good example of paying close attention to a style that will appeal to a target audience.

Figure 4.3. Style sample — Kimberly DiMarco (This theme-based Web portfolio works to demonstrate knowledge and experience fostering educational philosophy and teaching standards based curriculums.)

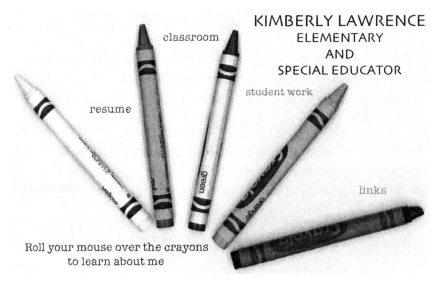

The style of the site was important to Mrs. DiMarco for several reasons. When discussing the history of the site, Mrs. DiMarco explained that the site was needed to act as evidence of professional growth and lifelong learning and would be submitted in the future when she applied for tenure and promotion. Also, the site would be viewed by parents in order to get to know her and to get a feeling of her style as a teacher. Because she understood her audience, Mrs. DiMarco was able to gather the appropriate content to meet her goals. Included in her Web portfolio are her teaching philosophy, examples of lesson plans, photos of her and her students (which she receive parental and district permission to use), a resume, and a short biography. This site was instrumental in helping Mrs. DiMarco when she graduated from student teaching and applied for real-world teaching positions. She explained, the advantages of showing a Web portfolio were evident in the positive comments she received during interviews. Having the Web portfolio gave her a competitive advantage when pursuing a teaching position.

www.richardkirkmills.com

Rick Mills is an artist and educator who is highly active in public art projects. When setting out to develop a Web portfolio, Rick was concerned with exhibiting the proper style that aligned with his personal mission as a public artist and appealed aesthetically to himself and his audience. The site opens with a simple flash animation showing a sequence of images complemented by a soothing soundtrack. The theme of the site resides in nature, and the natural feelings, emotions, and curiosities elicited by the art of Rick Mills. Visual content and its tasteful yet efficient presentation was paramount to Professor Mills when he planned the site. A fluid style is achieved through the use of color that uses soft tones on different pages. Photographs of art work alone and with natural environments constituted a large portion of the site's content. Professor Mills uses simple navigation which included contact, history, projects, a professional section, and finally a link to important resources. Additionally, a resume rounds out the site to make it an effective vehicle to communicate the accomplishments, ideas, and artwork. When I interviewed Professor Mills about his experience during the Web portfolio design process he stated that, as an artist, style and content were critical. As a professional designer, Professor Mills was able to create navigation and sub navigation that was elegant and simple. Rick Mills's Web portfolio site is a success because it fits the needs of

Insert Figure 4.4. Style sample — Richard Kirk Mills (This artist's Web portfolio provides an open interface that engages the user with photography and artwork. Notice the compact drop down menu to list projects.)

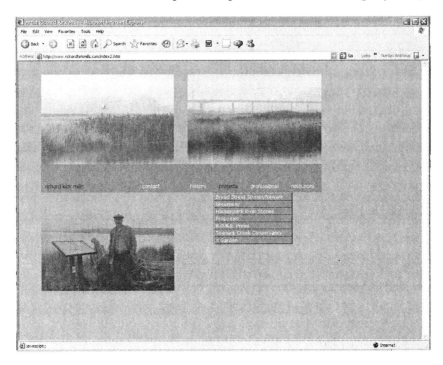

an artist, educator, and designer while providing a visually beautiful and intuitively engaging experience.

When planning your Web portfolio, think about your strengths. How can they be evidenced? What is the most important message left behind from your content? In my case, I want the user to feel that my site portrays a professional educator who has strong design sense and has paid attention to make his Web portfolio a great user experience. In addition, I need the user to navigate through my Web portfolio with a feeling of intuitive confidence while enjoying the work. To achieve this, I tried to impart a style that is organized and clean. My stylistic focus will be on integrating images and other work into an open portal with strict typographic and design consistency. Header graphics for each page will include a personal logo. Each page will have a consistent Web safe color for the page backgrounds.

You might want your portfolio to utilize a style that is based on your personal themes. Maybe you like nature and want to use earth tones and nature images to provide a theme throughout the site. Maybe you want classical music to load with the site and play throughout the user experience. That might be good if you are a music teacher. Either one is okay, but it should fit the context of your audience. If you are trying to land a job as a recording artist or a production person, a rock theme might work well. However, if you are a preschool teacher, that would not help you persuade and communicate with your audience in a positive fashion. Using a metaphor that relates to teaching would be more persuasive. Remember, the style should appeal to the audience in some way. Otherwise, no one will have a chance to learn about your skills and experience because they are turned off by the theme of the site.

Think about style seriously. Don't worry if you feel like you don't have a grasp on a style yet, you still have time to make stylistic decisions. In fact, your style decisions may be altered during the Web development process. It is okay to be without a concrete theme at this point. You will create style identity by using consistent visual elements including color and typography and themes. Thinking about certain elements in the site, you can focus on one common theme and then extended through at the site. As with the site examples that we showcased previously, you too can develop a style based on a theme. These examples portrayed styles of cutting-edge popular culture of a designer, the postmodern artistic vision and multimedia prose of a professor and artist, the fun and creative kindergarten teacher, and a beautiful exploration into the life and public art of an artist in residence and professor. Use these cases as inspiration in developing your own style. Venture out on the Web and seek out styles that appeal to you. From your research, gain vision and insight and then make decisions about your own style.

Style is great and it gives a look and feel that comes memorable to your Web portfolio. Now that we have discussed style a bit, let's move on to composition and some visual design principles to get a better foundation for arranging our Web portfolio pages. Style is useless if composition is weak. When composition breaks down, order is lost and ultimately so is the user. Composition Web pages becomes challenging because there are multiple elements which need to be included in the arrangements. The development of each of these multiple elements needs to be performed so that each is unique part which fits into the composition without causing visual disturbance.

Composition and the Web Portfolio

Speaking in visual terms, composition is the arrangement of elements to create an effective visual product. The proximity, weight, continuity, scale, and repetition of items in a Web page have an impact on how the page is perceived and acted upon. Composition takes these factors into account. By giving the user a well thought-out composition, the pages and interface structure become transparent and the user can intimately focus on your content. So like navigation, composition is seen by the author and is natural to the user. When composition is flawed or inconsistent throughout Web pages, it causes the entire Web portfolio to suffer.

Composition brings all the elements together. Imagine you shot five photographs: these are your elements or assets. You then took the photos and arranged them on top of a piece of cardboard. You overlap each photo a bit to create a layered look. Or, you could change the composition and butt the photos up against each other side by side so that they arrange a grid. You have changed the composition, and thus will change the communication and the reaction fed back by the receiver. Composition refers to the individual pages and how they are assembled, as well as the entire site and how it is assembled.

There are many techniques to assist you in composition. One of the main things that we want to focus on when we are creating a visual composition is placement of elements including text and graphics. Without training in two-dimensional design, this process is not an easy one to master. Because there are so many possibilities in two-dimensional design, no one can really master it. We only can hope to develop good visual habits and be open to criticism, revision, and redesign.

One technique that is effective to help with two-dimensional composition is to use a grid. Using a grid is a common practice to develop composition. Grids are utilized in all forms of art and design. In computer art and multimedia applications, grids are easy to set up and use. Design Web pages, also known as screens on paper first. Use regular graph paper or draw your own grid. The grid will help you arrange the elements on the page with balance, unity, and emphasis. Then, when you begin to use digital production tools, you can reproduce the grid electronically in your applications. Dreamweaver, Fireworks, Flash, Freehand, and Photoshop all have grid setting and guides to help make composition a bit easier.

Figure 4.5. Composition grid in Macromedia Dreamweaver (Macromedia Dreamweaver provides a scalable grid to help you with visual layout of Web pages. The content layer is positioned according to the grid.)

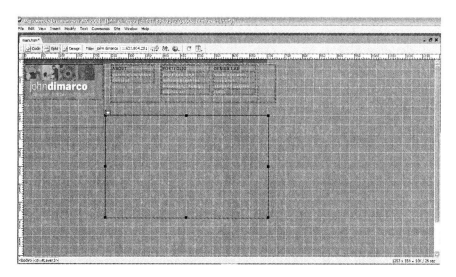

Space

Every digital design medium has parameters or boundaries. The boundaries are located within the space. Units measure boundaries. The common units of measurement in computer graphics are pixels.

Paper and print mediums are measured in inches or metric units. Paper is considered a two-dimensional space: width and height. Letter size paper has a space of 8.5" by 11" inches. The screen is measured in pixels, short for picture elements. In general terms, a pixel represents one small bit of information which is combined with other small bits on a computer screen. These bits fool the eye to create an image. A Web page can typically occupy a space of 640 pixels wide by 480 pixels high. The screen is two-dimensional space. Space has some important characteristics, which are highlighted as follows.

Format

Two-dimensional space traditionally has vertical and horizontal formats. Portrait, which is tall, is the vertical format and landscape is the horizontal or wide format. Formats for two-dimensional space can also be varied in shape or size.

The format for Web pages is can be horizontal or vertical. Keep in mind that vertical formats will require scrolling. For this reason many designers strive to create fewer vertical format scrolling pages. Horizontal design is better for pages containing a majority of large graphics. Horizontal design provides a format that is wider than it is taller. Horizontal pages do not work well with long sections of text, such as with a resume. Are horizontally designed Web page may be 800 pixels wide by 600 pixels high. Vertical, scrolling pages are better for text intensive pages. A vertically designed page may be 800 pixels wide by 1024 pixels high. Vertical format is taller and than it is wider. If a document will exceed the browser window, as in the case of an 8.5 x 11 page, you should use of vertical scrolling page. Web portfolio pages can be any site you wish. You should however keep in mind that the content must fit the format.

Think about format and page content. Come to conclusions about common page formats that will be used for specific content. One example would be to plan to have a vertical scrolling page for your Web resume. You want to make sure that the format of pages is consistent with the content. Page formats can be mixed but, you must do it cautiously so that you do not damage the style or the functionality of the site.

Space and Dimensions

The concept of space and dimensions are something that is common to artists and designers, but may not be common to students, academics, and professionals in other disciplines. Understanding dimensions and space will help with visual design of Web portfolio pages. Spatial dimensions can be quantified in several different measures. Space can be two-dimensional as with paper and the screen. Two-dimensional space is measured by height and width. Space can be three-dimensional design as we see in a building, sculpture, or 3D graphic model. The dimensions for three-dimensional objects are height, width, and depth. Volume also is involved when the space is not virtual. Space can also be four-dimensional and include the dimension of time. Web sites, interactive CD ROMs, and performance medium such as stage, television, and film are four-dimensional due to the fact that they span time. Computer applications that allow design within the fourth dimension of time all have one thing in common: they have timelines that allow dynamic time-based design.

So to add these definitions to the Web page, we must note that a Web page when it is being created is a two-dimensional space. The space provided in a

Web page can be measured by height and width using the unit of pixels. When the Web page design leaves the two-dimensional design application such as Adobe Photoshop or Macromedia fireworks, it is brought into a four-dimensional application such as Macromedia Dreamweaver or Macromedia flash. In these four-dimensional applications, objects including text and graphics can be added and manipulated on timelines which bring the elements into the fourth dimension. In the fourth dimension, objects can be animated with motion over time.

Actual Space

Actual space refers to the real space we have to develop our design within. It is the working space or the live area. The actual space is a product of our project specifications. It always has defined dimensional requirements. Most computer design tools allow a working space in addition to the actual space. For example, digital illustration programs utilize a page and a pasteboard area to lay unused graphics and type. If they are not on the page/actual space, they will not be printed. Only the actual space is output. The same concept of working space and actual space is seen in four-dimensional computer applications such as Macromedia flash. In flash, objects are created in a symbol editor that is external to the working flash movie. When we begin to create storyboards where going to define areas that constitute actual space and live area for our content. The actual space encompasses the entire Web page, the live area is a place where content will be inserted and changed. We must make sure that graphics and text that are created to fit in actual space meet the size requirements of that space. We do not want to scale content when it is in actual space. We only want to work on content, scale it and manipulate it when it is in working space, before final output. In our Web portfolio pages, the actual space is the space that we define when we create our content. The Web page has boundaries outside of actual space which sit inside of actual space. This sounds confusing but, what I mean here is that a Web page can scroll on and on with content. However, at some there needs to be an end. A new page should continue content. Forever scrolling pages can be ineffective in displaying a quantity of information that has multiple categories and needs multiple spaces to present the content exclusively. So keep mind that actual space in a Web page is based on the size and quantity of content. Once content is placed in a Web page and is live within a browser, you as the author need to control the user's navigation throughout the space.

Negative Space

If we talk about actual space, we must balance it out by covering the concept of negative space. Negative space refers to the empty space within the actual space. It is void of objects and elements. Its usage is vital to proper visual design. It is always the starting point for our design. It may be a blank piece of paper or a new file in an application ready for content to be placed. When you begin to create a Web screen in Macromedia Fireworks, you begin with negative space. Negative space also goes by the name white space. The term white space was coined in traditional 2D design. It is a frequent term in graphic design. In Web design, white space is just as important to composition as content is in many instances. Visually, negative space provides visual relief as well as gives intelligent organization to elements on a page by highlighting and separating text and graphics with the use of white space. Just think, between characters, between lines, between everything, is white space. Effectively using white space means that you do not crowd content for no good design reason. Occasionally, a design may call for no white space or rely on negative space for the design, but in Web design, particularly in situations such as the Web portfolio, we want to utilize white space in our interface and typography. Doing so will create invisible order and will enhance readability of the Web page.

Proximity and Containment

Proximity and containment become important considerations when you are designing within a two-dimensional area such as a Web page. Keeping navigation items located consistently and strategically is of high importance. Menus should be contained to upper regions of the page when they are of high importance. Sub menus can be lower on the page to reflect the hierarchy of the two navigation items. Personal logos and page headers should be contained in the upper regions of the page to command immediate recognition and to establish page to page identity and style.

To expand on proximity and containment, we need to think about how our user will move around our Web pages. It is important that we put the most important navigation elements within quick reach and without clutter. That's where proximity and containment common. The ability to put white space around a logo or the ability to separate navigation elements properly so that each is independent and can be clicked on by the user without error exemplify using proximity and containment to enhance the Web page.

Containment of content within Web pages is critical to showing off your best work. Pop-up windows are good examples of content containers which set off work from the rest of the Web site. Containment also offers organization to a Web experience. An example of this would be PDF files that may contain external documents for viewing or downloading. Isolating documents within a Web site gives priority to them and allows the user and effective method for gaining access. Larger documents that do not convert well to dynamic Web pages are perfect for containment within the PDF browser environment. Containment also occurs within flash movies. The movies act like containers for multimedia content which gets placed inside the framework of a Web page. The flash movies are developed and saved as self-contained, self running multimedia snippets that can be swapped out for new content quickly and easily without affecting the overall stability of the Web page. Containment also helps in hierarchal structure and the management of overall content presentation.

Weight

Weight refers to the visual value placed upon the items on your Web page. A heavy weight graphic could be over sized, distinctively colored, or oddly positioned to imply that it has dominance in the visual space. We want to establish strong weight to our portfolio pieces and work items and a light weight to our navigation items. Logo and headers should have light to medium weight so they have impact, but do not overwhelm the page or distract from the impact of the work. The overweight nature of many interface designs seen in my research leads me to believe that focus is not as centered on content as it needs to be.

Another way to exhibit weight is to use bold text within large text blocks or for links. Bold text is also effective when used in rollovers to show visual feedback when the mouse goes over the navigation. Weight can be seen in borders and rules used in Web page designs. These items can be effective in distributing weight and breaking up white space within a design. Make sure the weight of borders and rules is consistent and not overwhelming to the eye. Rules and borders should be kept under two points to avoid a heavy look.

As you begin to perform visual design on paper and using computer graphics applications, think about weight and how will have an affect on your Web portfolio pages.

Scale

Scale refers to physical size. Large scale images on a page can result in dominance of that page. Small-scale graphics can represent lack of importance or in the case of text; they can be iconic or representative of a single navigational or representational item. Small scale also implies order, as with a set of thumbnails. Scale affects composition because it takes the eye to something or confuses the eye in determining what to look at first. We want to make sure that we use scale effectively in a Web portfolio pages. During this requires us to have visual contrast between scaled items or it may require repetition of items at the same scale to portray a series or a visual list.

In the portfolio we want to make sure that our content items that are specific work pieces get represented properly by being created at the proper scale. We don't want our project samples to be too small or too large. Both cases cause problems due to scale. Images that are too large, may be difficult to decipher, or maybe disproportional to the space. Images that are too small may be difficult to see simply because of physical size and lack of resolution.

The best rule I can give you for scale relates to a technical point not a visual point. The rule is to create graphics to the scale you need for the final Web page. Visually, experiment with scale to get appropriate visual contrast and to give elements on a Web page prominence or order.

Repetition

Repetition refers to repeating elements. Sounds elementary, but sometimes inexperienced designers one non-designers use it the wrong way. Repetition is used for several different purposes within a design. Repetition can be good or it can be bad. Mostly, I think repetition should be used to remember things easier and allow the user not to think so hard when encountering common elements. Repetition should act as an intuitive guide for the user. We want to repeat certain things such as typefaces, positioning of elements, and procedures that the user communicates with while interacting with the site.

Good repetition should help establish identity, such as when a personal logo is used on a Web portfolio. However, when the logo is blinking on the page, or is placed on the page several times, the repetition becomes bothersome and distracting to the user. Good repetition is when you place all the page headers in the same exact location on every page. Good repetition is when you use consistent navigation systems in your site.

Bad repetition happens when things are repeated for no good reason than simply to repeat them. As with the case of blinking items and putting four instances of a logo on one Web page. Another event that exemplifies bad repetition is when navigation is repeated in the exact same way on the same page. Navigation can be repeated on a Web page. It is a good idea to have main navigation which is graphical or text-based at the top of the Web page and if the pages are scrollable, main navigation should be located at the bottom of the pages in a simple, small scale text-based navigation bar. Components to the Web portfolio page such as a contact button should be repeated in the same place on every page, but not multiple times on the same page for no good reason. When you begin to design your Web page screens think about the role of repetition in your designs. Once you decide that an element should be repeated, make sure that it is repeated consistently throughout all of its occupied pages. Before duplicating items on a page asked the questions: Why am I doing this? Will this be effective or bothersome to the user? Is this repetition needed to benefit the user? Will this repetition help guide the user when they are navigating through the site? Will this repetition help promote my personal identity and add value to my public appearance? These questions are given to you so that you consider them when you begin visual design. I offer them to you so that you can begin to eliminate common visual mistakes that I made one non designers and new designers begin to create visual work.

Continuity

Continuity is a term that is defined as consistency and adherence to structure. Continuity within the Web portfolio relies on keeping pages in the designed site structure. Technical snafus sometimes cause us to let continuity fail. For example, if we forgot navigation item after we were well into the design what should we do? Should we throw in anywhere? Or, should we redesign the navigation to integrate the missing piece? Sometimes we can add last-minute items and navigation to the Web page. In most cases doing this will disrupt continuity. Therefore, it is important that we establish continuity and consistency before we spend the bulk of our time physically creating completed Web pages. As a rule, you should not move navigation items to accommodate content. Establish minimum and maximum content sizes so that you can adequately fit the navigation and content proportionally on the page. Content should dominate 80 percent of the page and navigation should be replicated exactly throughout the site. Different page levels should share the same navigation features. Meaning, the pop-up windows you create may have a slimmed down or different menu system than you home page and main site. That's all right; just keep each level consistent with navigation and content placement. Continuity means keeping site the same throughout. We can't let consistency slip at any stage of the design if we want to achieve maximum quality and visual value.

Type

Type is crucial for communication but can also be an engaging visual element. With that in mind, let's define the two conditions of Web type.

1.   Web pages can have plain editable HTML text, or
2.   Text can be created in a digital design application such as Adobe Photoshop, Adobe Illustrator, Macromedia Freehand, or Macromedia Fireworks and then saved as a graphic for inclusion into a page. This is called graphical text.

The most effective Web pages generally combine both graphical and HTML text. **Here are some general rules to follow in your dealings with text:**

- For lots of text, text that must be edited frequently, and for faster loading of text intensive pages, **use HTML text**.
- For page headers, buttons, and strong visual emphasis, **use graphical text consistently and mostly on items that change infrequently.** A header would not change frequently, but a paragraph head might.
- The type style, font, size, and condition of type you use in your Web portfolio really depend on several factors. Here are some general rules to choosing text attributes.
- **When using HTML text, try to stick to one typeface only.** It will help with readability and consistency. You can vary style of the typeface. This

means you can add bold, italic, and caps to certain text blocks to add emphasis. However, you should use these type styles consistently and keep them to a minimum. Fight the urge to use blinking text, lime green text, and other painful HTML text attributes that might detract from your credibility or the user experience. Black or white should be your dominant HTML text color. Highlight important information by using one other color only. You should create a color scheme. We talk about this more later on in this chapter.

- With regards to Web type, you have only these choices: Helvetica, Arial, Times, Times, New Roman, or Verdana. Type on computer browsers is limited to a set number of fonts. If you use fonts outside these, you risk the good possibility that the user will not have the typeface on his or her computer, thus serving up unknown fonts on the Web page. That would have negative impact on the visual design of the page, the user's perceptions, and ultimately we would lose the persuasive pitch that we had intended.

- **When using graphical type, keep it simple and consistent.** Don't overdue it with drop shadows, glow, and outlines, and gradients — all applied on the same piece of type! Many people new to art and design tend to over use the bells and whistles that exist in applications like Adobe Photoshop. Try not to feed into the temptation. "Overdone" type, as I call it, is a distraction from the most important part of your Web portfolio, the project descriptions and credentials. Fancy effects that draw attention from the meat and potatoes of the Web portfolio are actually obstacles to clear communication.

- It is important to use HTML type on the home page in some fashion other than navigation. Perhaps add brief introduction paragraph about the site. This is a good Web communication strategy. It will also provide your site with text-based retrieval words to be picked up by the search engines. We will cover this more when we talk about Meta tags later in the book.

Images and Graphics

The use of images also known as graphics in the Web portfolio provide a high level of communication that cannot be achieved with text alone. Presenting graphics in the Web portfolio is not only attractive but is necessary to provide the best multimedia narrative possible. The images you use should back up your theme and your work. The images should not be sprinkled frivolously throughout the site. Build a library of good images to use on your Web portfolio will be part of the learning process that comes along with the design of any type of electronic portfolio. Collecting images from different sources becomes an area in which you must recognize copyright laws and visual style. I highly recommend that you try to use a minimal amount of clip art and stock images and a maximum amount of your own work samples. Clip art and stock images can be effective when used properly. Navigation items, page headers, and images that follow a theme are all good uses of stock images and clip art.

When it comes to telling a story of your effectiveness, your personal narrative needs to be backed up by samples of the work. Images such as photographs from your gallery exhibition or your classroom are appropriate. Images that you create as art, design, or some other project deliverable are great. Photographs from your last vacation may not be appropriate. However, if the vacation was coupled with an interesting learning experience or valuable historical exploration, the photographs may be effective in telling your professional or academic story. Other images that you may not think of are charts and graphs that you have created. PowerPoint projects can be used as standalone graphics by taking individual slides and saving the content out as a JPEG image. So keep your presentations in mind when thinking about images.

Another area of text documents that may become graphic images later on are letters of recommendation, evaluations, and lesson plans. These items may be scanned as graphics and exhibited as tangible assets. They will be exhibited on the Web portfolio as graphic images rather than downloadable documents.

An easy way to add graphics to your site is to use ready-made clipart or stock photography. These items are good for establishing themes and visual skins for the Web portfolio site. However, they do not constitute your work. Stock photography and clipart should not be the only images within your Web portfolio. These images should be used only if they are considered royalty-free. If an image is not royalty-free, care should be taken when deciding on usage. Copyright infringement is serious and has detrimental effects on the value and appearance of your Web portfolio. We will try to give you some insight here as to the usage guidelines you might want to follow when using images and graphics that are not your own.

Borrowing graphics from authors is a touchy subject. Author Miles Kimball (2003, p. 89) sites that rules are loosely defined the copyright law are translated by the Consortium for Educational Technology in University Systems as being based on fair use within four criteria:

1.   the purpose and character of the use including whether its commercial or nonprofit,

2.   the nature of the copyrighted work,

3.   the amount and substantiality of the portion used in relation to the copyrighted work as a whole, and

4.   the effect of the use upon the potential market for or value of the copyrighted work.

Kimball also states that it is difficult to find fair use of images and graphics. However, one good rule to follow that is cited by Kimball is that in most cases if the images used for educational purposes, which means that it is engaged in learning rather than selling, it is deemed fairly used.

Metaphors and Image Maps

Metaphor can be a productive conceptual tool for visual communication. Use of metaphors in visual Web design is quite popular, definitely on home pages. When we use the term metaphor and image map we are referring to image based navigation systems employed in Web pages.

Metaphors provide theme based image maps with contextual value. Metaphors must have meaning. The image map/metaphor will guide the user action. For this to happen, the user must be familiar with the metaphor (Kristoff & Satran, 1995).

Identity

Identity is a crucial element to developing a strong visual relationship with the user. Personal touches whether business worthy (a department logo) or not (your hiking photo), should be part of your sites overall visual plan. Don't go overboard with extensive clutter. The user will be bored and not persuaded. The identity elements help establish recognition of name and brand as well as providing a stable design element to enhance overall site consistency. You can incorporate a personal logo (we will do this later in the book) and develop simple page headers that are consistently placed on each page. By consistently putting the same graphic, in the same location, at the same size, in the same color on each page, identity and recognition are established. These are important elements in persuasion. We want the user to remember our great credentials.

Color Schemes

Color schemes are important in establishing credibility, mood, experience, and page readability. It is important to use colors that work to project identity, promote information, add style, and set a mood. Don't pick colors that are annoying to look at — bright lime green, for example — unless they explicitly fit the theme of the site design.

Colors change user perceptions because they make a significant emotional impression on the user. Bright vibrant colors give users the impression of excitement or maybe even youth. Conversely, bright colors may be seen as loud or immature, or uncultured by some users who are from different backgrounds or disciplines. Muted or dull colors may be seen as conservative or possibly be viewed as boring to a certain user population. Users may make emotional judgments on a sites content based on the color schemes employed. Keep your audience in mind when you think about color schemes. It is important that you prepare the Web portfolio color schemes to fit the audience preferences and possible perceptions as best you can (Kimball, 2003). To get color scheme ideas you should explore different Web sites to find color schemes that appeal to you. Remember keep colors simple and geared to the specific audience you are trying to connect with during the Web portfolio experience.

Navigation Systems

You have established the functions and the structure of the site up to this point so developing a visual approach to a navigation system will be easier. As you have learned in past text passages, Web portfolio navigation should be simplified to provide seamless usability and serve to communicate a functional hierarchy.

There are several types of navigation systems that you can use in your Web portfolio pages. They all perform the same function, to get the user somewhere quickly and easily. Text-based navigation systems are easy to use and easy to update. They are great for bottom-page navigation and for simple communication. Keep the text styles consistent. You can accomplish this by using CSS (Cascading Style Sheets). A lesson in how to create styles and style sheets appears later on in the book.

Graphical based navigation systems use gif or jpg graphics to trigger events instead of text. Using metaphors and image maps are typical ways to integrate graphics. With these designs, you should be sure they have functional hierarchy, they have to mean something and be in the correct order of overall functions. Graphical navigation systems are more difficult to create and maintain due to the fact they originate in a digital imaging or digital illustration application. You must design the artwork separately and then export it to your Web site directory. From there, you would need to import the graphics into Dreamweaver or whichever Web development application you use. With text-based systems, you create the menu directly in Dreamweaver with text tools.

Backgrounds

Have you ever gone to a Web page and seen one image repeated consistently as a background? Visually, this is not very appealing. You need to know what background image is so that later on he can avoid using one. Backgrounds, better known as background images, are resource hogs that serve no communication purpose than to provide anguish to the user while waiting for them to load. The only time that background images seem to be needed and can be used are when non-Web browser safe colors are used in a design created in Adobe Photoshop or another image-editing application. In this case, solid colors are used for the background and although loading time is slowed down, the background keeps an aesthetic decency due to the fact that solid colors tile seamlessly. You still want to use them very rarely.

Alternatively, the horrible tiling of one image creates an annoying pattern that ruins anything else placed in front of it. Bottom line: avoid background images.

You can and will use a background color on your pages. And, you will use plenty of images. They just won't be nested in the background tag of the Web page HTML code.

Pop-Up Windows

Windows and pop-up windows are the shells of Web pages. They should be considered and their use should be planned out when designing a site. The pop-up window can be used as a micro site to add another level of accessibility and functionality to your site. Or, it can be used to provide an exclusive visual space to isolate and present artwork, video, animation, motion graphics, database the applications, lengthy text blocks, and your specific portfolio content. As mentioned before, pop-up windows provide containment. This exclusive containment can be important to showing off your most critical project samples.

We will be using pop-up windows in the Web portfolio site designed in this book. I feel that using exclusive space for showing off important content is vital to isolating the attention of the user. The trick is to make each window a valuable piece of the user experience. Pay close attention to details such as keeping window sizes consistent. Be sure that you are providing navigation inside the window that helps the user navigate the work and close the window. All the things we're discussing here surrounding pop-up windows will be fleshed out with a technical instructions later on in the text.

Storyboards

Now that we have discussed some of the visual principles and elements that are important to the look and feel of the Web portfolio, let's create a rough draft of how we want the information to look on the Web page. More importantly, we should make notes on the drafts of what multimedia, navigation, and visual elements we want to include in the page design. Also, we should create a rough draft of all types of pop-up windows that exist in our site.

The drafts that I am referring to are storyboards. In simple terms, the storyboard blocks out a set of actions for each screen, what the user sees when arriving at the Web page, what navigation or other controls are available when the user gets there, and the sequence in which events will occur (Kristoff & Satran, 1995).

Creating the storyboard does not require intense artistic talent. Actually, very little detail is show in paper storyboards. Paper storyboards are all that is needed to block out the Web page sequences. Button and other page locations only need to be approximate and you should only show Web pages that change. For each screen you should show:

- Approximate and tentative image locations
- Text position
- Motion graphic or animation locations
- In the margin, write in audio track or sounds to be played and in the storyboard show how audio is controlled
- Navigation, sub navigation locations
- Pop-up windows with sub-navigation, captions, and close buttons

Now it's time for you to create storyboards. Take a piece of paper, 8.5 x 11 is fine, and turn it sideways to a horizontal orientation. Use the whole piece of paper as if it was one Web page. This is your actual space. Start with your index page also known as your home page. Don't worry about color right now, just think about where the elements such as navigation, text, and images need to go. Just think in the simple terms for now. As you build the storyboards, you can begin to integrate in other elements such as animations and audio controls. But for now just concentrate on where the navigation is going to go, where you're going to place the text inside of the page, and how the images are going to be positioned in relationship to the text inside the actual space. This won't be a process that is easy and you will succeed at on the first try. Different storyboards for one page are common. Once you work out one-page, you should have some visual elements which can be carried through consistently to the other pages which gives the site continuity. You can get inspiration by looking at other Web portfolio sites and even other Web sites. You can take a screenshot of a Web page or simply print the page from the Internet and use tracing paper to outline the existing positions of the elements on the Web page. At first, it will be difficult to develop consistent Web pages. But you must put forth in your mind that consistency will help make the Web portfolio organized an effective.

Start the storyboard from the top down. Rough out the space for a banner or personal logo. Rough up the space for the navigation items and position them on the page approximately where you feel they should go. This decision is critical because it will be followed through on other pages. Without consistent navigation from the start, you and your user will be lost.

After establishing the identity and banner considerations, you should designate the live area for content placement. This live area will hold text, graphics, and multimedia items that reside on the page. Once you have established a home page, you want to follow the navigation design throughout the rest of the storyboards to establish continuity. If you need additional navigation items, you can sketch in sub navigation which can be customized as content and needs dictate.

You should be creating storyboards for each page that changes. As you are beginning to create your storyboards you may want to rough out as many as you can to practice this conceptual process. Remember, the storyboard needs to tell the story, not be a high level illustration. The time you spend creating storyboards should be utilized in the process of thinking, analyzing, and designing the visual framework for an engaging Web communication experience.

Conclusion

At this point, you should have thought about and possibly completed conceptualization, information design, and visual design of your Web portfolio. This chapter has given you some ideas as to what can go into a Web portfolio and given you some instruction on how to assemble the site visually, on paper in the form of storyboards. You should have established a tentative layout for the Web pages and you should be able to assume where the content will reside inside the Web page designs. The content items must be formatted to fit into the Web page layout you designed in the story boards.

With an idea about what you want the Web portfolio to look like and how it will work, all of the items for the Web portfolio must be gathered and manipulated into a Web-based format. In some cases, artifacts and assets may need to be developed from scratch or converted from paper or application formats. We will explore these processes and tasks in the next chapter.

Chapter V

Content, Collection, Development and Management

Introduction

It's time to hunt and gather. In a large part, the Web portfolio design process relies upon you as the author to be an investigator. What this means is you have to go back into your own personal history and find all of the assets and artifacts that will help you tell your story in the Web portfolio. Remember, this story is wrapped around the content. The content must be collected, processed, and refined so that it is technically and visually suitable for publishing on the Internet. Content will be scattered all over. To make things easier during the content collection process, refer to your content outline. By doing this, you can cycle through a list and gather all available materials. Some items might be lost or not worthy of the Web portfolio so they should be deleted. You can also leave space for items that will be complete and ready for presentation in the future.

The Web portfolio is dynamic and will be updated throughout its lifetime. Developing content requires you to be creative and make things. New projects, sample items, school projects, and professional work are items that you will be developing as your Web portfolio is growing in size and credibility. During this metamorphosis the Web portfolio will act as a container for you to manage your content. Management of your Web portfolio and ultimately your assets and full spectrum of publishable content will be available to you at all times through the Internet.

After the content is captured and created, it must be described in the Web portfolio. This requires you to write consistent, thoughtful project descriptions that give the essence of your role and accomplishments during the project process.

This chapter presents the optimization process needed for Web content development. We will examine how approach and prepare various asset types including MS Office files, Adobe Photoshop and Illustrator images, Quark documents, photographs, and paper-based documents. Also provided are suggestions on photographing and preparing three-dimensional artwork for Web presentation. Web resumes and CVs are discussed, and finally, development of project captions is examined and examples are provided on effective formats for describing projects developed all disciplines.

Revisiting the Content Outline

Previously, you made a content outline that contained your text, images, and project items that you plan to include in the Web portfolio. Now, it is time to accumulate your content and get it ready to be put on the Internet. To get your work into Web pages and up on the Internet it has to be converted to a few select file formats. Without proper file formatting, page elements will show up as missing.

Gather up all your digital and paper documents, your artwork, programs you created, design work you have done, case studies you have written, and all the supporting images and text. Once gathered, you can begin to prepare the content for the Web page design process. Next, we will set up our folder structure and look at the image types and the methods needed to optimize each for the Web.

Figure 5.1.   Folder structure (This folder structure is important to organization and to successfully posting your site to the Internet. Make sure that you are putting files in their designated folder location. Moving items after you create your Web pages may cause some problems later.)

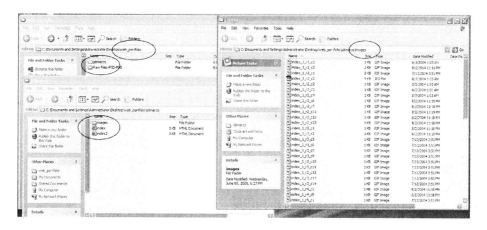

Setting Up the Folder Structure

The Web portfolio is a big project that has several different parts. To be organized and to have the Web site work, you must employ a folder structure that remains constant. Here is the structure I recommend for the Web portfolio project…

On your desktop, create these folders:

1. Create the SITE folder: no spaces or punctuation characters: name it: **Web_portfolio.**

2. Inside the site folder create your ROOT Folder: **johndimarco** or **jdimarco** (first initial last name — no spaces). All Web pages go in the ROOT folder.

3. Inside the ROOT folder create the RAW-PSD-PNG folder: **RAW Files** (all raw files go here).

4. Inside the ROOT folder create the HEADERS folder: **headers** (all Web page headers go here).

5.   Inside the ROOT folder create the IMAGES folder: **images** (all Web images go here).

6.   Inside the ROOT folder create the FLASH folder: **flash** (all flash files go here).

Image Types

As we discussed in Chapter IV, images play an important role in our Web portfolio. There are three formats for graphical images to be seen in Web pages on the Internet. GIF, JPG, and PNG are the formats for Web portfolio graphics. Typically, GIF and JPEG and the most widely supported by Web browsers so it is a good idea to stick to using them and avoid PNG for live Web pages. PNG has other uses as we will see later.

PDF

You probably have a bunch of documents that are paper or electronic that need to be presented individually and may need to allow the user to download them. As well, many of your documents may contain formatting and type styles that cannot be reproduced on the Web. In order to keep the document visually compelling, true to its original nature, and printable on any computer, use the Adobe Systems Portable Document Format (PDF). A PDF is a universal file format that is created using Adobe Acrobat software or any number of applications that print to PDF. PDF files are viewed, navigated through, and printed from the **Acrobat Reader**, a free software application that is directly installed on every computer during operating system installation. Acrobat reader also runs through Web browser. This allows a guaranteed universal platform for external document exchange on the Web. Here are a few things you should know about the Acrobat reader. First, the Acrobat Reader (also called the Adobe Reader) can be downloaded for free from http: www.adobe.com. The Reader does not allow you to make PDF files. To do this, you need Adobe Acrobat, which uses the Distiller to output PDF files.

As I mentioned before, many popular software applications provide a feature that allows you to print directly to PDF file format. The Microsoft Office applications allow PDF output from Microsoft Word, PowerPoint, and Excel. By using this feature, you can use existing applications to generate a library of portfolio pieces in PDF format. The nice thing about this workflow is that it allows you to stay within your native applications and not have to venture off into graphic applications to prepare the bulk of your work. If you like, you can output elements from your Microsoft Word and Microsoft Excel documents to bitmap file formats and then manipulate the graphs, charts, spreadsheets, and diagrams within Adobe Photoshop or Macromedia fireworks. Getting graphical elements from your Microsoft office applications is easy. You can do it several ways. First, you can select any graphical element such as a chart and right-click to copy it. Then, open up a new document in Macromedia fireworks or Adobe Photoshop and the document space will automatically be the correct size to accommodate a copied image. Paste the image into the image-editing application and now you have the ability to scale, crop, and correct the graphic if needed. You now have the ability to incorporate freely the graphic into other Web page layouts using a powerful image-editing environment. As well, you have the graphic in a new space where you can add a caption and perform visual layout, something that you can't do in the Microsoft office applications very effectively. Another method for outputting Microsoft office documents for Web publishing is to right-click on individual charts and graphs and save them as bitmap graphics in GIF, JPEG, or BMP formats. BMP formats need to be opened image-editing program and saved as JPEG or GIF files. BMP (short for bitmap) file formats are not acceptable for Web publishing. Finally, it is important to note that Microsoft office applications also allow files to be saved as HTML Web pages. Be careful if you decide to use this feature. It may cause technical problems or a lack of continuity with other Web of pages that are developed using other methods. If you're going to output Web pages from Microsoft Office applications you should use those pages in pop-up windows or blank target browser windows that load on top of your existing Web portfolio and are contained in their own browser window. By separating the documents you will minimize a lack of consistency if it exists. As well, you will isolate the documents so that the user can focus on reviewing them without distractions of other content.

Another alternate route to PDF and Microsoft office Web output is to perform screen captures of your documents from your desktop and open them in Adobe Photoshop. After taking the screenshot, you will open a new document Adobe Photoshop or Macromedia fireworks and paste the screenshot from the clipboard onto the canvas (this technique is explained in more detail next).

From there, you can crop out the desired area using the crop tool. The external area will be gone and now you can use the power of the image-editing program to manipulate the graphic image. After manipulation in Adobe Photoshop you have the option to save the file as a PDF. Photoshop handles the PDF creation task quite easily. As described with the Microsoft products, many graphical and page layout software packages now have direct menu items or a menu bar button for you to output directly to PDF file format. The page layout applications QuarkXpress and Adobe InDesign have such capabilities.

You should convert any formatted documents that you want your user see in original form to PDF format. You can link directly to PDF files from your Web portfolio pages using a standard link.

You can also link to native documents in your Web portfolio such as Microsoft PowerPoint, Excel, and Word documents. This is where you actually upload the Microsoft Office documents directly to the Web server. Internet Explorer will allow Microsoft office users to view native documents in a browser. If the individual is a Netscape user, the process isn't as easy. The Netscape download scenario may present a few obstacles to the user. First, the documents must be downloaded to the user's computer. Another problem may exist with fonts. If the user does not have the same fonts and same version of the application, there could be problems viewing the document.

With PDF format documents you don't have to worry about color. PDF documents are converted to be viewed on the Web regardless original colors used. This is not true for other Web graphics and Web pages in general. The visual and technical aspects of color must be looked at as you begin to create content that needs to be browser friendly.

Web Color

There are many books that cover Web color in detailed scientific terms. However, for our objectives, let's briefly discuss Web color and how it will be used in the Web portfolio. You will need to develop a color scheme for your Web portfolio pages. This means that you will designate colors for your page background, the type used on the page and any other static elements that reside in the page. There are two types of color that can be used in Web graphics. The colors can be associated with the Web graphic file formats we just mentioned: GIF and JPG.

GIF

GIF files use index color. Index color consists of 216 common colors found on all computer monitors and within all Web browsers. These common colors reside in a Web palette. The Web palette of colors is available in Macromedia Fireworks and Adobe Photoshop so they can be used in design of Web screens without variance of color when the pages are on the Internet. Also, the Web palette is the standard color palette in Macromedia Dreamweaver and Macromedia Flash. This allows us to achieve consistent color across Web applications and Web browsers.

We use Web colors for:

- Web text/HTML text
- Web page backgrounds
- Web page colors used for table or layer backgrounds
- Web links
- GIF files

JPG

JPG files use red, green, and blue (RGB) for graphical color. RGB color is also known as full color. Full color items include bitmap graphics or photographs. We want to utilize photographs as much as we can within a Web portfolio to add to the visual rhetoric and the narrative that we are trying to present.

Extensive use of photographs, especially their manipulation in programs such as Adobe Photoshop, require a brief description of the RGB color model. RGB color is known as additive color because of all colors, red green, and blue were added together at their full intensity that would create pure white. The mixtures of the relative strengths of these colors, "create the millions of colors computer monitors can show" (Kimball, 2003, p. 95). The strength of these colors is set in from zero to 255 with zero being the least intensity and 255 being the highest intensity. When red, green and blue are combined at zero intensity the result is black. At full strength, high intensity, where the values are set at 255, 255, 255, the result is pure white. To remember this, here is a simple metaphor. Think of the red, green, and blue as light switches. Each light switch using a slider has a range of zero to 255. When all the white switches are set at zero the room is dark. What all the light switches are set to 255, the room is lit at full intensity. Once you begin to use image-editing applications such as Adobe Photoshop and Macromedia fireworks, you begin to explore computer color within your graphics and photographs.

When discussing color usage, full color or RGB color is present in photographic JPG files and other created artwork. Full color images should not be saved as GIF files because of the limited number of colors. By having limited colors, the full color image will represent the true colors using the existing Web palette of 216 colors. This creates a poor, dithered, and ugly image. That is why it is very important to use the right file format for each specific graphic.

When converting print images to the Web, it's important that you do not use the CMYK color model for anything including graphics. The CMYK model is not a monitor friendly color space. The CMYK graphics cannot be seen in CMYK on the Internet. They can only be represented by the RGB color model or the Web safe (indexed) color model.

Here are the rules for Web color:

- Full color images (RGB palette) and photos are saved as JPG.
- Flat graphics (Web 216 palette) with limited color are saved as GIF files.
- For Page backgrounds use the Web safe palette (Web 216 palette) in all computer graphics, multimedia, and Web development applications.

Now, let's discuss Web page and graphic size.

Size

Web pages are measured in pixels. Pixels are the unit of measurement for the screen. A Web page can literally be any size. Standard Web pages usually fit into a few sizes:

- W × H
- 600 × 800

- 640×480 (Dreamweaver default)
- 1024 × 768
- 550×400 (Flash default)

The default Web page sizes provided in Web friendly applications and listed earlier are a great place to start. You will probably use a smaller, custom size for pop-up windows. The Web page size you choose is up to you. Remember to use actual space for the Web page effectively so that the content is in the proper proximity to the user's navigation patterns. Web page size affects the way users move around the Web pages and the Web portfolio site.

One rule: Pick a size for all main screens and stick to it. Consistency in page size should be used on each level of the Web portfolio design flowchart.

You will need to understand size in the image editing application when you develop screens and Web graphics. We must keep our graphics within the page size guidelines otherwise they will over extend the Web browser and the user will need to scroll to see them. That is not a good thing and will definitely turn off the user.

When you are looking at Web screens and graphics in an image editing application such as Macromedia Fireworks or Adobe Photoshop, you can see the exact size the image will occupy on a monitor when the view is set to 100 percent. This means that you can get an accurate indication of how a page will look before going through the process of making it an HTML Web page. This helps with design and production. It helps eliminate guess work when developing pages. Size also depends on resolution. Let's discuss resolution next.

Resolution

Screen resolution refers to the number of pixels a screen can display in a given area. The standard resolution for Web graphics is 72 dpi for Macintosh and 96 dpi for Windows. This means that all graphics should be saved to their needed exact size at 72 dpi. If graphics are larger than 72 dpi or 96 dpi, they need to be optimized and exported using Macromedia Fireworks or Adobe Photoshop. Remember, all graphics should be 72 or 96 dpi to scale. Typically, 72 dpi works well for both platforms. By using the lower resolution for graphics on

Windows and Macintosh platforms, Web page loading performance is improved. The quality between 72 dpi and 96 dpi cannot be seen when examining Web site pages. With a high-bandwidth connections of today's Web users, 96 dpi will not cause too much of a performance issue. However, we want to try to make all Web pages as efficient as possible. So, 72 dpi for all graphics is not such a bad idea.

Using Photography to Develop Content

The use of digital photography for content development is highly effective for Web applications. For obvious reasons that include speed of transfer from the camera to the computer and the ability to shoot photos at will without laboratory development costs make digital photography an important part of Web portfolio development. Digital photographs used on your Web portfolio can present any number of imaginable images of your work. You may have sculpture, package designs, or student work that you want to show in the Web portfolio. If three-dimensional objects need to be captured, photography must be performed. Digital photography is effective in the creation of Web portfolios for any discipline. A landscape designer may have photographs of completed terrestrial projects. A natural scientist may have photographs of a field expedition or research subject matter. A social scientist may have photographs of research environments and historical artifacts. In addition, simple things like personal photographs of classrooms and conference presentations can make a tremendous impression on the user and potential audiences. Keep this in mind as you go through professional situations. Keeping a photographic record of these events and presenting them on your Web portfolio further validates your credibility and adds an engaging element to your site.

Digital Photography Shooting Tips

Using a digital camera, set up physical works (sculptures, 3-D design, bulletin boards, and classroom shots) and take several photos in good light, preferably outdoors. Use a tripod and the camera's macro setting if available to get a photo that clearly defines the subject and provides as much detail as possible.

Bad photos should not be included in your Web portfolio. Out of focus images, distant subjects, and poorly lit should be eliminated from inclusion. All photos need to be opened in an image editing application to be cropped, color optimized, and set to 72 dpi or 96 dpi. We will cover how to do this later in this chapter. Images stored and transferred from a digital camera are typically in JPG format so you will not have to save from another file format. However, when you open up the files from the digital camera in Adobe Photoshop and you start to edit them you may save the file as a Photoshop document (PSD) in order to perform editing and other digital imaging functions that require layers in Photoshop.

Scanning Your Work

If you need to capture flat artwork and paper assets, you must perform scanning. Scanning hard copy work and flat artwork can be accomplished using a flatbed scanner. Keep in mind the size and resolution when scanning files for the Web.

- Scan all images at 150 dpi and then optimize to 72 dpi or 96 dpi (in Photoshop or Fireworks) and save to exact size that will be placed on the Web page.
- Scan photos using 24 bit full color scan settings.
- Scan b/w and line art images at 8 bit settings or Web color settings.
- Save your files as .JPG for photos & full color or .GIF for line art/clipart Web colors respectively.

Taking Screen Captures

Capturing samples of Web pages, page layout documents, and animations may require you to get screen shots. This can be accomplished by viewing the document on your monitor and then taking a screen capture (shot) of the entire desktop. After taking the capture it is your job to crop, optimize, and save the graphical piece you need.

Screen captures are always grabbed at a resolution of 72 dpi on MAC and 96 dpi on WINDOWS computers.

On the Mac, you press **shift + apple + three** and you get a camera shutter click. The captured file is placed on the root directory of your hard drive and is saved as a PCT file that can be opened in Adobe Photoshop or Macromedia Fireworks.

On a Windows computer, use the Print screen key (PrtScrn) and the desktop is captured to the clipboard. When you create a new file in Adobe Photoshop or Macromedia Fireworks the default page size is the same as the captured document. This size will be equal to your screen resolution setting. You want to capture at a high screen resolution so that the detail is clear when you scale and crop the desired image portion. To do this, set your monitor resolution to a high resolution, 1024 x 768 or above before doing the screen capture.

Once you perform a screen capture, you should crop out any unwanted areas of the desktop that were grabbed. Then, the image should be saved or exported as a GIF or JPG. We look at this task later on in this chapter.

Image Preparation, Crop, Scale and Save

Getting your images ready takes time. It is a process requiring acute detail, but it must be done. Image editing software makes preparing images relatively easy. There are several things that you should be aware of when preparing your images:

1. **Set the resolution to 72 dpi**

    To set the resolution of a bitmap graphic in Adobe Photoshop:

    With the file open in Photoshop, go to **Image>Image Size.** Set the resolution to 72 DPI then set the pixel height and width sizes. Be sure to keep **Constrain proportions** are checked on to keep the aspect ratio of your graphic true.

    To set the image size in Macromedia Fireworks, go to **Modify>Canvas>Image Size.**

Cropping a graphic eliminates wasted image area. Using the crop tool in Macromedia Fireworks or Adobe Photoshop allows you to drag the crop tool around the image section that you want to keep, and then adjust the parameters of the crop with adjustment handles located on the crop box. Once the crop is complete, press the enter key and the crop will take effect. Cropping will also make file sizes smaller and decrease load times. Use the crop tool to surround the desired area, then press enter.

2. **Set the color palette of the image to 24 bit RGB or 8 bit** (NO CMYK) (this is done automatically when you export or save as a GIF or JPG in Fireworks and Photoshop's Web exporting function). Note: conversion from CMYK to RGB must be done manually on files saved as JPG in Adobe Photoshop. If you use Macromedia Fireworks, the color conversion process is completed regardless of file format, all you need to do is decide on whether you will use JPG or GIF

3. **Set the background color of the image to what you want in the image editing program.** You can not edit images in Dreamweaver. Placing background colors is part of the image editing process.

   In Fireworks, select **Modify>Canvas Color** to change the background color of the image. If there is bitmap information in the background, say a white border, you would use the **magic wand tool** of the image editing program to select the white portion pixels and then press delete to eliminate them. The background color should show through. It will become bitmap data when the file is flattened and saved as a JPG or GIF.

   Export or save as JPG or GIF file format.

   Fireworks automatically assigns GIF or JPG file formats to any exported graphic. If you use Photoshop, you can save for Web to create an optimized Web file. Or, you can manually save a JPG or GIF file from Photoshop and export a GIF or JPG file from Fireworks.

   In Fireworks, **saving means saving a PNG file.** PNG is a Web format that has layers and transparency, much like the native Photoshop format. PNG is the proprietary format of Fireworks. Exporting in Fireworks gives you the Web graphics needed for Web sites.

   In Photoshop, saving can be done with any file format including PSD, the native file format for Photoshop.

   Scaling graphics is done in the image editing application. Open graphics and use the **free transform tool (CTRL+T)** in either Adobe Photoshop or Macromedia Fireworks. The graphic can be adjusted using handles for scaling and rotating. Once scaled, use the crop tool to eliminate extra space around the graphic. Then save or export the graphic as a GIF or a JPG.

Text-Based Content

The following sections on Web resumes and project descriptions can initially be created in Microsoft Word and then copied and pasted into an HTML file in Macromedia Dreamweaver or in the case of the resume, be saved as a PDF. The important point here is that you want to write the project descriptions first so you have a chance to write them, proof read them, and edit them. This shouldn't be done while you are creating Web pages. It may cause you to spend less time and consideration on the information included in them.

Web Resumes and CVs

Web resumes and curriculum vitas (for teachers) are simply text-based content that can be represented in your Web portfolio in the form of a PDF file, an HTML file, or even a graphic file. The techniques for handling the various formats have been discussed in this chapter. However, we will give some extra attention to Web resumes and CVs because they are critical components to the self promotion, credibility, and persuasion of the Web portfolio.

The Web resume or Web CV can be interactive and have links from HTML-based text. Or, you can use the image map tools on the properties inspector in Dreamweaver or Fireworks to create linkable hotspots anywhere on the resume (you'll learn about this in later chapters). You could link from jobs listed on the resume directly to projects in the Web portfolio. Using these content techniques, prepare your resume and have it ready for the Web functionality and Web development techniques that you will be learning later in this text.

Project Descriptions

Project descriptions are important to framing the perspective of the project and to explaining your involvement to the user. Captions are sometimes sufficient, possibly in the case of artwork or design, but in the case of technical projects, a full description may be needed. Descriptions should be catered to important aspects of an individuals discipline or field. For example, a salesperson might describe a project success and roles as revenue generated or accounts secured. While in the same portfolio project context, a musician might describe a project in terms of collaborators or performance venue. There are some possible constants that can be used as a foundation in beginning to describe projects in a wide range of disciplines.

Carliner (2005, p. 71) describes several important items for commentary in a showcase portfolio:

- Name of project
- Role played
- Major contributions to the project
- Issues to consider when reviewing this piece

I mostly agree with Carliner's suggestions on project description; however there a few pieces of information that might be included:

- Chronology
- Tools and or techniques employed
- Media (for arts and entertainment portfolios)
- Publication or exhibition/performance date
- Collaborators or contributors

Keep in mind that you will develop your own template for project descriptions. Think about the narrative around the project and write a succinct narrative that gives only the most salient and persuasive points.

Review and Conclusion

This chapter has provided a mix of technical and organizational information that will help us move along in the Web portfolio development process. Discussion has included content optimization, Web formats, resolution, and transforming Microsoft assets into Web accessible graphics and text files.

Setting up folder structures and understanding where files go locally will help as you create the Web portfolio and publish it to the Internet later on.

Critical attention must be paid to resolution of content. Graphical files must be 72 or 96 dpi maximum to scale. Adobe Photoshop and Macromedia Fireworks are the premier tools for creating Web graphics. You had a chance in this chapter to read and hopefully use some basic graphic manipulation tutorials in both applications as well as learn about the graphic file types used in Web pages: GIF and JPG. We discussed the advantages of using the portable document format (PDF) to publish content in its exact native visual appearance without distortion of fonts or color.

Getting your content together may include digital photography, screen captures, scanning, and using export and saving techniques in Microsoft Office products. Regardless of the format, graphics must conform to Web color or RGB standards to be viewable on the Internet. The size of Web graphics is critical to formatting Web pages and to visual appearance and communication effectiveness of Web pages.

Lastly, Web resumes and CVS needs to be output in all formats to be used in a variety of situations. PDF output is best for keeping visual integrity. HTML output is linkable and allows fast browser loading from directly inside the Web site. And a graphical Web resume or CV might be best when the resume is illustrated or uses color extensively.

Let's move forward in the Web portfolio production cycle and begin to develop our Web portfolio page designs. The next chapter brings us to laying out Web pages using Adobe Photoshop and Macromedia Fireworks.

Chapter VI

Web Page Design

Introduction

This chapter focuses on digital design for the Web using Adobe Photoshop and Macromedia Fireworks. It's time to review the storyboards that you created in Chapter IV. Your goal at this point is to use the storyboard designs that you sketched to create Web page screens. You want to utilize the content you gathered and developed while working in the last chapter. After successfully completing this chapter, you will have Web page screen designs that will be output into table- or layer-based HTML files. The files you will generate are going to be HTML files, but will not be functional Web pages. They will not have working links, pop-up windows or multimedia. The pages that are generated in this stage come from Macromedia fireworks or Adobe Photoshop. In this chapter, you will learn how to develop screen designs that will be turned into Web pages. When we open these pages in Macromedia Dreamweaver, we will be able to an extensive Web functionality and integrate flash-based multimedia. The main thrust of this chapter is to provide you with enough basic skills to get your portfolio pages designed and exported using professional level tools. Once you have completed the process, you'll be empowered to continue to develop Web pages throughout your career. As a learning tool, the Web portfolio makes you get involved with digital tools.

So far, we spent a lot of time working on paper. This is a good thing, because otherwise there is a good chance that we might be highly confused when we begin to use digital tools. Web portfolio design and Web design in general cannot begin simply by using digital tools. As we have stressed in this text, there must be conceptualization and content development. We need to have the ideas and materials available, before we manipulate those using digital tools.

Digital Tools

Computers give us choices in applications and in workflow methods. We see this in the sheer number of different companies that produce the same software. You can use Microsoft Word or WordPerfect for word processing. Each yields a text document, but the difference lies in the preference of you, the user. You might think Word is easier or more intuitive. Or maybe you are used to WordPerfect from a previous job, so you make it your tool of choice. The point here is that there are many software packages available for Web design and development. There are also many ways to approach designing Web pages on a computer. The processes I will be demonstrating and using for the Web portfolio design presented in this book are used in professional design shops. Most importantly, they are tools and techniques that I have used and taught successfully. I am a designer, so I take a designer's approach more than that of a programmers approach. That is not to say that we won't be doing Web programming. We will be using JavaScript, ActionScript, and some basic HTML to enhance functionality of our Web pages. On the design side, we will use image editing software and Web optimization software for front end design. I know this sounds very daunting, but it is a simple compact method for creating impressive Web portfolio pages. As your learning grows, so will your confidence.

In this chapter, we will spend some time discussing how to create Web pages from scratch in Macromedia Dreamweaver without working extensively in an image editing application first. This method may appeal to you if you have a Web portfolio that is filled with text and text documents as opposed to a more graphics-filled Web portfolio. If graphics are the majority of the content or the design is complicated, using an image editing application for Web screen layout and design is a better method than simply using Dreamweaver.

For multimedia and motion, we must use specialized applications. You will learn more about multimedia applications and have an opportunity to execute some techniques later on in the text, but in this stage, you will be planning and assuming positions for multimedia items in the screen designs. The multimedia items, which are Macromedia Flash movies will be added later on.

Eventually, you will work to discover new methods and tools on your own. Then, you will adapt to the techniques and applications that you feel provide the easiest workflow to creating Web pages.

Here are some of the digital tools we will be using to create Web pages for the Web portfolio:

- We will be creating our graphical Web page designs and individual graphics using Adobe Photoshop and Macromedia Fireworks.
- We will be using Macromedia Dreamweaver to perform Web development and to add functionality to our Web pages.

For motion graphics and multimedia:

- We will be using Adobe Audition to edit audio.
- We will be using Macromedia Flash to create motion graphics and multimedia.

Digital tools are important to master, but it is also important to pay attention to the visual aspects of the Web portfolio. Too many times I have seen bad designs that alienate the user with blinking text and horrific color choices. The look and feel of the Web portfolio should not be intimidating, it should be inviting.

Visual Design of Web Screens

A Web page is a collection of digital media elements that resides in a programmable framework, it also is a screen. The term "screen" refers to the fact that Web pages are presented on screen and not on paper. Web screens need to be built; initial design needs to be created before Web coding can be done. The goal when designing screens in an image editing application is to create only the graphical elements and layout. Concentrate on graphical elements only, leaving space for Web text (browser based text) and multimedia components.

Screens can be created in any image editing program that optimizes and outputs Web pages. Keep in mind, the screens you design will become Web pages in your site. The reasons we create screens in an image editing application and use this technique are many. We use a two-dimensional design program to create Web pages because it provides an accurate view of what our page looks like in size and color, allows us free-form design with type and graphics, and most importantly, because the screens we create will be composed of layers, we can edit graphical content pages quickly and easily. In this book, I will use Adobe Photoshop and Macromedia Fireworks to create screens.

The screens you create in Fireworks become Web pages in the following manner. Screens get optimized, sliced, and exported into HTML tables using Macromedia Fireworks. The resulting Web pages with tables are opened in Dreamweaver. Then, the tables can be converted to layers or kept as tables. The tables hold all the graphics. More tables or layers are added for the text elements and additional graphics if needed. An easy technique is to use layers placed to float on top of the page. Layers can be positioned easily. Tables, when they are freely placed on Web pages, may need added HTML editing savvy and can be more challenging than simply using layers. Especially, when you are new to using Macromedia Dreamweaver. Tables are easier to manipulate when they are inserted into layers. This approach is a useful technique for positioning elements freely in a Web page.

The screens we create may change during the design process. We may improve something or realize that something is not quite right. That's okay, design is a dynamic process. Also, we will not be creating all pages using the Fireworks screen slice techniques; we will be using Dreamweaver to create Web pages "from scratch". We will also touch on static page design combined with some simple JavaScript and HTML tweaks. I approached the tutorials for Web pages this way because I wanted to provide multiple techniques for assembling Web pages. You will adopt the techniques which you feel most confident using.

Previously, you completed some storyboards that represent your Web pages in very simple sketches. When you create your screens, you will refer to the storyboards and begin to create the pages that you planned out during the visual design process.

To review, the basic components that you should have included in your storyboards are:

- Image location
- Text
- Motion graphic and animation locations
- List audio track or sounds to be played and explain how will be controlled and positioned
- Navigation, sub navigation (refer to your content outline and flowchart)
- Sketch pop-up windows with sub-navigation, captions, and close buttons)

When designing screens, think about these elements and begin to design the graphics and layout of your Web pages. For Web text and other Web development items, simply leave a space for anticipated elements. For example, you would leave space for a paragraph of HTML text in the body of the page. Later, in Macromedia Dreamweaver, you would type in the text using a Layer. Only graphical text will be designed into the screens in the image editing application. Any text that needs to be edited or searched should be HTML-based and inserted into the page after the screen design is created and optimized for the Web. We add the text in Dreamweaver.

Pop-Up Windows

Pop-up windows are also screens, they are Web pages. If your pop-up windows are simple in content, you can create them as Web pages in Macromedia Dreamweaver. If they carry lots of graphics or graphical buttons, then you may want to use an image editing program to create a Web page

Figure 6.1. Pop-up window (The pop-up window allows isolation from the rest of the site without abandoning it. You should consider using pop-up windows for showcasing project work. Keep the design simple and add functionality with next, back, and close buttons if needed.)

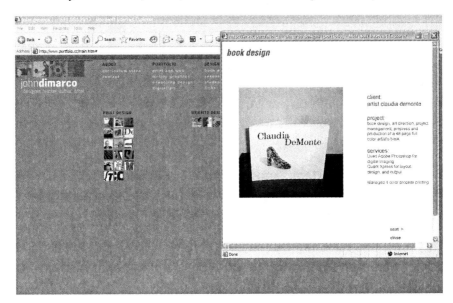

screen. You cannot create Web graphics in Macromedia Dreamweaver. Dreamweaver is used only for Web page authoring. We will talk about pop up windows in detail later in this text.

Text Decisions

There are two kinds of text in Web pages.

- **Web text or HTML** text is editable text that can be seen in browsers using limited system resources including font, size, and color. Web text is processed by HTML and can be explicitly controlled by using Cascading Style Sheets (CSS). Web text should be used for text that will have future updates and also for searchable text. All text in a Web page can be HTML text. Many sites employ only HTML text to increase performance, searchability, and to make future edits easier. For the novice graphics person, starting with Web pages that are less populated and use HTML text as opposed to graphical text is an easier approach.

• **Graphical text** is a typographic image. It is a bitmap graphic that uses type. It is an image, not character based text in the digital form. In a communication form and from a design standpoint, graphical text is very valuable to attaining style, identity, and visual impact. Graphical text is used mostly in Web page headers, Web logos, buttons, icons, and motion graphics. The best sites employ both HTML text and graphical text. HTML text is almost always used for updateable information and graphical text is used for items that do not change. That is the approach we will take in the design of the Web portfolio we work through in this book.

Icons and Logos

Page icons and logos can be designed in Macromedia Fireworks or Adobe Photoshop. Or, they can be created using a vector illustration application such as Adobe Illustrator or Macromedia Freehand. The advantage to using a vector file is the quality of the graphic and the ability to edit the graphic in the illustration

Figure 6.2. Converting vector text and logos to curves (Converting vector based text in programs such as Adobe Illustrator and Macromedia Freehand makes the item a graphic. The text is no longer editable and the font appearance is preserved.)

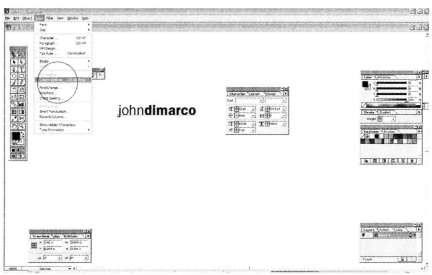

application without loss of quality. The edited file can then be re-imported into an image editing program. By creating a vector graphic and importing it into an image editing application, the font data is preserved and the font appearance remains unchanged. The graphic can then be saved or exported as a Web-friendly format, as we mentioned several times already, GIF or JPG.

I created a personal logo for my Web portfolio using Macromedia Freehand. The logo type was designed and then **converted to curves** when complete. By converting the file to curves, the font data is not needed and the editable text turns into an un-editable graphic. The file can now be saved as an .eps file. Then, it can be opened in Fireworks or Photoshop and eventually exported or saved to GIF or JPG format.

Navigation and Buttons

One great way I found to create graphical buttons is to make them in Macromedia Fireworks and then slice and export them out as a Web page containing a nice neat table. Then the table can be copied and pasted into a layer and positioned anywhere on the Web page freely and easily. The visual advantage to this is that you can work directly in Macromedia Fireworks, make a Web screen, and see how the navigation fits into the Web page itself. You can create shapes using the shape tools in Macromedia Fireworks and place type on the shapes to create individual buttons. Or, you can make complete navigation panels that incorporate all site controls.

Remember, navigation also can be HTML Web text only.

A Word About
Slicing and Exporting Pages

Both Macromedia Fireworks and Adobe Photoshop provide image slicing and exporting functions. However, I prefer the slicing and exporting tools found in Fireworks better than in Photoshop. On the other hand, I like the typographic effects, image editing features, and overall design control I get with Photoshop.

Figure 6.3. Navigation and button bar in Macromedia Fireworks (You can make navigation bars and buttons in Macromedia Fireworks quickly and easily. Buttons can be sliced and exported to make navigation bars for use in Macromedia Dreamweaver.)

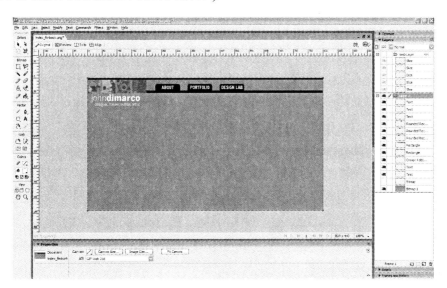

As well, in many cases, I have legacy documents that are in Photoshop file format. My point here is that I use both applications when I design Web site screens. You might favor one over the other. But for slicing, exporting, and integration with Dreamweaver, Fireworks wins hands down in my opinion. Not to worry though, Fireworks opens native Photoshop files with layers and the text is completely editable. As long as versions are up to date, the integration is seamless. You could design all your pages and navigation graphics in Photoshop and then open them in Fireworks to optimize, slice, and export. If you create pages in Photoshop, you can save the files as PSD format. Then, you can open the PSD file directly in Fireworks. You can tweak the page and slice and export. Lastly, you can save the file as PNG so that it is easily edited and re-exported in the future.

Macromedia was purchased by Adobe in April 2005, but Fireworks and Photoshop still remain individual products. In the future, it will be interesting to see how Adobe integrates the applications to create a Web graphics tool that will enable even the newest Web portfolio designer to create Web screens and output them to Web pages quickly and easily. The process is good now, however there always be improvements made to digital workflows as technology progresses.

We have overviewed various pieces in the Web production process up to this point. We covered several approaches to creating Web pages. Web screens and using Dreamweaver for creating Web pages from scratch are main points that we discussed. Also, we covered various graphic file formats used for Web images and we establish which formats to use for various types of artwork. We also established basic designs for our Web portfolio pages and developed storyboards to guide us through the development process.

In the next sections we take a closer look at the tools and explore some of the most important techniques used to create Web portfolio pages. Don't expect to learn the applications and each technique immediately after reading the tutorials. You should become familiar with techniques by reading about them and then attempting to execute them repeatedly on your own while tackling a Web portfolio design project. As I mentioned previously, you will develop your own personal workflow and technical approach as your practice and experience preparing assets and creating Web pages expands.

With that said, let's begin by using Macromedia Fireworks to design, slice, and export a Web page.

Make a Web page layout in Macromedia Fireworks MX 2004:

1. Open Macromedia Fireworks and immediately go to **Window>Properties** and **Window>Tools** to show the tool bar and property inspector. Both palettes may be open on start up.

2. Go to **File> New** and create a document at the size you want your Web pages to be: use 800 x 600.

3. Set the resolution of the document to 72 dpi and choose a Web safe background color from the palette.

4. Start by creating a page header and navigation bar. If you are using HTML text-based navigation, you can skip this section. Your navigation will not be graphical. That's fine and very appropriate for a Web portfolio. But if you want get a bit fancier, the following are a few steps on how to create page headers and graphical navigation buttons.

   To make a page header, create a box that spans the top of your Web page (800 wide by 75 high). Set the header box to the desired color and then add text to the bar or open an image and drag it into the Web page document directly from its window (see next). Scale the graphic accordingly in the Web page document and then place it on the navigation bar.

The header text should state the page name, for example bio or resume would be typical headers (categories).

To make the navigation buttons, create boxes or circles (around 50 x 50 pixels) and align them vertically or horizontally. Then overlay the corresponding category text. Be sure to align the text and the buttons correctly so that the visual appeal is consistent. If you need help with alignment, you can go to the menu item

View> Grid

and

View>Guides — Drag guides from the rulers on to the page. Align elements using the guides.

Leave the rest of the page blank. We will add layers to this content area later on when we open the newly sliced Web pages in Dreamweaver.

5. If you want to push the pages further in Fireworks, you can open the Web graphics you created into your screen designs by dragging and dropping from window to window, copying and pasting, and by importing. The easiest way is to drag and drop. You can open images in Macromedia Fireworks and drag from one window to the next. Each image comes over on to its own layer. Use the scale tool or simply click CRTL+T and you will get a free transformation bounding box around the graphic. Hold the corner node and shift key and scale the graphic; hit return to complete the operation. You can design pages with graphics completely using Fireworks or place the individual images on the Web pages later using Dreamweaver. We will show both techniques in this book, the choice of design methods will be yours.

Slicing Pages

Once you have designed the Web page or opened up a page saved as a Photoshop or Fireworks document, you are ready to begin slicing. The slice tool in Fireworks allows you to slice a graphical screen design into an HTML page.

When using the slicing process to create a Web page, the first step is designing the page. Then, using the **slice tool** (located below the main tools on the toolbar

Figure 6.4. Sample Web page design in Macromedia Fireworks (You can design entire Web pages in Macromedia Fireworks.)

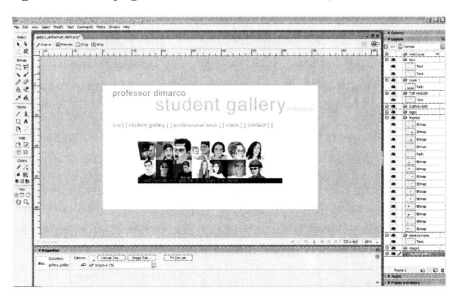

in Fireworks), the page is sliced into rectangular boxes that have a green overlay. Sliced elements should include any item that needs to work as a link and any element that is a separate graphic on the page. When the slices are **exported,** all the graphics are optimized and converted to either a GIF or JPG file and assigned a sequential name. Each slice is placed within an HTML table and the resulting output is an HTML file and all the supporting graphics. The HTML file is a Web page. Although Fireworks has some tools for adding functionality to the Web page, Dreamweaver is far better suited to perform the Web authoring functions needed. The HTML page you generate from Fireworks can be opened in Dreamweaver and all the Web functionality can be added.

Optimizing and Exporting
Pages and Graphics

Optimizing graphics means choosing a color palette for the slice. We stated before that all photos and full color images need to be JPG files and that all flat color logos and icons need to be GIF files. In Fireworks, you can click on each

Figure 6.5. Sliced page in Macromedia Fireworks (Slices create a table with placed graphics in each cell.)

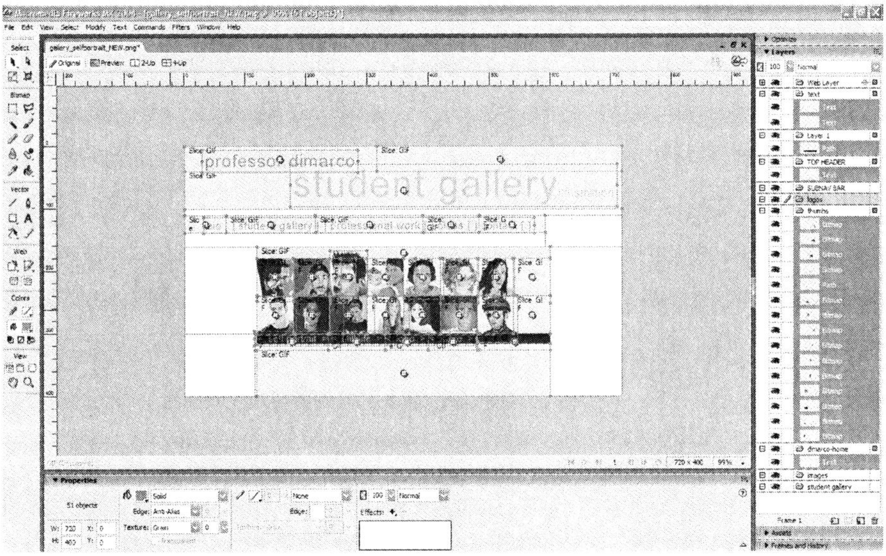

slice and use the properties inspector to change the file optimization format used upon export. This means that some slices are exported as GIF and some are exported as JPG. This is all based on your decisions when slicing.

Upon exporting, Fireworks will ask you where to place the new graphic files and the HTML file that supports them. You'll need to refer back to the folder structure you previously created.

The most important thing to remember when exporting is to put the files in the correct folders. Be consistent and place files in their proper locations.

For this site we are using this structure: **All HTML pages are exported to the root folder: jdimarco (first initial, last name).** Name the .htm pages descriptively. Bio.htm, .portfolio_menu_page.htm, cases_1.htm, cases_2.htm, are all good name conventions. Don't use spaces or odd characters in file names. Underscores are good for separating words in file names. Do not use extra periods in filenames—except at the end before the .htm file extension. The files will not work if they are named incorrectly.

All images are exported to the images folder: jdimarco/ images. Your home page or "first page" of the site is always named index.htm. After export and optimization, you will save a native Fireworks file complete with slices, layers, and text. The file may be used for editing and exporting later on.

Figure 6.6. Optimization in Macromedia Fireworks (Graphic files can be optimized for GIF or JPG exporting.)

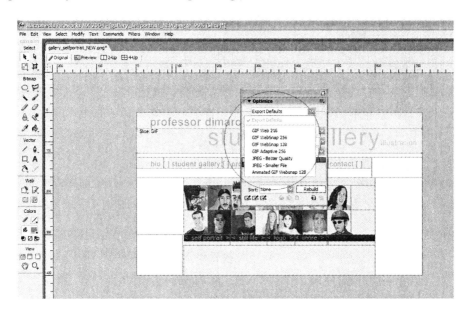

How to Export individual JPG and GIF graphics in Macromedia Fireworks MX 2004:

You can create your content and artwork in Adobe Photoshop, Corel Draw, Photopaint, Adobe Illustrator, or any other graphic art application. However, we know that all Web graphics need to be converted to the proper format so that they can be viewed on the Web. To do this exercise, find an image on your computer or the Internet that you can use.

Open Macromedia Fireworks and immediately go to **Window>Properties** and **Window>Tools** to show the tool bar and property inspector. Both palettes might be open on start up. Open a graphic file in any format (TIFF, EPS, PSD, PNG, JPG). Scale, crop, add to it, and then **use the slice tool** to slice all the parts of the image in Fireworks. Click each slice and then using the **properties inspector, set the Default Export Options file type to GIF Web snap 216** or **JPG (better quality**). Remember that GIF is best for flat line art and logos while JPG is best for photos and full color images. **Go to FILE> EXPORT.** Export the graphic files only into your images folder. Save the file as native Fireworks PNG file for use later.

The exported graphics can be placed into layers and tables on your Web pages in Dreamweaver by going to **Insert> Image.**

Figure 6.7a. Root directory after exporting (The .htm files (Web pages) should be in the root directory of the Web site. Notice index.htm is the homepage.)

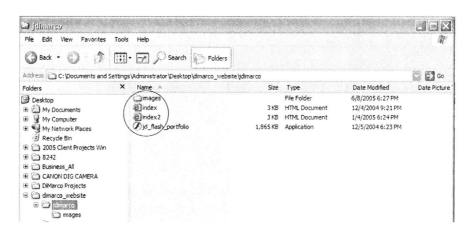

Figure 6.7b. Images folders after exporting (The image files should be located in the images folder of the Web site. Notice the naming conventions: r for row and c for column.)

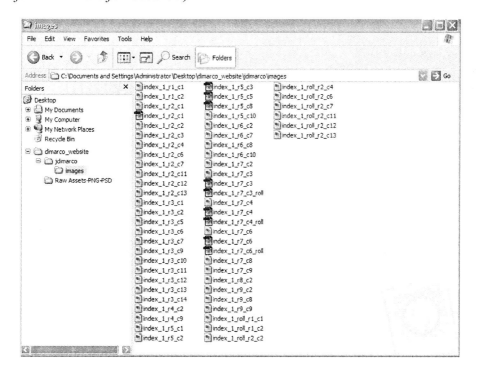

Saving files for editing and archive:

Once you have a basic screen layout, you can experiment with placement and color. After screens are complete, you can save the file as a PNG (Portable Network Graphics) file in Fireworks. PNG is the native format for Fireworks. Portable Network Graphics are full color files that support transparency, unlike JPEG which does not. The great thing about PNG in Fireworks is that all images and text remain editable and on layers. It is very important that you save a PNG file for every screen and Fireworks file that you make. If the page elements need editing, the Fireworks PNG can be opened, edited, and re-exported. This is an important step in the production process. If you have native Photoshop files, you can save a PSD file in layers as your editable document. There is one simple rule for color: no CMYK color files. CMYK graphics are built for printing, not Web output, as they will not show up in your Web pages.

Let's review what we have covered in the Web portfolio design process so far. Overall, we stated that the Web portfolio needs to be content driven, easy to navigate, persuasive, and dynamic. The steps we have tackled so far include:

1. Conceptualization of the Web portfolio
2. Creation of a rough content list
3. Creation of a content outline
4. Creation of a flowchart
5. Creation of storyboards
6. Collection of content items (assets)
7. Development of Web screens
8. Slicing of Web screens
9. Exporting sliced screens into HTML pages, and GIF and JPG graphics
10. Exporting individual graphics to the images folder

Our Web pages complete with tables and graphics are now ready to be opened in Dreamweaver so we can add a multitude of Web functionality to our site pages. Specifically we will need to edit and add these items:

- Navigation links
- Color

- Page titles
- Web text
- Pop up windows
- Secondary navigation
- Functionality buttons (window close, sound off, etc.)
- E-mail link contact link
- Content

Review and Conclusion

In the next chapter, you begin to explore Macromedia Dreamweaver and some basic things that you need to know about tables and layers. These basic Dreamweaver tutorials should give you a foundation for editing and creating functional Web pages. As you move forward to begin using Dreamweaver, your skills in brainstorming, content creation, graphic development, and screen design will have yielded enough content to start to see the Web portfolio come to life. Moving into Web development, you will begin to push your technology skills and learning further and further. You will see that there will be times when you are a bit confused and may have to repeat steps several times to begin to understand them, that's just natural. It takes a long time to make Web development skills and intuitive part of your abilities. However, another great thing about the Web portfolio design process is that it makes you repeat the same steps over and over again. The repetition that is needed to learn and perform Web portfolio design is instrumental in building real skills. Now let's move forward and continue to build Web pages using Macromedia Dreamweaver.

Chapter VII

Web Authoring

Introduction

Web authoring is the process of developing Web pages. The Web development process requires you to use software to create functional pages that will work on the Internet. Adding Web functionality is creating specific components within a Web page that do something. Adding links, rollover graphics, and interactive multimedia items to a Web page creates are examples of enhanced functionality. This chapter demonstrates Web based authoring techniques using Macromedia Dreamweaver. The focus is on adding Web functions to pages generated from Macromedia Fireworks and to overview creating Web pages from scratch using Dreamweaver. Dreamweaver and Fireworks are professional Web applications. Using professional Web software will benefit you tremendously.

There are other ways to create Web pages using applications not specifically made to create Web pages. These applications include Microsoft Word and Microsoft PowerPoint. The use of Microsoft applications for Web page development is not covered in this chapter. However, I do provide steps on how to use these applications for Web page authoring within the appendix of this text. If you feel that you are more comfortable using the Microsoft applications or the Macromedia applications simply aren't available to you yet, follow the same process for Web page conceptualization and content creation and use the programs available to you. You should try to get Web page development skills using Macromedia Dreamweaver because it helps you expand your software skills outside of basic office applications. The ability to create a Web page using professional Web development software is important to building a high-end computer skills set.

The main objectives of this chapter are to get you involved in some technical processes that you'll need to create the Web portfolio. Focus will be on guiding you through opening your sliced pages, adding links, using tables, creating pop up windows for content and using layers and timelines for dynamic HTML. The coverage will not try to provide a complete tutorial set for Macromedia Dreamweaver, but will highlight essential techniques. Along the way you will get pieces of hand coded action scripts and JavaScripts. You can decide which pieces you want to use in your own Web portfolio pages. The techniques provided are a concentrated workflow for creating Web pages. Let us begin to explore Web page authoring.

WYSIWYG Applications vs. HTML Hand Coding

"What you see is what get", or WYSIWYG, refers to software packages that use intuitive interfaces and menus for user initiated functions, in other words, application specific software. In contrast is traditional programming and specifically HTML (not really a programming language, but a mark up language). HTML is a hand coded method of creating a Web page. Hand coded methods are considered tedious by some and require the expertise of an experienced programming practitioner. As well, if the HTML writer is low or moderately skilled, there is a strong chance the Web pages will be poorly constructed and visually weak. In this text, we will find that common ground between the two methods focuses mostly on WYSIWYG applications including Macromedia Dreamweaver. In the real world, the professional Web designer needs to have strength in one main method and should have some moderate knowledge and skills in the other. For example, you may be a strong designer and have extensive expertise using Web applications including Macromedia Dreamweaver and Flash. However, you want to try to achieve some level of moderate skills and knowledge in ActionScript, JavaScript, and HTML. Developing Web pages, you will use the knowledge in these areas frequently and should dedicate learning time to these areas in order to build a more rounded skill set.

This chapter provides some techniques and information on JavaScript and HTML. JavaScript is a programming language that allows you to add extended functionality and interactivity to Web pages (Negrino & Smith, 2004, p. 2). Here is an example of a JavaScript to close a browser window:

JavaScript:self.close()

HTML is hypertext markup language. It is the language used in Web pages. It is a written text file consists of tags containing varied attributes. I do not focus in this authoring chapter on creating HTML Web pages by writing the HTML. However, you need to understand that HTML is the underlying engine that drives you a Web page on the Internet. A basic example of how to write an HTML page using only hand typed code is provided in the appendix.

Now let's start to develop the functionality in our Web pages. First, we will dissect our sliced Fireworks page and then briefly discuss why we are focusing mainly on using Web development software and only touching upon hand coding methods.

Opening Sliced Web Pages from Fireworks

I have found the integration between Macromedia Fireworks and Dreamweaver to be seamless. Exported HTML pages and associated graphics files are placed in your desired folder structure. Now you are ready to open the HTML (the files will be named .htm or .html) pages in Dreamweaver and add Web functionality such as HTML text, links, JavaScript, and simple motion using Dynamic Layers. When you open .htm pages in Dreamweaver the sliced page will be in a nested table. The table is constructed of rows and columns that hold a piece of the Web page. Each of your slices became part of the table upon exporting. Your images and buttons are nested in the table and consecutively named with a _r _c suffix, with R representing row and C representing column.

The table can be edited and manipulated. However, tables are sometimes challenging to work with if you are new to Web design so I have decided to show you an alternate method on how to utilize floating design using layers. You can learn about both, and use which ever one you feel most comfortable with. Now, you are probably saying what will you do with this big complex table?

Tables

HTML tables allow you to arrange data. Data in the form of text, preformatted text, images, links, forms, form fields, and other tables is assembled into rows and columns of cells. When used with graphics, tables may force users to scroll horizontally to view a table designed on a system with a larger display. To minimize these problems, authors should use style sheets to control text layout rather than tables.(http://www.w3.org/TR/REC-html40/struct/tables.html#h-11.1). To add to this, style sheets and layers are great for controlling data in a Web page. I find that complex tables are effective to use and easy to manage

Figure 7.1. Table in Macromedia Dreamweaver (Tables are containers in the form of rows and columns. This table contains the text based navigation to my Web portfolio.)

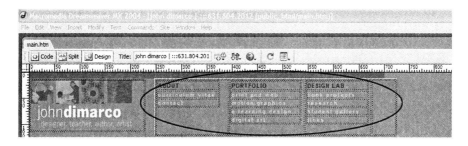

Figure 7.2. Page properties in Macromedia Dreamweaver (The appearance of background color, font, links, margins, and headings can be set in page properties.)

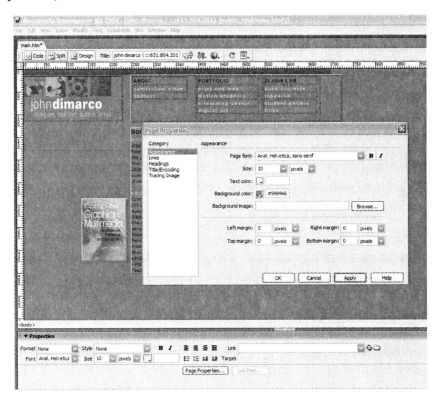

when they are made using the slice tools in a Web optimization application such as Macromedia Fireworks. Slicing seems to be easier than hand coding table rows and table data. Also, the slicing method allows the table to be edited using the table properties in Macromedia Dreamweaver. Editing a complex sliced table is easier than creating a complex table from scratch in Dreamweaver. You can use both methods as you build your Web authoring skills in Macromedia Dreamweaver.

The table creation abilities of Dreamweaver are great for making simple tables and for nesting tables inside of each other. To insert a table on to a Web page, you can use the menu item **Insert>Table.** To nest a table, simply click inside of a table cell and insert a table.

As I have mentioned before, techniques described throughout the book can be mixed and matched. Or, you can decide which is most comfortable for you and stick with it for your page designs.

Figure 7.3. Editing a table using the properties inspector (The properties inspector in Macromedia Dreamweaver controls the attributes of the HTML components on the page such as tables, layers, links, and navigation elements.)

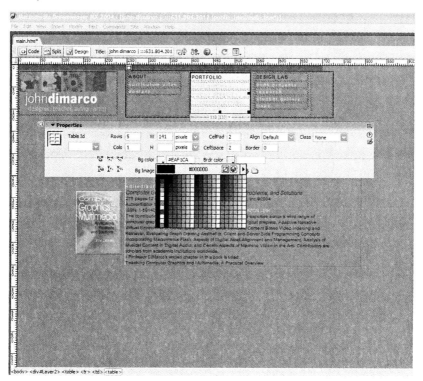

Creating a Web Page Using Macromedia Dreamweaver

Creating new pages requires you to perform a process. As we have discussed previously, Web design processes can vary. So you should find one you like, use it to get work done, and constantly explore and learn new processes to grow your skills and portfolio. We have identified and defined the process for creating, slicing, and exporting a Web page using Macromedia Fireworks. The process for creating Web pages using Dreamweaver starts with you creating a new .htm page.

File>New>HTML page

This will create a new Web page. It will be a blank white page. HTML pages are rather simple when created in Dreamweaver. Think of a Web page in Dreamweaver like a word processing document. You can type and place graphics inline. You can change type color, page title, and page color by going to **Modify>Page Properties.** Don't worry so much about setting any other parameters than page title and background color.

Once you have created a new page and set the page properties, you are ready begin to add content. To add content, you must insert a layer. To control the content more effectively, insert a table inside of the layer.

Properties Inspector

The properties inspector is an important tool palette in Dreamweaver. The inspector will change depending on the page element that is selected or highlighted. For example, when a table is on the page and you click inside of a cell, the properties of the table cell are active. You can experiment with created tables to see how you can edit the data they contain and manipulate their form and attributes. There are two places to edit tables, inside the table and outside the table.

The outside cell table properties that can be edited are:

- Rows and columns
- Width and height
- Cell pad (space outside) and cell space (space around content)
- Alignment
- Color attributes (border, background)
- Background image

The inside cell table properties that can be edited are:

- Font
- Style
- Link
- Color attributes (border, background)
- Vertical and Horizontal alignment within the cell

Figure 7.4. Layers and tables together (This main page uses layers for precise layout. Inside are nested tables that contain content. (A) The table is nested inside of the layer. (B) The layer has resize handles for easy manipulation.)

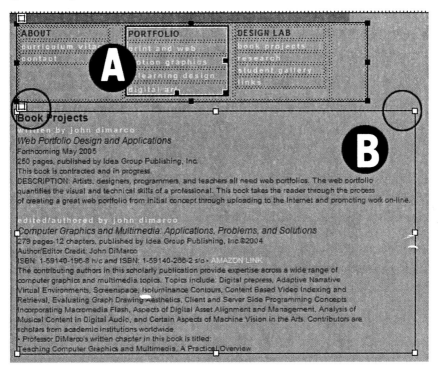

Remember, text, images, and other content elements can reside in either a layer or a table. For the best positioning and control, use tables inside of layers.

We have discussed using traditional HTML hand coding and working from scratch in Dreamweaver for creating your portfolio Web pages. I have shown you several production shortcuts using Fireworks and Photoshop that allow you freedom of design in the familiar environment of digital imaging and efficient optimization. Although we may or may not utilize the slicing and exporting techniques for every page, we will be using Fireworks to optimize individual Web graphics as we need during production. As well, we might find the need to slice up a navigation bar or desired page to fit into our site at the last minute. The point here is that we have overviewed and discussed several tools and techniques so far and you should keep them in mind as we move forward. Now we are going to continue into the Web development and multimedia stages of the Web portfolio site. To begin, we will focus on DHTML with layers and timelines.

Figure 7.5. Converting tables to layers (Tables created by exporting from Macromedia Fireworks slices can be converted to layers for simpler handling.)

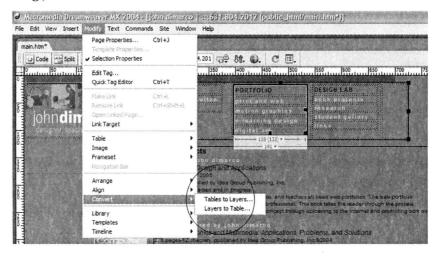

Utilizing the Content Holders

Tables and layers both hold content. However, there are specific differences between the two. Ideally, you want to use tables nested inside of layers. This method provides several benefits. Layers can be moved freely on the page, tables cannot. When a table is nested into a layer, it has the ability to be positioned outside of the paragraph format that tables must follow when placed loose on a Web page.

Not to worry, Dreamweaver can do all the work and convert the table to layers. Now, each table cell has become a layer. Extraneous pieces will also be in layers. You may want to delete them to clear up the page a bit. After conversion, the layers are placed in a stacking order onto the layers palette.

Layers

If you are new to using Macromedia Dreamweaver or image editing software you probably are a bit sketchy on the definition of a layer. A layer is a container of HTML content. The container holds elements such as text, graphics, animations, color, and any other object or item that can be placed on a Web page (Towers, 1999). We said before that tables are great for controlling the items in a layer. Layer items can also be controlled by CSS attributes. Cascading Style Sheets allow items to be positioned absolutely on a Web page. For our uses and for people with little experience, CSS can be skipped over for now. We will learn about CSS later in this chapter.

Each layer occupies a separate, stacked position on the Z axis. Z is the axis of depth. Layers have a Z axis because they can be stacked on top of one another, thus creating depth. The Web page has X for width, Y for height, and Z for depth. Here are some of the virtues of layers:

- Layers can be added and deleted easily.
- Layers can hold any Web asset or object.
- Layers can be dynamically controlled (DHTML) using a timeline.
- Layers can be resized, colored, and positioned to fit conveniently into your Web page design.
- Tables can be nested inside layers to provide extensive content control.

Using layers with tables is an easy and highly effective way to develop Web pages from scratch, without using Fireworks to create an entire page. In this case, you would use Fireworks for optimizing and exporting individual graphics, instead of entire pages.

The layers inspector lists all the layers on the current page. Go to **WINDOW>LAYERS,** and the layers inspector will pop up. When you create a new layer, the layer1 name will appear in the name section of the layers inspector. You can click on the layer name and rename it descriptively. This will help when you have many layers on the page. The layer will also have an assigned Z index number. The Z index refers to the stacking order of the layers and to the load sequence on the page. The top-down stacking order is represented on the page in the same manner. The layer at the top is the highest number. It will always load at the top of the page, above other indexes. In sum, the highest number loads last and on top.

You can prevent overlaps with layers, but you might want to overlap layers in your page design process. So, you might want to leave the overlap button unchecked unless you need to use it.

To manage positioning of layers, you can use the rulers, properties inspector positioning fields, and the grid. The grid allows you to snap the layers to a predefined grid. Or, you can move the layers freely where you want with conforming and locking to the grid. The advantage to using the grid is that you can position items consistently and accurately on the Web page. Using a grid will also help you simplify your Web pages so that they are streamlined and built for the user to enjoy the content. Grids help you maintain visual integrity with the placement of your Web page components.

To insert a layer go to the menu item **INSERT>LAYOUT OBJECTS>LAYER.**

To scale a layer, click on it on the page or in the layer inspector and grab an anchor handle (use a corner to do two sides at once). Resize layers to snuggly fit their content. You can also type size numbers into the width and height field on the properties inspector to scale the layer precisely to a desired numeric size.

You can position a layer freely by clicking on its bounding box and grabbing the tab in the top corner. To position on an exact page location, use the properties inspector and type in the X and Y location values. For example, X = 100 and Y = 100 would move the top corner of the layer down 100 pixels and over 100 pixels.

Figure 7.6. Layer properties on the properties inspector (You can position and size layers precisely. This allows for a free form design of Web pages that is more difficult to achieve using only tables.)

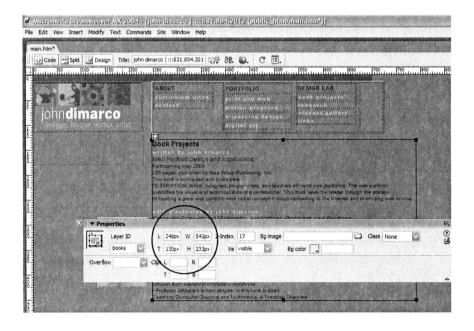

It's easy to get content into layers. Any Web content can be placed into layers:

- Text
- Images
- Tables
- Forms
- Multimedia (Flash)
- Other layers

To get content into layers you can **Insert > Images** into a layer or you can type directly into layer. We will be using layers more and more so you may want to practice creating a page and adding some layers, then adding some text or an image from your images folder.

Now that you have learned about layers, let's discuss how to make them animate and move.

Layer Motion with Timelines

The timeline inspector is a wonderful, powerful tool; it allows us to make HTML files dynamically move. They also provide a method of simple animation that does not require the experience and patience of using Macromedia Flash. We will examine some techniques using layers and the timelines in Dreamweaver. Now, this portion of the text will get a bit in-depth. If you feel that you are not ready to start with dynamic pages and want to stick to static, non-moving pages for now, you can skip ahead to using the properties inspector to position your layers and make a balanced Web page layout. Let us continue with layers and animation.

The basis for animation is change over time. The timeline consists of channels. Each channel contains frames, and the frames represent time. The timeline is best set to move at a certain rate over time. For example, if the timeline was set for 15 frames per second for a 10 second animation, assuming perfect performance conditions, the animation would run go through 15 frames per second until 10 seconds were met and 150 frames were run.

Animation channels are numbered and have a top down stacking order similar to layers. The only elements that can be animated and manipulated on the

Figure 7.7. Object on the timeline (A: The object "book_move" added to the timeline consists of a layer which contains a thumbnail graphic. B: The object book on the timeline has two keyframes (dots). The keyframes represent changes. In this case, the keyframes are a start and a finish point for motion across the Web page.)

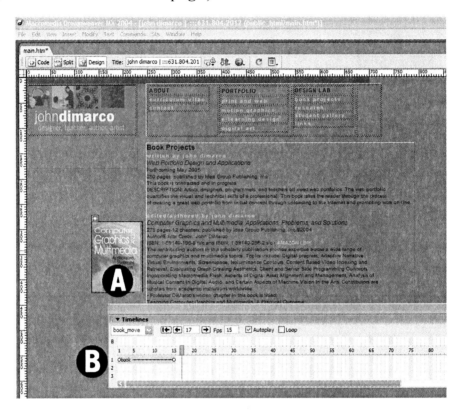

timelines are layers and images. The channel at the very top is the behavior channel. It holds JavaScript Behaviors that can be placed using the behaviors palette. We will talk more about behaviors later.

There are some key terms that you must become familiar with when working with timelines. These words will come in handy later when you learn about motion graphics and Macromedia Flash.

The animation channels are like rivers; they are pathways for content to flow. To stop and change the flow, insert a keyframe. Keyframes are points in time where change occurs. In the keyframe movement application to the layer and edits to attributes such as position, color, visibility, and size will execute. These changes must occur on a keyframe placed in the timeline. Layers can be set to visible and invisible at certain keyframes. And because the timeline animates layers and what is inside of them, you can experiment with animating content that you place inside of your layers.

Animating layers on a timeline requires several steps. Once you have performed the steps, you can add more timelines and more animated objects to your Web pages. You can place layers and images on timelines. Now that does not mean you have a free pass to the land of bad design. Quite the contrary, you need to use animation sparingly and strategically. The goal of the animation should be to provide extra emphasis on communication of an important point. For instance, you may want to have an animated biography that consists of a series of images and captions that show highlights in your career. At the end of the animation you would not want to keep animating your name over and over again in different type faces throughout each Web page. Why, it would be distracting to your real content and it would be perceived as annoying. Remember, your goal is to persuade not assault.

To Animate a Layer on a Timeline

Start with a fresh, clean practice HTML page. **FILE>NEW>HTML**
Open the timeline by going to **WINDOW>TIMELINE**.

Put a Layer on the Web Page

1. Go to **WINDOW>LAYERS,** to open the layers palette
2. Add a layer to the Web page by going to **INSERT>LAYOUT OB-JECTS>LAYER.**

Name the layer in the layers palette RED (Double click on Layer One and type in RED)

3. Open the **Properties Inspector** and change the layer bg (background) color to red.
4. Position the layer using the L(Left) and T(Top) fields on the Property Inspector (Use L=100 and T=100)

Add the Layer to the Timeline

Select the layer and go to **MODIFY>TIMELINE>ADD OBJECT TO TIMELINE**

You will see the layer name RED on the timeline in a grey bar (when selected it is purple) with a line and two dots. The dots represent keyframes. There is a start and an end to every animation. Keyframes represent the start, middle, and finish points of the animation. If you want to change the object during the span of time, you can add a keyframe in between the beginning and finishing keyframes. For now let's just get this layer to move across the page.

1.   Click directly on the last keyframe (dot) and move the layer across the Web page. You can extend the time it take the layer to move from start to finish by selecting and dragging the last keyframe down the timeline.
2.   Check off the auto play button and preview the Web page in a Web browser such as Internet Explorer or Netscape by pressing F12. You determine which browser is used for testing in the preferences of Dreamweaver.
3.   If all is correct, you should have seen the layer move across the page. It only moved once because we do not have it set to loop. If it did not work go back to Dreamweaver and check to see if you there is a check in the Auto play box located on the timeline. To loop the animation, check off the loop box. Now preview it in browser again—F12.

You'll notice that Dreamweaver announced that it was going to add a Behavior to your Web page code (after you checked LOOP) to allow the animation to go to frame one repeatedly. Behaviors are JavaScript based snippets that Dreamweaver supplies to help JavaScript programming become a bit easier on the novice and intermediate. Instead of writing hand coded JavaScript, Behaviors provide easy, intuitive drop down menus to allow you to use JavaScript functionality without extensive coding knowledge. We will be looking a Behaviors and JavaScript later in the text.

A Brief Review

You can set up the entire Web page with layers and then plug in your content. Or, you can slice a page, graphic, or menu in Fireworks and export a table, which you can leave as a table or convert to layers when opened in Dreamweaver. You can also combine the two methods by starting in Fireworks and creating headers and navigation menus. Then you can add layers with all of your content items after the pages are opened in Dreamweaver.

Links

Linking is what makes the Web an interactive (user-controlled) medium. Links allow the user to initiate action. When a link is clicked by the user on a referring page, it is directed by the HTML code to go to the target page. Links also can be called buttons or navigation items. Links make up the component functions of the interface. Technically speaking, on the code side of the Dreamweaver page, links are created using the **href tag.** Think of a href as short for a hyper reference.

Where can you link to?

- Web pages in your site
- Other Web URLs (Web site addresses)
- Images
- Multimedia items (Flash, Video, Audio)
- Downloadable programs
- PDF files
- Native documents on the server (MS Word or MS PowerPoint)

All of the items that you are linking to must reside in a folder or folder structure that does not change. I provided you with this folder structure:

- All .html pages are exported to the root folder: jdimarco (first initial, last name)

- All images are exported to the images folder: jdimarco/images (substitute your first initial and last name for mine)
- Your home page or "first page" of the site is always named index.htm

We can add a folder inside our Root Folder for downloads. Name it "Downloads." This is where you can put downloadable files including PDF and native Microsoft documents.

Linking Concepts: Absolute vs. Relative

Links can be written and directed two ways:

- **Absolute Links** are links that are outside the site. For example, if your portfolio site linked to your schools Web site, you would link absolutely — this means you use the entire URL address: http://www.eastlakeschool.edu.

- **Relative Links** are links that exist inside your sites directory (folder) structure. When you link relatively, you do not have to write out the entire path name. You can use just the page and any subdirectories in the coded link command.

Placing an external link in a Web page in Dreamweaver is easy. Go to **WINDOW>Properties Inspector.** The specific field for adding links is called LINK.

1. Add a layer or table and inside, type Go TO MACROMEDIA using Web text or place and select an image.
2. Type the link Web address or click the yellow folder to choose a Web page to link from in your site. Try this (http://www.macromedia.com).
3. Close the window and press F12 to preview in browser.
4. In the browser, click the item you added the link to and see if it goes to the Macromedia Web site. (You must be online for this to work.)

Figure 7.8. Graphic link (You can link from a graphic. Notice the circles. The graphic links to a student work illustration page named selfportrait.htm.)

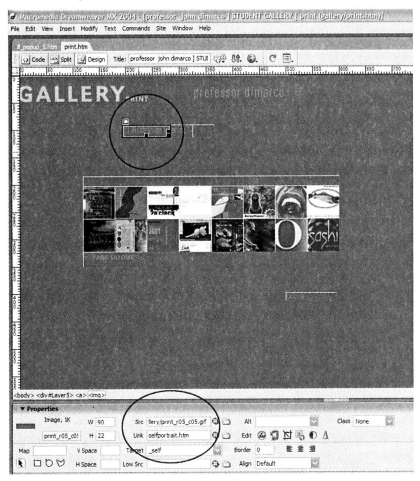

To link pages in your Web site you should follow the same steps but instead of typing a link location as in Step 2, click on the small folder next to the link button and navigate to your Web pages. Then, link to the desired .htm file.

Eventually, all navigation, buttons, and content downloads need to be linked from their page to a location somewhere. Linking insures a dynamic experience for the user. Broken links are not good. They can ruin the user experience, and most importantly they will act as roadblocks to your content.

You can change the color and size of your Web text using the properties inspector. Later we will examine style sheets to format text and page properties.

Figure 7.9. Text link (You can link from text. Notice the circles. The text links to a JavaScript that closes the browser window. The font is Arial.)

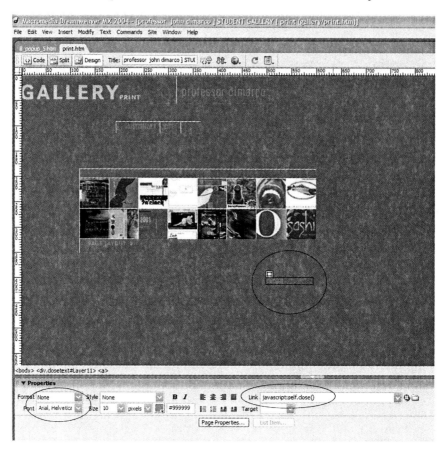

Alt Tags

Alt tags are text based labels that come up as you graphic or animation is loading. They are good to include as an etiquette item and to allow users with sight disabilities to be able to read the text only. Don't go overboard with wild descriptions, one to two words should suffice. You plug in alt tags on the properties inspector after selecting an image.

Jump Menus

Jump menus are form based drop down menus that give you a list of linkable items that when selected "JUMP" to the URL. Jump menus are good prefab-

Figure 7.10. Jump menu (You can link from a jump menu. Use this behavior-based navigation item when you have a long list of linked items (US States, for example) and no space, or when using electronic forms that auto fill and log data. Programming the jump menu with links is easy. Add the name that will appear in the menu and then the link destination.)

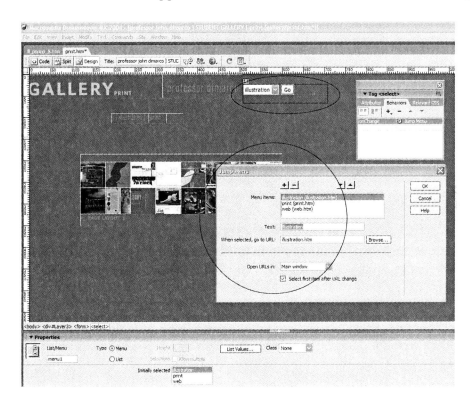

ricated tools that you can use in your portfolio. You might list your artwork or other content in a quick list for the user to jump immediately to the work without moving through any page gateways or introduction animations.

To create a Jump Menu, you must insert it from **INSERT>FORM>JUMP MENU.** You will see a red dotted line around the menu in Dreamweaver. Don't be alarmed, it's just a form tag that needs to be in place for the Jump Menu to work. To edit the Jump Menu, you should double click on it to reveal its properties in the properties inspector. The list values button provides menu name and the value is for the link that the menu name jumps to. Use relative paths for pages in your site and absolute HTTP:// addresses for Web pages and sites outside your site.

142 DiMarco

Figure 7.11. E-mail links (You can link to an e-mail from the properties inspector. When clicked, the link launches the user's e-mail client.)

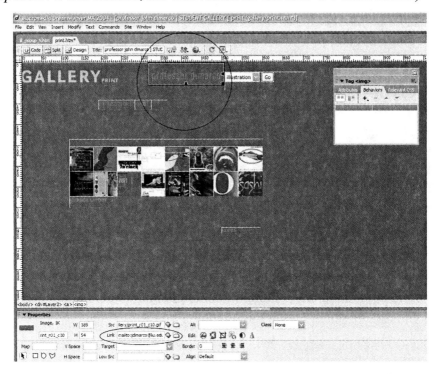

E-Mail Links

You will want your impressed users to contact you when the site has wowed them. To do this, you need to add contact information. The easiest, most intuitive method for doing this in a Web site is to provide an e-mail Mailto: link. It sounds a bit technical, but it's really quite simple.

All you need to do is type the words "e-mail me" on the page (try doing this in a layer). Now, highlight the text and go to the properties inspector, in the Link field, type mailto:[your **e-mail address].** Add your exact e-mail address behind the colon in mailto. When the user clicks the linked text, an e-mail client will pop up ready to send a message.

Named Anchors

Named anchors provide links within a Web page to somewhere in the same Web page. For example, you may want to have a navigation-based resume

Figure 7.12. Named anchor (The named anchor works just like a link, except it links within the page. Make sure to add the # before the named anchor when linking.)

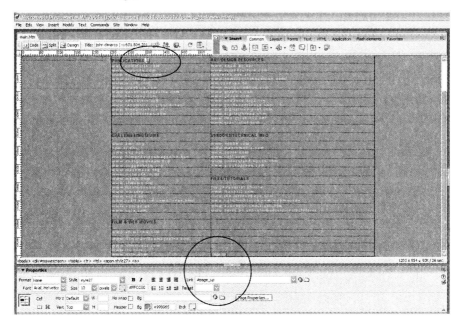

page in your Web portfolio. Rather than break the resume parts up on to separate pages, you decide to place them all on one page. To clarify the page contents you can create a menu of named anchors for each section on the resume. When the "skills" link is clicked, the page scroll would go immediately to the location of the skills section of the resume. Let's go through a quick tutorial.

To place a named anchor in your Web page, follow these steps:

- **Insert the anchor.** Put your content in layer on a new Web page. Pick a place on the page where you want the anchor, (or click some text or graphic on the page) and go to **Insert>Named Anchor.**

- The Insert Named Anchor dialog box will appear, type in the name of the anchor location: for example, "one." Choose a one-word name or use only a few characters — no spaces for the anchor name. Once you name the anchor, you will not see it unless you turn the invisible element viewing on (**View>Visual Aids>Invisible Elements**). This view shows invisible character in the body of the Web page.

Link to the Anchor

To link to the named anchor you will use the same method as we used to link to a URL and other Web pages. However, the named anchor will not be in the form of Web page (.htm), it will be a simple word consisting of a few characters with no spaces in the anchor name. Click on the text or graphic you want to use as the button for the anchor. Text works great for an anchor menu.

Click on the menu item that will trigger the link. Then, in the link field on the **Properties Inspector,** type in the anchor name you want the link to navigate to using a # in front (e.g., #page_up). When clicked, the browser will go to the anchored location.

CSS

CSS stands for Cascading Style Sheets. Although this name may sound like a setting on your washing machine, it is actually a standard of Web page design for controlling the attributes or "styles" contained in the HTML Web content. Style sheets add control to text, links, colors, and formatting. By using style sheets you can avoid the possibilities that might cause text in the Web page you designed looks different to the user. CSS overrides the user's Web browser default text settings so that what you design is what the user gets. Style sheets also allow universal updating of text attributes through the pages that contain the same style sheets (Towers, 1999).

You can create one style sheet for your entire portfolio. Then, you simply attach the style sheet to each page. When you attach the style sheet, Dreamweaver places the text styles you designated when you created the new style sheet into the **Properties Inspector** drop menu under styles.

Create a New Style Sheet

You can make and attach style sheets to your Web pages several ways. The quickest way is to use the **Properties Inspector** and go to the **Styles** field. Click on **Manage Styles**. From there, you can create a new style sheet. Creating a style sheet requires you to name the new style sheet and then set up

Figure 7.13. Style sheets (The new style sheet .css file (A) is created and then the individual styles (B) are developed based on attributes applied to page elements such as fonts and links(C). A page or site can use many styles inside of one style sheet (.css) file.)

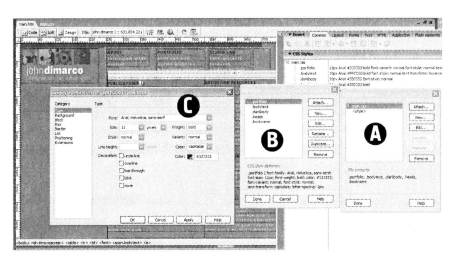

the specific attributes that you want available to you when you are formatting HTML text in your Web pages.

1. Click **New**

2. Name the style in the dialog box; be sure to keep the period in front of the name.

    E.g.: **.headers**

    Selector type should be Class and Defined in (New Style Sheet)

3. Save the style in your root directory.

    Now, you name the style sheet with the .css file extension.

    Style name: **portfolio.css**

    Root directory: **jdimarco (your first initial, last name)**

    Create a Type style for your page headers. Each time you create a new style for your text elements you will define the style in the **portfolio.css** style sheet.

4. To attach a style to a text element; highlight the text and go to the styles field on the **Properties Inspector** and choose the style. It is best to create

most of your styles before creating all your Web pages. You can add styles later on, but you would have to re-highlight and apply any new styles to the existing text. If you make a change to an existing style, it is updated through out its usage in the site.

5. To edit the style go to **Manage Styles** on the **Properties Inspector**

Behaviors

Dreamweaver's behavior tools let you apply common JavaScript actions without having to write any JavaScript. You can make something happen on a page when your users load a page, click on an object, or move the mouse around (Towers, 1999, p. 29). To open the Behaviors palette go to **Window>Behaviors**.

Behaviors provide a wealth of JavaScript features that are perfect functional compliments and necessities to your Web portfolio. For example, **Pop Up Windows (Open Browser Window)** are excellent for presenting your content in an defined window that isolates the work and allows the user to concentrate on the work and not on the other elements located on the Web page. **Rollovers (Swap Image)** are also important elements in Web page design. Rollovers in a Web page refer to the execution of a change of graphic or text color when "rolling over" a Web page hot (active) link.

The behaviors palette in Dreamweaver MX 2004 allows you to add several behaviors to the Web page's text and graphic elements.

Rollovers (Swap Image)

Rollovers provide feedback to the user when they mouse over an image by replacing the image with a "lit up" image or another image entirely (Towers, 1999). There are several ways to create rollovers in Dreamweaver. One way is to use the **Swap Image Behavior.** Another is to use **Insert>Image Objects>Rollover Image.** Either way is effective, so we will describe both techniques. You can choose the one that you are most comfortable using. The Insert Object technique seems to be a bit simpler. Both techniques accomplish the same thing, setting up a rollover image on an HTML page.

The simplest or two state rollovers require you to create two graphics. One is the graphic that will be "rolled over". This is usually a navigation button or a graphic that triggers the appearance of other graphics. The second graphic is the replacement image that shows when the mouse over occurs. In the case of a navigation bar, the second graphic usually has visual contrast to the first graphic. Graying out or adding borders around the replacement graphic are typical techniques.

Multiple state rollovers can also be created. You can assign a different image for each occurrence of mover over and mouse down. In this case you would need three graphics. One for the button also known as the mouse out state (the mouse is not on the graphic), or the beginning state. The second graphic is for the mouse over state, and the third graphic is for the mouse down state.

To create rollover graphics you can use the PNG file you created in Macromedia Fireworks, hide your slices in the layers palette and alter the existing buttons you created. Maybe change the text color or add a color border around the shape. You can also lower the opacity of an image to show a rollover effect. Try one of the mentioned changes to the graphic. Don't worry about style and visual impact, just try it. You will be making many buttons and many rollovers as your Web portfolio design evolves.

Then, show your slices again and then right click (CTRL+click) on the image to **Export Selected Slice. The name will be same as the slice you exported. Add the suffix _roll before the .jpg or .gif file extension.** This will allow you to see the rollover image quickly when you are creating the rollovers in Dreamweaver. Save the files to your **firstinitiallastname/images folder.** (Use your root directory, images folder.)

Keep in mind that if you use the existing table that you exported from Fireworks in Chapter Six, you must keep the images the same size; otherwise the table will scale the graphic to fit the space. The result is less that eloquent and should not be a part of your Web portfolio design. The rule here is that if you create rollovers in a table, both images must be the same size. You can create rollovers that affect different images other than the source image. This means that one image can trigger the change of another. This effect is great for menu previews of your work. The user rolls over the menu item RESUME, and below in a blank or populated area swaps in a thumbnail image of your resume.

Figure 7.14. Export selected slice in Macromedia Fireworks (A slice can be individually exported to create a second "state" for the rollover. The exported slice will act as the graphic triggered by the rollover.)

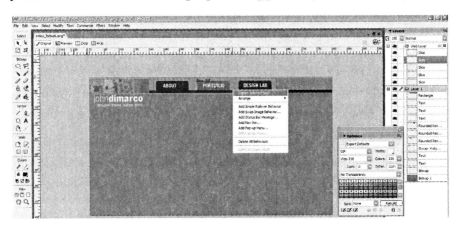

Creating Rollovers with the Swap Image Behavior

Before we begin making the rollovers, we should name the images that are going to be used so that we have easy references to images in the behaviors swap image dialog box. The names should be descriptive and simple. That is the reason we name the images. Dreamweaver will use predefined names if we do not attach a name. Assigning a name to an image is performed in the **Properties Inspector**. Click on each image and name it in the naming field located to the upper left of the Properties Inspector. If the button is the bio button, use the name bio. Keep it short and clear.

Next, we add the Swap Image Behavior.

1. Click on the + in the Behaviors palette and choose **Swap Image.** The Swap Image dialog box will open and you will be prompted to choose an **Image** and **Set source to.**

2. In the **Images** section, click and find the name of the image you want to swap from. The image you select is usually selected by default so you do not have to touch this if you are doing a single state (two images) button.

3. In the **Set source to**, browse to the graphic **that you exported from Fireworks.** It should have a **_roll** suffix before the filename. After setting the images, Click OK.
4. In the Behaviors palette, set the event to **onClick or onMouseOver.**
5. **F12 to Preview in the Browser. Test the Rollover.**

Here is another way to create a Rollover in Dreamweaver.

*   In the menu go to **Insert>Image Objects>Rollover Image.**
*   Choose the original image
*   Choose the rollover image
*   Add a link destination.

This method should be used when you are creating a Rollover without an existing image on the page. If you are starting from scratch and have no images on the page, use this method. If you have existing images on the page and have the rollover images waiting in your images folder, then you should use the Swap Image Behavior in the Behaviors palette. The Swap Image technique is required

Figure 7.15. Naming graphics for rollovers (A name can be applied to a graphic in the properties inspector to identify it easily inside of the swap image behavior dialog box. This is especially helpful when creating multiple state rollovers.)

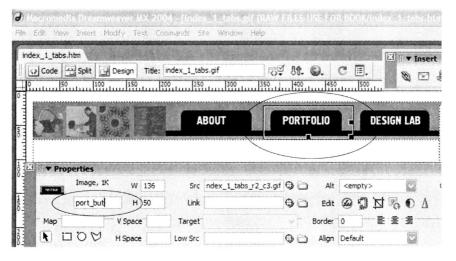

Figure 7.16. Swap image behavior dialog boxes (Notice how the file we named with the _roll sticks out among the other file names. Using techniques like using naming strategies can help you with design and production.)

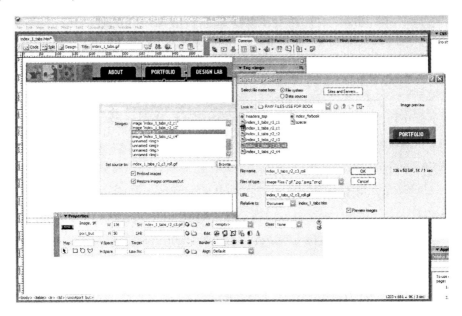

for doing multi state rollovers. In that case, you would perform the process inside the Swap image dialog box. You must pick a source image twice and then set the **behaviors panel** event to **onMouseDown** and **onMouseOver.**

Pop-Up Windows (Open Browser Window)

I am using the term pop-up window. In the behaviors palette, Dreamweaver refers to this JavaScript function as **Open Browser Window.** I'll use the Browser Window reference for clarity in this section but I will continue to use the term Pop Up window throughout the text.

As I have state previously, using Browser windows to isolate your work is an effective design strategy. Here are few items of importance for you to consider when working with the Open Browser Window Behavior:

Pop-up windows should typically be smaller than the Web page that launched it. It does not have to be, but it makes good design sense to apply the idea.

These sizes can vary. Here are a few suggestions. Try 600 x 400 for showing off graphics and image related work. Use 400 x 300 for smaller work that requires smaller windows. Try 600 x 800 for long text-based pages such as an interactive Web resume. Let's use the background color white.

Each of these pop-up windows has a unique link address (URL) that links to a distinct HTML page that you must create separately (Towers, 1999). What this means to your portfolio is that you must create a separate page for each "piece of work" that you put into the portfolio. You are probably thinking that this will complicate and lengthen the production process. Actually, it will shorten it. You can use your flowchart to assume the number of pages needed for the work going into the Web portfolio. Work on one page until you are completely happy. Then use Save As to save the page again and again as a template for each piece of work.

The pop-up window should be kept simple with minimum graphics and text. Navigation should be included but it can most definitely be text-based. The layout can consist of a few strategically placed layers that will contain a work layer and a navigation layer. No other content is needed. We do not want to distract the user away from our content. In addition, we use other techniques inside the pop-up windows such as jump menus and named anchors. Both of which we spoke about in previous sections.

Apply the Open Browser Window Behavior

This JavaScript needs to be applied to a text or graphic button to trigger the event.

1. Highlight the text or graphic that will trigger the event and go to the behaviors menu.

2. Click on the + in the Behaviors palette and choose **Open Browser Window.** In the dialog box click **Browse.** This will open up the navigation widow showing your computer. Click to where your Web portfolio resides and choose the .htm page that you want to load in the Pop up window.

3. Set the event to **onClick.**

Calling JavaScript

You can "call" JavaScript with or without using behaviors. JavaScript can be typed directly into the link field on the Properties Inspector. We might call a JavaScript to perform some sort of function. This book is not about JavaScript, nor am I a qualified expert on the subject, but what I am about to explain to you is pretty simple to understand and very functional to have in your Web page design arsenal.

When your user opens a pop-up window displaying your work, you want to be sure that you have an easy and intuitive method for the user to close the window and return to the home page. You can rely on user to click on the window's title bar and close the window by clicking the X. But, it's kind of nice give the user a close button somewhere in your pop-up window page designs. This is where some simple JavaScript comes in.

Make a Close Button

In a pop-up window (don't put this on your home page—it will close it!) make a new layer and type the words **close window** and apply a style (or make a new one for closeout). Highlight the text and in the **Properties Inspector** go to the **link** field and type: **JavaScript:self.close().** Now preview the Web page in a browser by pressing the **F12 key and Close the window. You must preview the page in the browser to execute the JavaScript and see it run.**

Congratulations, you have successfully written JavaScript. You can explore some more on your own; for now this little JavaScript morsel will help you make your pop-up windows a whole lot more user friendly.

To use Behaviors to call JavaScripts in Dreamweaver, type **close again** in the layer you made before. Highlight the text that will trigger the JavaScript (in our case, the close again button), now click on the + in the Behaviors palette and choose **Call JavaScript.** Set the event to **onClick.** In the dialog box type self.close() and press F12 to preview in the browser. Thus, the same result as when we typed it into the Link field on the Properties Inspector.

You use the close button with forward and back buttons in your pop-up windows to provide user navigation. This navigation system should be very discreet and should not interfere with portfolio work in any way. The navigation should be in the same location on every page.

Figure 7.17. Open browser window behavior dialog boxes (The open browser window behavior allows you to specify the size and window attributes. This is effective for controlling window sizes on pop-ups without having to write JavaScript code.)

The list of techniques provided earlier are only a small sample of the Web authoring techniques available using applications such as Macromedia Dreamweaver. Hopefully, you are beginning to understand how the Web portfolio design process involves some technical skills which will be beneficial to you throughout your professional career. These techniques can be directly applied to any Web development process and are some of the most common items used by Web authors. By experimenting with them in your own Web pages you will begin to see how each component may enable user functionality or limit functionality.

Meta Tags and Keywords

Meta tags provide author information and other attributes of a Web page. Meta tags are located in the HEAD section of the Web page. In addition to the Meta tags, the keywords reside in the HEAD section and are invisible when they are placed in Web page code. Search engines use the keywords to index pages. When you type in a keyword in a search engine, it looks for all occurrences within Meta tags of Web pages. It is a good idea to add keywords to your Web pages. The Macromedia Dreamweaver Help screens explains that:

> *Many search-engine robots (programs that automatically browse the Web gathering information for search engines to index) read the contents of the Keywords Because some search engines limit the number of keywords or characters they index, or ignore all keywords if you go beyond the limit, it's a good idea to use just a few well-chosen keywords. Enter your keywords, separated by commas, in the text box labeled Keywords. (Macromedia Dreamweaver online Help, 2004)*

To add keywords to your Web page, open the page in Dreamweaver, go to the Macromedia Dreamweaver Menu:

1.   **Insert>HTML>Head Tags>Keywords**
2.   Add words that describe you, the disciplines, and projects you are involved in—here is an example: design, art, multimedia, dimarco, Web portfolio, e-portfolio, computer graphics.
3.   After inserting these keywords, your Web pages will look and function the same. However, they will be more likely to be seen in search engines when information seekers type in the keywords you listed.

Review and Conclusion

Reviewing the chapter, it is important to point out how the technical processes are authored to program the Web page's capabilities for the user. After opening a sliced page from Macromedia fireworks, we see that the designs we created have been neatly placed into a table based on our slices. Each slice is a graphic which holds space within a table cell. Each table cell was generated from a slice. Tables can be converted to layers for easier movement and manipulation, or you can simply use the existing table. Table cells can be manipulated using the Properties Inspector. Each table and cell with it has specific attributes that can be changed using the Properties Inspector.

The most important navigational element seen in the Web portfolio is the link. Links provide an interactive experience and are the basis of all hypermedia. Linking occurs between pages and other Web sites for the purpose of providing an easy path to locating content. Broken links cut the user off from the content, so they must be thought out structurally and checked during testing phases. Links need to be consistent throughout the Web portfolio both in visual style and hierarchal position. Top-level navigation and links must stay at the top level on all pages. This is true for sub-navigation as well.

Other navigational elements that were discussed include jump menus and drop-down menus which are effective when there are lists of items that need to be accessed by the user.

Isolating contact may require you to create a pop-up window. The pop-up window is simply a Web page that has launched from a JavaScript attached to text or a graphic. Opening browser windows is a great technique for the Web portfolio because it allows you to control the window size and literally create a micro site for the portfolio work.

Visual feedback in navigation elements is seen in rollovers. Rollovers provide the user with a change in state of the button or linked graphic. The change of state is typically visual and lets the user know that the navigation element is live and linked to go someplace. Using rollovers should be planned out so that each time rollovers are used they have a purpose and are not simply added to the design for ornamental or entertainment purposes.

Discussion on timelines within Macromedia Dreamweaver showed us how we can add layers to timelines and then structure keyframes along the timelines in which change can occur. Timelines in Dreamweaver allow motion of layers across a Web page and also provides the ability to have a layer be visible or hidden at a certain point in time. Using timelines may not be needed for basic Web portfolios. But, as you start to experiment more and more with Web software applications you can begin to integrate what you have learned into your existing Web portfolio.

Finally, the basic JavaScript commands were discussed in the context of behaviors and handwritten codes. Behaviors are JavaScripts which are accessed inside of Macromedia Dreamweaver. Creating both Windows using open browser window is an example of using a behavior. Writing the JavaScript to close a browser window is an example of handwritten codes. Both applications were examined and you should practice in executing JavaScripts using behaviors and writing basic scripts similar to the close window one.

Once you have completed Web authoring using Macromedia Dreamweaver you should have a working, ready to publish Web portfolio. The Web portfolio would be considered an HTML-based Web site. All you really need is an HTML-based Web site. Loading times, user accessibility, space needs, and development difficulty are all lessened in the case of an HTML Web portfolio versus a flash based Web portfolio. The scenario is to have a stable HTML Web portfolio that integrates some multimedia components developed in Macromedia flash. The amount of flash components that you place in the Web portfolio is entirely up to you. The next chapter addresses motion graphics and audio development using Macromedia flash and Adobe audition. The chapter is somewhat technical in nature. But, again only the most important flash components for Web portfolio inclusion are shown. What I have tried to give you are some simple techniques that you can use to create flash text animations and a simple audio switch which allows the user to turn a Web portfolio soundtrack on or off.

Now let's go to the next chapter and examine motion graphics and multimedia production in the context of the Web portfolio.

Chapter VIII

Motion, Graphics and Multimedia Production

Introduction

This chapter presents motion graphics and provides simple lessons on creating text animation using Macromedia Flash. I will provide background information on digital audio editing and optimizing using Adobe Audition. We will cover how to make loops using Adobe Audition and export them for use in Flash. Also included in this chapter, the reader gets specific instructions on how to make an interactive sound on/off switch in Flash.

What I have mentioned earlier may scare you if you are not experienced using multimedia and motion graphics. You have a choice to include or not include sound and motion in the Web portfolio. The Web portfolio can simply be static pages with text and graphics or just text documents. Depending on your discipline you may think this is best for you. However, if you embrace multimedia, you may be able to find a whole new way to present your content in an engaging manner. One example would be to add music to a poem or photographic presentation. Using multimedia and motion on small scales at first will help you build confidence to continue to explore new applications and build your digital skill set. I recommend that you use this chapter as a resource for developing flash objects for your portfolio. This chapter is bare-bones in relationship to the plethora of materials available on using Macromedia flash. The goal here was to narrow down some nice multimedia techniques that can be explored by people of all levels and in all disciplines. Do not expect to tackle this chapter in an hour. Do expect to use these techniques piecemeal as you need or want them to be part of your Web portfolio presentation. Taking small steps and experimenting with some of the technical tutorials in this chapter you may find that you want to begin to explore multimedia and motion further. Again, this is part of the lifelong learning process fostered by making a commitment to develop a Web portfolio.

Overview of Web Multimedia
Applications and Design Processes

Multimedia delivers content through multiple media. For something to be multimedia, it would contain any combination of text, static graphics, audio, video, and animation.

We see multimedia in many communication channels, the most prominent being the internet, film, and television. Taking advantage of the multimedia capabilities

Table 8.1. Multimedia applications

MULTIMEDIA APPLICATION	Audio Editing	Audio Publishing	Video Editing	Video Publishing	Motion Graphics	Web App Pages/Sites
Macromedia Flash MX 2004	X	X		X (pro version)	X	X
Macromedia Dreamweaver MX 2004	In Web pages				X	X
Macromedia Captivate	X	X		X	X	X
Adobe Premiere	X	X	X	X		
Adobe Audition	X	X				
Adobe Live Motion	X	X			X	X
Adobe Go Live	In Web pages				X	X

of the internet is important in developing an engaging and effective Web portfolio. Embarking on multimedia design projects requires the designer and developer to call on several different applications to create the final multimedia product. We can get caught up the frenzy of new applications and toolkits, eventually completely confused, or worse, using the wrong tools and never getting the project finished. You will need plenty of time exploring multimedia applications in order to build a strong, varied skill set. To give you some insight into multimedia application choices, I have provided a matrix with a view of multimedia applications and what they can help you create. There are many more software packages to list with regards to multimedia applications. But, I wanted to list the ones most useful to Web portfolio development and the most accessible in cost and learning curves.

The Multimedia Process

We have addressed the multimedia design process in this book. The Web portfolio contains text, graphics, animation, and sound. That qualifies the Web portfolio as a multimedia project. The multimedia development process is basically the same process. The only exceptions are that we are not editing and preparing video. Otherwise, we created a concept, a content list, a content outline, storyboards, collected the assets, and designed screens in Fireworks. We then started development of the Web site using a Web authoring tool, Dreamweaver. Next, we will be adding animation and audio. To do this, we will use Adobe Audition and Flash. So, to create the Web portfolio, we need to use at least four to five applications. That is why teams typically handle multimedia projects. Each team may have an audio person, and animation person, a video editor, a programmer, a graphic artist, a digital imaging specialist, and a project manager who acts like a producer. Unfortunately, we do not have a team to work on our Web portfolio, but we will be empowering ourselves and building our skills while working towards completing an important career project.

Motion Graphics Defined

Motion graphics guru Hillman Curtis (Curtis, 2000, p. 01:04) describes motion as a universal language and he states his own communication theory in parallel with that of Marshall McLuhan. Curtis describes the notion that the *motion is the message.* He describes how moving a text object, slowing, and fading in and out of black will imbue that text element with a sense of drama, focus, and perhaps, stability. Or moving an object by spinning it around the screen might imply playfulness, or in most cases, annoyance (Curtis, 2000).

Curtis has done a strong job of deciphering the art of motion graphics and with it he implicitly focuses his design strategies on using motion for communication. His strategies are important to understand and exercise as you develop motion graphics for your Web portfolio pages.

> *Motion is a universal language. It's understood by everyone in varying degrees. Look at it this way: If something whizzes across the screen, it communicates "fast" or "urgent." And the slow move can communicate "calm." It's really about rhythm, and we all understand that language.* (Hillman Curtis, 2000, p. 4)

What you must take away from Curtis and his theories are that motion should communicate. Rhythm is a crucial component in successfully communicating with motion graphics. Moving objects should have intelligent function other than to simply experiment or show off. Keep a practice page on your Web site to post things that you are trying out. Get the opinion of others on the value of the communication. As with all design, the design of motion graphics needs to be consistent and persuasive.

Motion graphics spans across many four dimensional mediums. You will see motion graphics in television, film, video games, marketing & training CD ROMs, and of course Web sites. The use of motion graphics varies from simple text animation to full scale animations with music tracks and character voice-overs.

There are many computer applications designed to author and output motion graphics. Macromedia Flash is the premier tool for creating motion graphics on the Web. It is not a simple application to master, but if you focus on a few small foundations, you can build up a very functional skill set that will help you add impressive motion graphics to your Web portfolio.

Basic Concepts in Macromedia Flash

Although, the multimedia functions next are introductory; they are robust and require some time and experimentation to develop solid skills. There are many books on the market that discuss Flash multimedia concepts in high detail. If you aspire to add video or enhanced multimedia capabilities to your Web portfolio, you should consult these sources. Flash has some basic editing tools for editing audio, video, and for optimizing images, but they only provide low level features. To edit multimedia files properly, you must use dedicated software tools. Later in this chapter, we will use Adobe Audition to edit audio files that will be imported into the library in Flash.

Macromedia Flash is the topic of many books dedicated to the application and the use of motion graphics. This book is focused on Web portfolios. Using Flash can add value to the Web portfolio, so we will explore Flash in a limited capacity. We will examine several key techniques and some principle foundations that are needed to get going with the program and we will provide basic lessons in animation of text, graphics, and shapes. We will also discuss exporting Shockwave Flash files (SWF) so that they can be imported into Dreamweaver and inevitably have a place on the Web in your Web portfolio. SWF, Shockwave Flash files are played from a Web page through a plug in or through the Flash player. Macromedia states that 98 percent of all internet users have the Flash player installed on their computers. This means that practically every user that may encounter your Web portfolio will have the Flash player on their computer and will be able to see your motion graphics.

Flash is a tool for multimedia production. Flash files can be viewed on the Web, on video or TV, on handheld devices, and on DVD or CD Rom based products. Flash provides an authoring and design environment that allows the designer or programmer to integrate text, graphics, audio, video, and motion into one file or a series of files that can call upon each other to execute multimedia and programmable functions.

The Flash application interface consists of several key components. Content resides in the library. Objects are assigned to the library after creation or importation. The objects that reside in the library can be any sort. Graphic files can include bitmap files (JPG, BMP, PNG, GIF) and vector files(AI, EPS, FH). Audio format Flash supports includes AIF, WAV, and MP3. Flash also allows importation of MP3 and QuickTime video.

Figure 8.1.   Flash application interface (Flash has several key areas within the software interface. (A) Timeline, (B) Layers, (C) Stage, (D) Scenes panel, (E) Properties inspector, (F) Tool palette, (G) Library panel.)

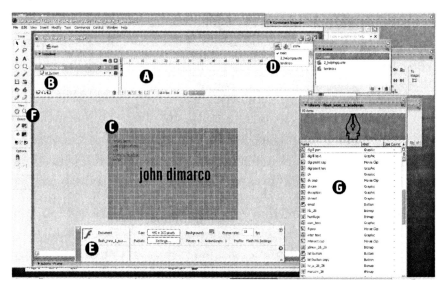

Flash has three main object types. Objects in Flash are referred to as **symbols.** Symbols are the building blocks of Flash movies. Symbol types are graphics, buttons, and movie clips. Each one serves a different purpose in Flash. When you create a new symbol in Flash (**Insert>New Symbol**) you are directed to a new timeline area that looks quite similar to the main stage and main timeline; this is the symbol editor. Symbols are reusable objects in Flash and they posses their own timeline that can be controlled and manipulated. The timeline of the symbol executes when the symbol is placed on the stage. Using a process called **instancizing**, you can create instances of movie clip and button symbols for use in ActionScript. By having independent timelines, symbols can also be nested with each other to raise control and interactive functionality within the objects.

Graphic symbols are used for simple animations and static graphics. Graphic symbols are the lowest level symbols because they do not have the ability to be controlled with ActionScript. **Graphic symbols** can be animated and used effectively in simple Flash movies. However, to use the real power features of Macromedia Flash MX 2004 Professional, **button symbols**, and most importantly **movie clip symbols** need to learned and utilized. These symbols take full advantage of the ActionScript language.

The Macromedia Flash MX 2004 Tutorial (Macromedia, 2004) provides this condensed version of the important components in the Flash interface.

- The **Stage** is the area that represents how your published content will appear.

- The **Timeline**, above the stage, displays a layer for the art and a layer for the effects in the document.

- **Layers** allow stacking content within the timeline.

- **Scenes** act like scenes in a play or movie, each piece can be acted out separately and collectively the scenes encompass the movie.

- **Panels** in Flash assist you in working with and assigning attributes to the document or to objects on the stage.

- **Tool Palette** provides raster and vector based drawing tools.

- The **properties inspector** allows you to view and change attributes of a selected object. The Properties inspector changes to display information about the tool or asset you are working with, offering quick access to frequently used features. (Macromedia Flash MX 2004 Tutorial)

- The **library panel** stores reusable items such as graphics, sound, and video clips. When you want to use a library item, you simply drag it from the library panel to the stage. (Macromedia Flash MX 2004 Tutorial)

The **stage** is the rectangular area where you place graphic content, including vector art, text boxes, buttons, imported bitmap graphics or video clips, and so on. The stage in the Flash authoring environment represents the rectangular space in the Macromedia Flash Player where your Flash document is displayed during playback. You can zoom in and out to change the view of the stage as you work (Macromedia Flash MX 2004 Tutorial). Typical sizes for the stage are 550 x 400, the standard Web page sizes: 640 x 480, 1024 x 768, and Web banner sizes: 468 x 60. You can create a Flash movie at any pixel size you desire. You can set the stage color and movie frame rate to begin building your movie.

Layers in a document are listed in a column on the left side of the timeline. Frames contained in each layer appear in a row to the right of the layer name. The timeline header at the top of the timeline indicates frame numbers. The **play head** indicates the current frame displayed on the stage (Macromedia Flash MX 2004 Tutorial).

The timeline holds **frames.** When content is added to stackable layers in the timeline, objects appear on the **stage** (the live area), and keyframes are filled on the timeline. **Keyframes** are where change occurs on the timeline. To add an object or script to a frame, a keyframe must be inserted. Objects are changed from keyframe to keyframe, either manually (frame by frame), or automatically using **tweening**. By using tweening, you designate the start and the finish keyframes of an animation, position or size changes for example, and then Flash makes all the changes **in-between** automatically.

Layers are like transparent sheets of acetate stacked on top of each other. Layers help you organize the artwork in your document. You can draw and edit objects on one layer without affecting objects on another layer. Where there is nothing on a layer, you can see through it to the layers below. When creating a text animation, you need to use layers efficiently. Each part of the animation should be placed on its own separate layer. This allows for editable content that is easier to manage. For example, you might place a word on each layer for the text animation. Then position the words in sequence so that they are shown over time. By using separate layers for each word, you can control each word as an individual element in the motion (Macromedia Flash MX 2004 Tutorial).

As you draw, paint, or otherwise modify a layer or folder, you select the layer to make it active. A pencil icon next to a layer or folder name indicates that the layer or folder is active. Only one layer can be active at a time (although more than one layer can be selected at a time).

When you create a new Flash document, it contains one layer. You can add more layers to organize the artwork, animation, and other elements in your document. The number of layers you can create is limited only by your computer's memory, and layers do not increase the file size of your published SWF file. You can hide, lock, or rearrange layers. You can also organize and manage layers by creating layer folders and placing layers in them. You can expand or collapse layers in the timeline without affecting what you see on the stage. It's a good idea to use separate layers or folders for sound files, actions, frame labels, and frame comments. This helps you find these items quickly when you need to edit them. In addition, you can use special guide layers to make drawing and editing easier, and mask layers to help you create sophisticated effects (Macromedia Flash MX 2004 Tutorial).

INSERT FIGURE   ActionScript CODE SAMPLE

ActionScript allows custom scripting to be integrated into movies by adding scripts to frames (frame actions) or objects (object actions). ActionScript can be applied in an easier context than hand coding by using behaviors in Flash. Similar to behaviors in Dreamweaver, **Flash behaviors** allow easy access to basic scripting functions that add interactivity and enhanced multimedia capabilities to Web pages.

Unit Values in Flash

The **timeline** in Flash is where all the elements in the Flash movie are positioned over time. Time needs be involved when motion and animation is involved. Animation is defined as change over time. Motion graphics is a form of animation. The unit of measurement that is used in Flash to represent time is the **frame**. A series of frames with objects runs over time to present an animation. The frames are designated a speed rate when the designer creates the movies. The FPS (frames per second) is typically set for 12-15 FPS for Web based animations. The timeline status display at the bottom of the timeline indicates the selected frame number, the current frame rate, and the elapsed time to the current frame.

The higher the FPS rate the faster the animation will try to perform. However, the animation has other factors that affect its performance. The first is the speed of the user's computer. The second is the speed of the internet connection. The performance attributes that you design into your animation also affect the way the motion graphics play. For example, bitmap images with heavy file sizes tend to animate slowly. Bitmaps must be optimized correctly and they also must be scaled appropriately for the Web so they perform and communicate. Vector images and shapes drawn in Flash animate quicker than bitmap images. For this reason, we will examine text based animations that are small in size and big in communication. Gradually we will learn about bitmap basic bitmap usage while creating an animated banner.

Thinking about the Text Animation

Creating even the simplest text animations in Flash requires creative planning. It is essential to develop a compact, persuasive message that will translate well in the realm of motion graphics. To do this, you should write out your ideas in a brainstorming session. Think of a core message that you want your Web portfolio to communicate to users. You examined this same question when you conceptualized the Web portfolio. Focus on that same message or develop a new message. Make it one statement that defines you. Once you have the statement, think of five to seven words that support the statement. Each word can be animated to present a full statement in motion across the users screen.

Creating the Text Animation

Creating the text animation is simple good beginning project to get acquainted with the Flash interface elements and to create an interesting multimedia element for your Web portfolio. We will make a **splash page** to open our site. The page will have an animation and an entrance button. We will also build this animation up by adding sound.

Start by creating a new Flash document. Let's use the default size of 550 pixels wide x 400 pixels long. This size will provide us with plenty of room to use motion and it will fit nicely into the content layer on our homepage. Pick a background color for the movie that will work within the color scheme of your site. You do not have to use the exact colors; you can use variations such as light or dark shades and complimentary tones. All the colors are Web safe in the palette so they will reproduce accurately on the users monitor. Save and name it the movie **splash_intro.fla.**

Now we should get some good Flash housekeeping issues. It's a good idea to organize your layers before beginning to work. Organizing layers means naming the layers consistently throughout your projects. When your projects begin to get larger in scope, you will appreciate naming your layers in advance. In the timeline, create new layers with this naming convention:

- Guides
- Labels
- Actions
- Sound
- Button
- Name

- Word_one
- Word_two
- Word_three
- Word_four
- Word_five

Now that we have established our work area, we can begin to create our objects. Because we are just beginning with Flash, we will use graphic symbols to animate on our timeline.

Start by creating the graphic text symbols that will be animated. In this animation, we want to create text fades using our name and five words that describe our abilities or work. At the end of the animation, a button with our name appears, ready to trigger the Web page. Our name and the words will be placed on their respective layers in the timeline on the main stage.

1.   Create a the name symbol by going to **Insert>Symbol** create a graphic symbol called **name_graphic**

2.   Type your name using the Text tool from the tool bar. Use 40 point text. Any legible font will do. We want to make a symbol, but will add motion to the symbol in the main timeline.

3.   Now we must align the graphic with the stage so that when we place it on the main timeline it is not off center and difficult to work with. Go to **Window>Design Panels>Align** to open the align palette. This palette allows you to align objects to each other or the stage. We want to align to stage because we need to center this graphical text. Set the **To Stage** button and the align horizontal and align vertical buttons to position the item directly in the center of the symbol editor, therefore aligning it with the center of the stage. Close the symbol editor by clicking the Timeline text up in the Timeline panel.

4.   Repeat the process from earlier and create five graphic symbols with the five words you brainstormed. Keep the size to 28 points for each word, and use the same typeface. Remember to be consistent with the fonts and sizes. Each symbol from steps three and four will be located in the library panel. Now that we have our graphic symbols prepared, we can begin to add motion to them on the main stage.

5. On the main stage (timeline), click on to the layer name and drag the name graphic symbol from the library on to the stage. Next, align it to the stage so that it is centered.

6. Repeat step five for the remaining words. Place each word on its corresponding layer. If you make an error, click CTRL+Z to undo. You get up to approximately 99 undos in Flash.

7. At this point, you should have your name and all the word symbols neatly placed in the center on the stage. The words should be overlapping each other with the name layer on the top of the stacking order. At this point, we can begin to add motion to the text symbols. To make things easier, we can hide the layers we are not using in the timeline by clicking off the dot under the eye for the corresponding layer. Hide all the layers except for the name layer.

8. Click on the text symbol and lets click on **Insert>Timeline Effects>Blur.** This effect will automatically provide an interesting motion effect for you to use. The blur effect dialog box will pop up. Set the **duration to 24, the resolution to 10, and the scale to 10.** Update the preview to see the results. The frame duration bar will now be extended out to frame 24. To preview the animation, click **CTRL and ENTER at the same time.** This will launch the Flash Player.

9. Now repeat the process with the five words. Move the words to different locations on the stage. Then, move each set of frames for each word down the timeline. The animation should not exceed 125 frames in total (five 24-frame single word animations). Be careful to work with each word individually. Pay attention to each word by hiding the other layers. For now, utilize the easy to use timeline effects provided by Flash.

Finally, we need to save the proprietary .FLA file and then export the Web-ready SWF file. To do this we go to **File>Save** and save the Flash document directly into our root directory. We could have made a new directory folder for the flash files but because we only have a few, we can manage them just as easy from the root. When we save the FLA, we are saving the editable Flash file with layers in tact. This is important because when we need to update the file we can have the source to make the job easy. To create the SWF file, we go to **File>Publish.** When we publish from Flash, Flash generates an SWF file and an HTML file. SWF files a Web page as a container or they will play directly in the Flash Player. SWF files should be embedded in an HTM page. They run nicely and independently from all Web browsers, but they still need the structure of HTM and an **Object Tag** to have them show up in your Web portfolio. Don't worry, you can **Insert>Media>Flash** to add a SWF to a Web page in Dreamweaver. Disregard and eventually delete the extra HTML file that Flash generates. Some designers use this file as a test page before placing the SWF into the live Web pages. If you want to eliminate the generation of the HTML page, however, you can go to **Publish Settings** and uncheck the HTML file box. After you do this, Flash will only generate the SWF file in your root directory.

This animation will loop in the Web page. To add our button, we open the existing FLA file.

We add a **stop action** and a button to enter the portfolio site.

- **First, we stop the animation.** We can make the animation stop by placing a stop action in the timeline. A stop action is an ActionScript that stops the timeline. It is the most basic and most used action available.

- To add a stop action, click on the timeline and select a frame right after at the end of the animation (frame 145 or 146):

- Insert a keyframe (F6)

- Open the ActionScript panel **Window>Development Panels>Actions**

- Click in the Actions panel and type **stop();**

- Or in the left side of the Actions panel,

- Click **Global Functions>Timeline control>Stop**

The action can be written or assigned from the Actions menus. For a simple stop, there is no real need to use the Behaviors panel. The ActionScript panel works just as easily.

Let us review what we have done so far in the creation of our text animation. First, we brainstormed content for a text animation that highlights our name and five words or phrases that define our abilities. Next, we set up our Flash document so that we can work efficiently and intelligently on the piece. To achieve this, we descriptively named our layers before we began working on the nuts and bolts of the animation. Then, we animated our words. Finally, we inserted a stop action so that the animation stops.

We are now ready to design our button. After we create the button, we will place it on the stage in its appropriate layer and then publish and test our movie. When we see that the movie is operating, we can then move on to sampling some sound that will be used in the splash page animation.

Defining Buttons in Flash

When we first prepared our Flash document for this animation, we created a layer called "button". On this layer we will place a button that will hyperlink the user to the homepage of the Web site. The splash page containing the Flash text animation is technically the first page that is loaded when the user hits the site, and therefore the file must be named index.htm. The splash page does not contain our navigation menus or a path to our content. We must have a proverbial "home page". This page may or may not be the first page seen by the user. In our case, we will be naming our first page—the splash page index.htm. We will name our second page index_2.htm. This page is the real home page in terms of hierarchy and user guidance. This page is also our main navigation page. The button we create will take us from index.htm to index_2.htm, straight from the Flash animation.

Setting up a button in Flash requires you to create a **Symbol.** When we discuss buttons, there are several important points that must be made. Buttons or interactive components are handled by Flash as event-driven objects. Being event-driven means that some occurrence (an event) must trigger ActionScript to execute a command. Events occur when the user clicks the button or when the play head reaches a certain frame. You can program ActionScript to occur when events happen in a Flash movie. For example onClick, go to Frame 5. Or, another example, onEnterFrame 5, play movieclip xyz. These are pseudo (fake) code analogies. ActionScript is very powerful and provides for complex programming is the developer is so inclined. ActionScripts can be very long and complex and customized or they can be a simple staple such as the stop(); action that we discussed earlier in the text.

Movieclips Can Be Programmed as Interactive Buttons

The reason we briefly covered some initial points behind ActionScript is because without it, buttons and movieclips are just like graphic symbols—not interactive and not very prominent in the overall scheme of dynamic Flash content creation. We are using the term button to define an interactive object that has a hyperlink attached to it. Button and movieclips are programmable in Flash. Programmability means that ActionScript can be attached either button or movieclip symbols. In essence this means that movieclip symbols can be used as buttons in Flash. Programmable, movieclips allow ActionScripts to be attached to their instances on the stage so that they can act as interactive buttons. Movieclips are contained objects that run a movie. The movie inside the movieclip can have all the properties and elements that are seen on the main timeline. However, movieclip symbols are different because they can be controlled on the main stage and they occupy only one frame in the main stage. Their unique timelines are inside the movieclip. The movieclip can contain an animation that is 200 frames. When the movieclip is placed on the stage, the symbol occupies a single frame, but executes the entire movie on the stage. Movieclip symbols have independent timelines that can be controlled by ActionScript on the main stage or by ActionScript contained in other movieclip symbols.

Another technique that is frequently used to boost the multimedia characteristics of a button is to nest an animated movieclip inside of a button symbol. This technique allows the unique timeline of the movieclip to play inside of the button during and event.

We will examine both programming possibilities, buttons and movieclips, in the context of a splash page in the next tutorial section. First, we will make a button symbol and program it. Next, we will make the same interactive element, but will use a movieclip symbol instead of a button.

Symbol Editor

When you insert new symbol, Flash changes the screen and switches to the symbol editor. Now this can be confusing to Flash novices, but once you understand where you are and how to operate there, creating symbols in the symbol editor will be easier. You tackled making a text animation on the main stage previously. Now we will venture into the symbol editor to make the hyperlinked button at that will occupy the last frame of our text animation on the stage. Then we will explore another way to accomplish the same task and we will create the button using a movieclip symbol. These tutorials will give you some basic knowledge on creating buttons and movieclips, but most importantly this section should help clear up some of the confusion that exists when Flash newcomers get into the symbol editor.

Make a Linked Button for the Splash Page

Buttons are symbols. We learned before that symbols reside in the library after they are created and then are placed on the stage when they are called into action. Bitmaps, shapes, and type can be arranged on the stage and then selected and converted to a grouped symbol or separate symbols. Making symbols by conversion on the stage is not a very good strategy for development. The best method for creating symbols is to make a new symbol — **Insert>New Symbol.**

Make a Button Symbol

The button symbol must be created in the symbol editor. When we **Insert>New Symbol>Button,** the Flash interface takes us to the button symbol editor. The button symbol editor does not look the same as the symbol editor that shows up for movieclip and graphic symbols. Inside the button symbol editor you will see four states. Buttons maintain an up state, an over state, a down state, and a hit state. The first three states can be animated (DiMarco, 2004, p. 183). Let's examine the states to understand what a state is and what each state does.

Insert > Figure > button symbol editor

A button state is literally the position the button is in at a given point in time. The up state of the button is when the button is up or on top. This means there is no mouse over the button or there is no mouse pressing down on the button. The other states are responsible for those situations. Over and down are based on the user's mouse control. Is the user rolling the **mouseOver** or is the user pressing the **mouseDown?** The individual states occupy one frame each. There is no need for extra frames because the event (over or down) triggers the state. Each state of the button can be unique. For example, we make a button that is a red circle with a grey border (stroke) when the button is static (up) it is exactly the same as when we made it, red with grey border. When the user rolls over the button the over state is triggered and in that state you change the red button to all grey. The visual feed back conveyed by the mouseOver lets the user know that this is an active button and that it should be clicked. Graphic rollovers provide feedback just as text links with color rollovers alert the user that there is more on if the link is clicked. The mouseDown state occurs when the user clicks the mouse. Here is another case where visual feedback can be used to guide or entertain the user. In the down state a new graphic or even a sound effect can be place. The first three button states can hold text, images, movieclip symbol animations, and sound files. All of these multimedia elements can be exist in the button in any state. To summarize; you can create interactive multimedia buttons in the button symbol editor. Now we have to discuss the most important function state, the hit state.

The **hit state** in the button symbol editor is an important part of Flash. This state is the hotspot that makes the button programmable and interactive. A button can be made with the hit state missing. When the button is on the stage, it will only execute the first three stages of the button symbol. If there was an ActionScript attached to it, it will not execute because the hit state is missing.

Making the hit state is easy. We will do it shortly. Here is a quick fact about the hit state. By using only the hit state, you can make **invisible buttons** that are programmable. Invisible buttons do not contain an up, over, or down state, thus making them invisible. Invisible buttons can be used to quickly and easily program movieclip symbols. Programming invisible buttons are easier in simple ActionScript cases because they allow the novice to attach the script to the invisible button, instead of the movieclip symbol. The ActionScript coding for the invisible button does not require reference to the movieclip object, which becomes a more complex task. The only requirement is that the invisible button is laid on top of the movieclip symbol and then actions are set to the invisible button symbol instead of the movieclip symbol.

Using the Personal Logo as the Button Symbol

The button that leads the user into the Web portfolio should be something that has some meaning — not just a red circle. To make our identity visible again, we will use the personal logo we created in Freehand to be our interactive button. We can lower the opacity of the logo on the up state and fade the logo in on the over state. To do this we have to embed a movieclip in the over state. We also can add some text to the over state, something like "Enjoy the portfolio". For the down state, we can leave this state blank. We can always edit the button and add something into the down state later. Let's move forward and get into the button symbol editor.

Flash can import a wide variety of file formats into the library. Eventually, each file is converted into a symbol and used in the Flash movie. Flash can import vector, raster, audio, and video files. The major bitmap file formats that are most commonly used are PNG files (native Fireworks,) JPEG images (JPG), and bitmap graphics (BMP). Vector graphics are Freehand (FT and FH) and all PostScript files (AI, PDF, EPS). Audio file formats include MP3 sound (MPG), WAV, and AIF. Video formats include QuickTime (MOV), Video for Windows (AVI), MPEG Movie (MPG), and Digital Video (DV, DVI).

To make our button we need to import or drag and drop the personal logo into the library. On the graphical side, there is tight integration between Freehand, Fireworks, and Flash. What's nice is that you can drag and drop artwork directly from Freehand or Fireworks right into Flash. Or, you can export your Freehand Files and Fireworks files and then import the files into Flash.

I love the quick and easy production shortcut so I will open Fireworks and Flash simultaneously. Then, I will drag my personal logo into Flash on to the stage. Immediately, Flash converts the item to a movieclip symbol and places the symbol in the library. This is terrific functionality for getting graphics into Flash. Now that the personal logo is a movieclip symbol, you can scale, position, and tween it. We will animate the logo with a fade in effect on the over state and add the phrase **enjoy the portfolio**.

1.   After dragging the personal logo to the stage from Freehand or Fireworks, delete it from the stage and rename it (from **Symbol One** to **logoart**) in the library. We need to make a movieclip symbol that fades the personal logo. **Insert>Symbol>Movieclip.** Name it **logo_mc.** The movieclip logo_mc will act as the container for our animated personal logo. Once the animated logo is complete, we can embed it into the button symbol.

2.   In **logo_mc**, name the first layer actions. Add a second layer and name it logo. Now click into the first frame of the logo layer and drag the logoart symbol on to the stage. Use the align panel to position it centered to the stage.

3.   On the layer with the logoart, layer two, click on frame five and insert a keyframe (F6). The logoart symbol will be automatically inserted in the frame by Flash. To indicate the keyframe, Flash adds a dot to the timeline. With that done, lets click back to Frame one to set the **alpha.**

4.   **Alpha** is transparency. Transparency refers to the ability to see through an image. For this effect, we want to lower the alpha at frame one and then make it 100 percent opaque in frame 10. When we embed the movieclip into the button, the result will be a fade in when the user mouses over the button. Click on frame one and select the button. Using the Properties Inspector, click the **Color** drop down, choose **Alpha.** Set the alpha to **40 percent.**

5.   Now we must tween the logo. Tweening allows the designer to set the keyframes in the timeline and then Flash will create the motion or shape tweens "in-between". To create a motion tween, simply click between two keyframes and the go to the properties inspector to **Tween.** Drop the arrow down and choose **Motion.** You will see several options appear on the properties inspector. **Ease** allows easing the motion in or out. This means that if a minus value is set, **ease in** is selected, the animation will move slower at the beginning and then becomes faster at the end. The opposite is true for **ease out.** With a positive ease out value selected on the slider, the animation starts quickly and slows as it nears the end. For now, let's leave this at **-100.** This value will give us a nice subtle ease in. Our animation is short (5 frames) so the ease will not be very strong anyway.

6.   Drag the play head back to frame one and press ENTER. The logo should fade in.

7.   Lastly, we must place a stop action on layer on at frame five. This will make the animation happen only once. Go to Frame five on the actions layer and add a keyframe. Open the ActionScript panel and type: **stop();.**

Keep in mind that we worked entirely in the symbol editor to create this movieclip. Now, we must assemble the button. Get back to the main timeline by going up to the top of the timeline to the Scene Path. You will see Scene one, logo_mc open when you are in the symbol editor. The **Scene** indicates the main movie timeline. There can be multiple scenes in a Flash movie. Each scene has a specific stacking order in the movie and has a main timeline. Click on **Scene One**. Here's a quick shortcut for jumping to the symbol editor without searching for the symbol in the library. Simply double click the symbol on the stage and Flash will immediately take you to the symbol editor where the symbol was created. The symbol can be edited and its updated version will be automatically replaced on the stage in each of its specific instances.

Here is a brief summary of what we just did. We dragged our personal logo from Fireworks directly on to the stage in Flash. All objects dragged in to Flash from Fireworks are immediately converted to movieclip symbols. We renamed the personal logo to **logoart.** We created a movieclip named **logo_mc** that would act as a container for the faded logo animation. We created the faded logo animation. Next we will create the button.

To make the button, we need to **Insert>New Symbol, button.** Name the button **logo_btn.** The button symbol editor will open. You should recognize the **up, over, down, and hit** frame states that populate only the button symbol editor.

1.   Click on to frame one of the up state and drag the **logoart movieclip from the library** on to the symbol editor. Align it center to the stage with the align panel using the set **to stage icon.** This is the static movieclip that we dragged over from Fireworks. We will use it as the up state graphic. We need to lower the opacity to **40 percent** to match the **logo_mc** movieclip. Logo_mc contains the fade animation and will occupy the over state.

2.   In the second frame of the over state, drag the **logo_mc** movieclip from the library to the symbol editor. Align it center to the stage. This movieclip should be set in the exact same position as the logoart movieclip.

3.   Click into the over state and press **F6** to add a keyframe. Now delete the item in the overstate. We are doing this because we need to add the logoart movieclip in this state (align it) because we do not want the animation to run twice in two frames. It will give a jumpy look. Using the type tool, we want to add the text, "Enjoy the portfolio", right below the logo. Make sure that the type is not too large. You do not want it to overwhelm the personal logo.

4.   Now we must add the hit state. To make a hit state in a button symbol I typically use onion skinning to see the artwork that I am covering with the hit box. **Onion skinning** is located under the timeline next to the layer trash can and directly next to the center frame icon. It is an icon with two blue boxes, the underlying box is smaller and semi transparent, the top box is blue. That is the onion skin toggle switch. It switched onion skinning on and off. You are probably asking, what is onion skinning? Onion skinning provides semi transparent underlay of frames in an animation. It is useful because it allows you to see frames that come before the frame you are working in. We will use it to show us the up, over, and down states of our

button. We will use this as a guide for laying a hit box over the artwork. The hit state is invisible on the stage, but is quite important. It outlines the boundaries for the mouse actions. This means that when the mouse enters anywhere into the hit state region, the button will execute its ActionScript functions. The hit state is a hot spot for making the button interactive.

5.   Turn on **onion skinning.** Make sure that your are in frame four, the hit state, and you have deleted the artwork from frame four. Now turn on onion skinning and then make a rectangle or square tightly around the shown onion skinned logoart. Change the color of the box to a bright green. I do this to remind me that this is the hit box. I use green because it corresponds with the slice color in Fireworks.

6.   Turn off onion skinning by clicking the icon below the timeline again. Click out to Scene one and the main stage.

7.   Place the **logo_btn** on the stage. Align it center to stage. Save the Flash file to your hard drive in the root directory folder. Test the movie by clicking **CTRL+ENTER.** In the Flash Player, roll over the button and see the fade effect. Our last step is to add some interactivity with ActionScript. We need to link to our index_2.htm page.

8.   Click on the button and go to the ActionScript panel. Go to the left side of the panel to the **Action Books**. They allow you to begin the ActionScript code by using simple drop down menus. The Action Books still require you to plug in information and values that ActionScript needs to execute the function. For the ActionScript we are applying (**getUrl**) we need to provide the URL address (Web address) of the location we want the browser to go to when the button is clicked. The address we need is an easy, **relative address**. We want the button to bring the user to our main navigation page, index2.htm. To do this we need to program ActionScript to get the url index2.htm on mouse click.

9.   In the Action panel we must add the event that will trigger getting the url. The event is **on (press)**. We need to add this to ActionScript panel before we can place the getUrl action in the script. We need to do this because the button is an object and we are applying the ActionScript to the object. In other cases we could apply the ActionScript to the frame. In this case, when the playback head reaches the frame, it executes the getUrl action. We want the action triggered by the object so we must add the object specific event.

A word about ActionScript syntax:

It is very important to make sure that you follow the correct **syntax** when writing ActionScript. The syntax is the grammatical correctness of the written language. Similar to the punctuation do's and don'ts of the English language, ActionScript has the type of grammatical structure. It is much simpler that the English language.

- In ActionScript, a **semi colon** ends a line of code ;.

   stop();

- Words or **strings** of characters need to be in quotations when they are in **parentheses()**. The parentheses hold the arguments to apply to the statement.

   on(press){

   gotoAndPlay(scene1,2);

   {

- **Brackets** }{ break off sections of code to execute a sequence of commands.

   on(press){

   gotoAndPlay(scene1, 2);

   {

10. In the ActionScript panel type **on (press)**

   then we must set off the function from the vent by using brackets {

   so now the code should look like this:

   on (press) {

   From the action books choose **Global Functions>Browser Network>getUrl.**

   Now the code should look like this:

   on (press) {

   getUrl ()

   We need to add the url location and browser window method for the link.

   Here is the final code:

   on (press) {

   getUrl ("index2.htm", "self");

   }

The code is now complete and will execute the link to the main navigation page.

Now that we have created the flash button, we need to place it at the end of our animation on the main stage of **splash_intro.fla.** This is our animation. We need to add the **logo_btn** at the end of the animation. Somewhere around frame 125 would be a good spot to place the button. Align the button to the center of the stage and be sure that you move the stop action in the actions layer to the same frame number as the button. This will cause the playback head to stop and let the user click the button. If the stop action is before the button, the user will never see the button because the playback head will stop short of the frame that holds the button.

Once the stop action is positioned, you can now publish and test the entire intro animation movie.

As we mentioned earlier, publishing a Flash file, by default, creates two files from the flash movie. The FLA file should be saved in images and moved for archive before upload. This is the proprietary Flash file that has layers and scenes in editable form. When **File>Publish** is selected, Flash creates an SWF file and an HTML file. The SWF file is the Shockwave Flash file that gets placed on the Web page and uploaded to the internet. The HTML file is created simply act as a container for our SWF file. Flash does this in anticipation for the need of Web page to play the SWF movie. You can delete the HTML file Flash generates later. We only need the SWF file. It will be an embedded object in a Web page we create in Dreamweaver. **Publish all flash files to the root directory folder (jdimarco).** This is not the most organized way, but it is the simplest way to keep track of your flash files when you place them up on the internet. When you get more experience, you can begin to make sub directories for each component in the site you are creating. Such as "Flash" for all flash files.

When complete, your published files will be **splash_intro.swf** and splash_intro.htm (the HTM file can be deleted).

In Dreamweaver, we need to rename our main navigation page which may be named index, to index2.htm. We need to create a new index page in Dreamweaver. This page will hold your introduction animation and will be the first page the user sees when they hit your site. Be sure to set the home links in your site to the appropriate page.

After creating the new index page, go to **Insert>Layout Objects>Layer.** Then you need to position the layer on the page to where you want to place your Flash animation. After positioning, go to **Insert>Media>Flash. Press F12 to preview the page in the browser. Check to see if the button brings you**

to index 2.htm. If the button does not work, you need to check to see if you followed the steps correctly. Revise the Flash file and replace it into the layer.

Now we can move forward with our Flash exploration and create a simple audio movie that plays an audio clip and has an on/off switch that lets the user stop the audio if they do not want to listen. Before we make the audio switch, we need to prepare our audio sample. Flash is not built to edit audio fully. It can handle some basic jobs like adding fades and changing compression, but to have a lot more control, I will turn to an audio editing application. We will use Adobe Audition to perform some editing before we place our audio into Flash.

Preparing Audio in Adobe Audition

Audition is a software application manufactured by Adobe Systems that provides traditional audio editing capabilities in a digital format. This means that Audition provides a complete multitrack digital audio recorder for capturing external sound, an editing environment that provides cutting, filters, and a mixer for creating and combining audio tracks. Audition provides a multitrack interface that allows you mix various files into one compilation.

Figure 8.2. Adobe Audition edit view (Edit view is where you can edit individual waveforms in Audition.)

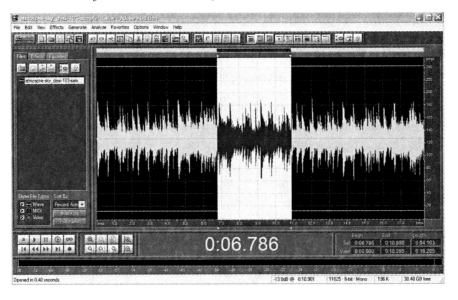

There is no way to examine an advanced application such as Audition in this slim volume. Also, I cannot claim to be an expert in digital audio editing. My experience is from the perspective of a multimedia designer with limited use on the full feature set of the application. However, I have managed to learn some great techniques using the software to prepare, compress, and output audio for use in digital video projects and motion graphics elements. I would like to help you do the same thing.

For this section, we will assume that you have some audio on your computer already. It can be any of the following file formats: WAV, MP3, AIF, or SND. Virtually all file formats are encoded and decoded by Audition. These listed formats are the most common. With a file available, you are now ready to enter Audition and begin to get your audio ready for Flash.

The Audition Workspace

Audition provides two main workspaces: **Edit View** and **Multitrack View**. Edit view works with a single waveform. In edit view you can edit one waveform at a time. You provide your digital alterations to one track and then you can view the track in multitrack view and mix it with other tracks. For example, you might have a music track and a voice over track. Each file is edited separately, but when the complete file needs to be output, both tracks are mixed down into one file.

Let's take a look at some basic editing features in Audition. First, you need to open the existing waveform residing on your computer in Audition.

In Audition go to **File>Open Waveform** to open a digital audio file from your hard drive. Choose the file, I used an .AIF that I transferred from my Macintosh computer to my Windows computer. The file will open in Multitrack View and reside on the left side in the organizer window (See Figure 8.4a). To edit the waveform, you must view it in Edit View. To do this, simply **double click** on the waveform. In edit view, you might need to delete a portion of the audio. Or maybe you want to add a **fade in effect** or **fade out** effect to the audio clip. Most importantly, Audition allows you to optimize and compress the audio to help determine the maximum quality in proportion to the smallest file size. There is always a trade off between performance, quality, and operability in digital media. The obstacles are decreasing with the influx of broadband into society, but there still must be serious considerations made when placing audio into your Web portfolio. We are striving for positive user experience, so we cannot make

Figure 8.3. Adobe Audition multitrack view (Multitrack view is where you can mix and assemble multiple waveforms on individual tracks in Audition. An example would be a voice track and a music track overlapped.)

the audio we use overwhelming or annoying. If we do not meet the particular tastes of the user, that is fine, we will provide an on/off switch that will kill the audio or start it up. Ideally, we would provide the user with a choice of audio clips that fit several different tastes. But we do not have the space or the need to go that far here. So we will concentrate on using one carefully chosen audio clip.

Grabbing chunks of waveforms is easy in Audition. It requires some mouse skills and remembering a few things:

- The yellow line is the insertion point. All pasted data is inserted at the insertion point or selected data portion.
- To select a portion of a waveform, simply hold the right mouse button down and drag across the portion you want to select. You can use the transport buttons (controller) to play the portion of the clip to insure it is what you want to select. If you want to add to the selection, hold the shift key and drag some more. If you don't hold shift, Audition will start another drag from that point.

There are many editing functions that can be performed in Edit view. To access them, go to the **Edit Menu.** In this menu, you will find basic waveform editing options that will give you common items such as copy, paste, redo and undo, as well as advanced features like **Mix Paste** which allows you to perform a quick and dirty mix on a pasted section of another waveform.

Let us explore several important functions from the Edit Menu.

- **Copy** allows you to copy a selected portion or all of a waveform form the edit view or multitrack view.

- **Paste** allows you to paste the data from the clipboard at the insertion point or it replaces the highlighted waveform data. If the formats are different, Audition performs a conversion to the format of the receptacle document.

- **Paste to new** creates a new file from the copied selection. It maintains the original file data information.

- **Mix Paste** allows for better pasting of waveform clips because it enables a small level of user control beyond the plain old paste. Mix paste lets you control the **volume** level of the pasted clip and insert or overlap the clip. **Insert** pushes the existing audio back to make room for the pasted clip. **Overlap** allows a mix of the pasted clip with the existing selected clip. With overlap, you can copy voice files and paste them directly into a single waveform with music to eliminate having to work in the more advanced multitrack mode. **Replace,** replaces the same time portion of the pasted clip in the edited clip.

- **Modulate** will modulate the clipboard data with an interesting effect that multiplies the waveforms. It is not a great effect for clarity of a clip, but is good for creating intro or exit effects.

- **Crossfade** applies a fade consisting of a set number of milliseconds to the beginning and the end of a clip.

- **Loop Paste** will paste the clipboard data a number of times in the inserted or selected area.

- The **Delete Selection** command will delete the highlighted selection from the wave from. Use this when you wan to chop off the end of clip to shorten the clip. The opposite command to delete selection is the **Trim command**. This command allows you to select a piece of the waveform and then trim away any data that is not selected.

The basic functions discussed in the previous paragraph will give you a start to editing audio in Audition. Once the audio is edited, you should **Edit>Convert Sample Type** to determine the best quality for the lowest file size. Converting the sample will allow you to optimize the waveform at a lower sample rate and determine if stereo or mono output is needed. Here is some information on sample rates and data resolution sizes.

The following Web sample rates are acceptable for Flash on low to medium bandwidth connections:

- **22,050 Hz** — great for voice-overs and monotone clips. Music can be optimized at this rate but it should be used for shorter clips if performance is an issue, which it is in a portfolio. (High end multimedia).
- **11,025 Hz** — great for smaller audio clips, music, and stereo. (Low end multimedia).
- For the Web, we can't go beyond here. These rates need very high bandwidth or dedicated devices such as your DVD player
- **96,000 Hz** — DVD quality
- **48,100 Hz** — DAT (Digital Audio Tape) quality
- **44,100 Hz** — Cd quality
- **32,000 Hz** — Broadcast quality

Data Resolution sizes:

- 8 bit used for simple music, monotone or voice data.
- 16 bit used for music
- 32 bit used for CD quality music

For Flash output, **11025 kHz and 8 bit resolution** would perform best and sound the worst. **22,050 with 16 bit resolution** would sound the best. You need to find a happy medium that sounds good and is relatively small in file size (under 1 MB, hopefully).

Try **22,050 and 8 bit** to accommodate clips that need quality. Use dither to reduce noise created by low resolution. Lower sample rate results in a lower pitch for the sound clip.

Experiment with different combinations of sample rate and bit depth to explore the outcomes. For our portfolio, let's shoot for a small clip with high quality (22/16). The small size will help performance. We can loop the clip in Flash if needed.

In the **Edit>Convert Sample Type** dialog box, choose **22,050 for sample rate** and **16 bit resolution.** Set to **Mono** for voice files and **Stereo** for music files.

You may be worried that this may lag when loading Flash objects with the audio embedded in the file. However, Flash has easy compression options that allow us to change the sample rate and bit depth as well as the export format of the audio file before using it in a Flash movie.

Then go to **File>Save As** and save the file as a WAV or an AIF within your **RAW** folder in the root directory. MP3 file format can also be used when saving audio for Flash. For most Web projects, WAV and AIF work best. You can optimize the sound file to MP3 after the file is imported into Flash if additional compression is needed.

Placing Audio in Flash

Audio files are external files. So are bitmaps and vector files. They all come into Flash the same way, through **File>Import.** The import menu command has three different options. First is **File>Import>Import to stage.** This command will allow you to import external files directly to the stage. Once imported, the file is automatically added to the library of the resident Flash file. If the imported file is deleted from the stage, the file still remains in the library and can be used repeatedly. The next menu command is **File>Import>Import to Library.** This command brings the file directly into the library, bypassing placement on the stage. This command is effective when you are beginning your Flash movie and need to gather your assets into Flash. If all the files were imported to the stage it may get confusing sorting through them all. You would need to delete most of them from the stage in order to get some structure. The final import choice is **File>Import>Open External Library.** When choosing a library file, simply click on the FLA file and only the file's library will open. This menu command allows you to use library file of other flash movies current movie. All symbols and assets in the library can be dragged into your current movie. You can mix symbols in movies easily. This provides some production shortcuts for you once you begin creating other projects in Flash. You could reuse a button that you liked from a previous movie.

To import the sound file you would use the **File>Import>Import to Library** command. Now that the file is in the library, we can begin to make our on/off audio switch. Once the switch is made, we can place the switch and the splash_intro.swf file together on the index page and we will have a nice simple text animation with audio and an interactive on/off audio switch.

Making the Sound Control in Flash

Now we will move forward into the realm of interactive multimedia and create a sound control button that will turn an audio clip on or off. This audio toggle switch is great for adding voice overs and music to any Web page. The switch sits independently in a layer anywhere on the Web page. You can change the background color and typeface of the audio switch in Flash to adapt it to the visual design of the other pages. As your skills and ambition grow, you can use the building blocks of the design to enhance the switch to include more than one soundtrack or voice over. The switch can evolve into a Flash Jukebox of sorts. Lets get started making a soundtrack switch for our Web portfolio.

Set Up the Movie

The first thing we need to do is set up our new Flash document. **File>New>Flash document**. Set the size to **125 pixels wide** by **25 pixels high**. You can adjust the size of the Flash file to fit your specific needs later. Set the background color to white.

Setting up the layers before work begins is very important in organizing and eventually editing your Flash document. Set up the following layers in your document:

- Actions
- Labels
- Sound
- Trigger
- Button Text

On the **actions** layer, we will be placing stop actions in the first two frames of the movie. Each stopped frame will have purpose in the interactivity. By isolating the actions on a layer, we can quickly reference our frame actions for editing.

- Insert a keyframe in **Frame 1** of the **Actions layer**
- Go to the **Actions Panel** click in the action area and type **stop();**
- **Repeat the stop() action for Frame 2**.

Set Up Labels

We will be using **labels** and an **invisible button** in this exercise. Both items are great for making interactive objects in Flash. A **label** is a reference point in the Flash timeline. Using labels allows you the freedom of naming points in the timeline descriptively, thus making references in ActionScript a bit more intuitive to program. For instance, you can make ActionScript take the play head to a certain frame in the timeline. Or you can have the play head go to a label point such as Start or Play. Maybe Stop or Repeat? Labels can be any name you like; the point is that they provide a higher level of control than frame numbers when programming an interactive movie. On the labels layer you will see red flags appear in the timeline at the label points. Don't worry, the flags are only markers to show where the labels are in the timeline. We will have two labels: **Play and Stop.**

- **On the Labels Layer,** go to **Frame 1** add a keyframe if the frame is empty(F6). On the **Properties Inspector,** under the word Frame, click in the field and type **Play.** This label is not seen on the timeline because the frames are so close together. If you roll over the frame slowly you will see the hint box appear with the label name. In the future, you can expand the frames out without changing the animation. Then you would see the label names in full view.

- **On the Labels Layer,** go to **Frame 2** add a keyframe if the frame is empty(F6). On the **Properties Inspector,** under the word Frame, click in the field and type **Stop.**

  We will use these labels for navigating the interactivity of our audio switch.

Make a Movie Clip of the Sound File for Easy Handling

Placing sound files on the main stage in Flash gets a bit messy. The timeline expands and now you can't really control the audio they way you might like. To solve this problem, you can place the sound file in a **movieclip symbol.** This will allow you to place the movieclip on the main stage and control the sound with ActionScript.

- Create a new movieclip symbol by going to **Insert>New Symbol>Movieclip.** Name the new symbol **sound_clip_mc.**

- Place a keyframe in the first frame, first layer. From the **Properties Inspector>Sound drop down menu** pick the sound. All the available sounds from the library will be showing here.

- Go back to the main timeline by clicking Scene 1 on the Scene path tabs above the timeline.

- In the **sound layer,** click on **Frame 1** and drag **sound_clip_mc** on to the outer part of the stage. The file does not need to lay on the stage because it is a sound file embedded in a movie clip that will play anywhere in the stage window it is placed.

- **Save and test the movie (F12).** The sound should play. The button is not created and will not show yet. Close the Flash player window and let's begin the next phase of creating the audio on/off switch.

Next we will make the button. The button will act simply as a rollover graphic. We will be coding the ActionScript to an **invisible button**. The invisible button is great for starting to develop your interactive tendencies in Flash. The button symbol we make now will have a text rollover that will grey out the on/off switch when rolled over.

- Make a button by going to **Insert>New Symbol>Button.** Name it **text_btn.** This will catapult you into the button symbol editor which has the **UP, OVER, DOWN, HIT** states that we discussed earlier in the text. We want to create a rollover only for this audio switch so all we really need are the up and over states. The hit state is not needed because it's job will be performed by an invisible button.

- Select the **text tool** in the Flash tool panel. Go to the **UP state** and type in the words:

- **music on / off.** Use the same color text for all the words.

- Go to the **OVER state** and press **F6** and create a keyframe. Highlight the on / off text and change the color to grey. Navigate out to the main stage.

- Place the **text_btn** on the stage in **Frame 1** the **Button text layer.** Align it to the stage. With the button in place and the sound file inserted, we are ready to make the invisible button, add some ActionScript to it, and publish our movie.

Making the Invisible Button

The invisible button is a hit state only. It is useful when you want to track your action scripts easily with visual clues. The invisible button is represented as a blue box on the stage and is similar to a "slice" in Fireworks. The invisible button acts as a hotspot for the attached ActionScript. It can be coded as any other movieclip or button symbol, but it requires less work because it has few attributes and is independent of the object it sits on.

- **Insert>New Symbol>button,** name the button **Trigger_btn.** This button will trigger the ActionScript that controls the sound clip on the timeline.

- In the button symbol editor, click on the **HIT STATE** and add a keyframe. With the **rectangle tool from the tool panel,** create a box that is 125 pixels by 25 pixels and center align it to the stage. Make the box color a bright green. Navigate to the main stage through the Scene Path above the timeline.

- Add the trigger to the button on the stage

- Place the **trigger_btn** on top of the **text_btn**. Align the trigger to the stage.

- Add a keyframe to Frame 2 (the one with the stop label) for EVERY LAYER

- This will extend the artwork across the two frames. The only item that will change in Frame 2 is the ActionScript attached to the invisible button (trigger_btn). All layers should have a dot (keyframe in them).

Insert > Figure > Screenshot > Audio Switch > Keyframes

Add ActionScript to the trigger_btn

We have done all the setup, now we must call on ActionScript to add the interactive functionality that we need to get this button working.

We want to accomplish two things:

- Stop all sounds (ActionScript) **stopAllSounds(); and gotoAndPlay("stop")**
- Start a sound (ActionScript) **gotoAndPlay("play")**

Here are the scripts

Click on the invisible button keyframe in Frame 1:

Add this ActionScript

```
on (release) {
stopAllSounds();
gotoAndPlay("stop");
}
```

Click on the invisible button keyframe in Frame 2:

Add this ActionScript

```
on (release) {
gotoAndPlay("play");
}
```

Hit **CTRL+ENTER** to test the movie.

Hopefully it worked. If not, check your layers and review the steps carefully.

When completed, save the Flash movie to the root directory of your site and name it music_switch.swf. Then publish the movie and the SWF file is automatically generated by Flash.

The Guts of this Flash Object

When the Flash audio button is launched the sound automatically starts playing. When the button is pushed the play head is sent to Frame 2 which it is told to stop all sounds and stop the play head. While in Frame 2 the button is pushed and the play head is sent to Frame 1 which starts the audio movieclip over again.

By adding audio switches, you can create a multi-track music player for your Web portfolio. For now, one soundtrack will keep your users entertained and allow them to shut the music off if they want to.

Now that we have the Flash audio switch you can place it in a layer on the index page of your portfolio. Here are the steps again:

- In Dreamweaver, **Insert>Layout Objects>Layer.** Then you need to position the layer on the page to where you want to place your Flash animation. After positioning, go to **Insert>Media>Flash.** Find the **music_switch.swf file and place it in the layer.**

- Press **F12 to preview the page in the browser.**

- **Add both .SWF files to individual layers on the index.htm page in Dreamweaver. Press F12 to test the page in the browser.**

You can also test Flash movies inside Dreamweaver pages by click on the green play button on the Properties inspector. This plays the movie without having to go into a browser.

Making Edits to the Flash Files

In order to make changes to a Macromedia flash document the need to go back into the Flash application. Dreamweaver gives you a quick way to do this by letting you access source files from within the Dreamweaver page. Whenever you insert a flash object into a Dreamweaver document you are using the SWF file and have the FLA file as source. The SWF is represented on the Dreamweaver page as a grey box with a Macromedia Flash icon in the center. If you right click on the image, you get a drop down menu that allows you to edit the Flash file. When this option is choosen, Dreamweaver will prompt you to navigate to the flash file (FLA) location. Once open in Flash, the source file can be edited and re-exported. In the case of the edited file and the old file, it is important to keep the file names the same after updating if you want Dreamweaver to update automatically the SWF in the Dreamweaver page. If the file has been updated for purposes other than a quick fix or typo, you may want to add a version number to the file so that you know that the file has had a major change (eg: intro_v2.swf). In this case, you would need to reinsert the new SWF file into the existing Dreamweaver page because of the name change.

Conclusion

With the Web portfolio coming together and multimedia being explored and possibly integrated into the pages, we are now ready to upload pages to the world wide Web. The completed pages need to be uploaded and tested to insure that the site is working properly. Next we will discuss the internet and how to secure a Web portfolio address, host space, and issues surrounding getting the portfolio live on the internet.

Chapter IX

Uploading and Testing Your Web Portfolio Site

Introduction

You have come a long way in your journey; the end is near, and it is time to take your Web portfolio site and present it to the world. This stage is a critical one. If the Web portfolio does not make it to the Internet, it loses its portability and fails as an on-demand communication. In this chapter we will explore the steps needed in purchasing a domain name for your Web portfolio, securing a host and Web space, and uploading site files using FTP. We will also cover how to set up a site in Dreamweaver so the uploading and future edits are easy. Finally in the chapter, we discuss usability heuristics and how they can be used to measure the effectiveness of the Web portfolio. We review some of the usability theories provided by Nielsen and Molich and adapt them to fit a model for the Web portfolio.

What You Need to Put Your Portfolio on the Web

Hosts and ISPs

To simply get access to the World Wide Web from your home or office, you need to have an **Internet Service Provider (ISP)**. You pay the Internet service provider for access to the Internet and they provide you with the connection you need to be wired to the Internet. The Internet service provider may give you access to the Web using a variety of methods. Each ISP charges you to use one method of getting on the Internet. This method is a hardware telecommunications channel that is paid by the user for access to a host server. Today, people get onto the Internet by using dial up, DSL (digital satellite line), cable modem, or dedicated T line. Geography dictates availability of different telecommunications channel's for Web access. Most metropolitan areas provide a choice of any of the channels listed earlier. Each service varies with location and cost. Speeds also vary. More remote areas may only have dial up access using standard telephone connections at 56 kb per second while metropolitan area Web users will have speeds from 1 MB per second on average from DSL to 1.5 MB and faster from cable modem connections. Access time is not only important when surfing the Web but also when you are uploading files or downloading files from the Internet.

The Structure of the World Wide Web and Hosts

The world wide Web consists of millions of computers that are interconnected over a distributed network. The population of computers is broken down into two groups: clients and servers. All servers on the Web can be hit by any client browsing the Web (Arpajian, 1996). This means that your Web portfolio needs a server to reside on so that clients can hit your Web portfolio site or any Web site. That's where **hosts** come in. Slice that we outlined earlier as hosts but are really specialized for Web portfolios. A true most provides a Web-based control panel which allows more extensive site manipulation and many technical templated features. These features may include SQL Server capabilities, chat rooms or message boards, hit counters, CGI scripts, and customized FTP settings for uploading files and securing folders. All hosts will provide server space for you to put your Web site up on the World Wide Web. But, reliability, price, and tools set these hosts apart from each other. You should do some investigation before choosing your host. Web host pricing is similar to Web portfolio site space. Hosting space is typically more expensive because of the toolset and the open flexibility. Again, some hosts provide low pricing for space, but for large amounts of server space for your site (over 1 GB) costs are in the hundreds of dollars a year range. Smaller space (50-500 MB) is typically well under $100 per month. A host will give you FTP access to upload your files to their server. Once you have a host, you need to have a domain name for the site if the host does not provide one. One solution to this is to purchase your own unique domain name.

Getting your portfolio up on the Web requires some steps. You will need a URL address, Web space, and an FTP program to upload your files to the host server. After the Web site is loaded on the host server you will need to test the site. Now let's look at each of these more closely.

You need to think about the name, or the URL of your Web portfolio site. You can go about this several ways. First, and most expensively, you can secure your own domain name. This means that you can have your own www.yourname.com. To get your own unique domain name you need to register the domain with a registrar. A domain name is a registered Internet address. Domains fit under different dot extensions. For example domains can be .com, .org, .biz, .cc, .net, .name, and .info for starters. There are more domain extensions available that correspond to countries such as .uk. Choosing a domain name can be a frustrating process if you do not have some general ideas as to what you want the Web address to be. That is because securing a domain name requires time, energy, creativity, and money. Finding the right domain name requires luck as well as creativity. Domain names are gobbled up every minute by Webmasters and entrepreneurs. The possibilities that all versions of your surname are taken is a good one. This is often the case if your name is common. To search available domain names, visit a registrar. Web registrars include network solutions.com, godaddy.com, and twocow.com. At these sites, you can search available domain names with most dot extensions. The prices for domains vary from registrar to registrar. Godaddy.com seems to be one of the least expensive registrars with domains costing around $7 or $8 per year. If the domain name you're looking for is not available, the Web registrars give you a listing of available names. If the name you want is not available, for example your surname is taken; there are other alternatives such as dedicated Web portfolio sites which provide subdomains and subdirectories.

A subdomain is a Web address that has a name, then a dot, and then a URL. An example would be mikesmith.portfoliovillage.com. Subdomains are effective because they are direct Web sites that are typically easy to remember because they are connected to an existing easy to remember Web address. Another advantage to using a subdomain is price. Typically, subdomains cost around $10 to $15, a one-time fee.

Where You Can Post
Your Web Portfolio

We have talked about Internet service providers and securing a domain or subdomain. Let's cover some of the real-world options that you will be making decisions about during the Web portfolio upload process. When it comes to posting your Web portfolio to a server, you have choices. The choices are based on price, flexibility, and hard disk space on the server. As hard disk space and flexibility go up so does price. As price comes down, server space dwindles and flexibility becomes stricter and stricter. Let's discuss a few examples. There are many places where you can get free Web portfolio space. Your institution may provide free space to students and faculty for the purpose of posting a Web portfolio or the instructor's case, course materials. The server space allowed by most institutions is typically unlimited. Obviously, there is a limit to everything. But, most academic information technology departments do not put stringent limits on server space for individual Web portfolio accounts. The only problem with the free Web server space is that it resides on the school server. The performances of academic servers are typically acceptable. However, what becomes a bit unacceptable are the long Web addresses that are given out to faculty and students. In the case of faculty, this is less of an issue. Faculty members already have positions in the professional world. Students, on the other hand, need the most effective promotional tools they can get to compete successfully in the knowledge age and in an age where technology rules the roost in marketable skill sets. Long addresses with ~ (tildes) and a lengthy line of subdirectory folders make academic Web portfolio addresses difficult to remember and less than impressive to give out in a professional scenario. A typical academic Web address may look something like this (www.myWeb.xyxcollege.edu/students/~jdimarco). Notice the deep subdirectories and the less than attractive tilde. Some employers with less computer savvy may not even know what a tilde is will be able to navigate to the address to see the Web portfolio. What a scary thought.

You can only spend money if you want to upgrade from an academic Web portfolio situation. There are many Web sites that provide portfolios for pay. These sites range from inexpensive to ridiculously expensive. Typical costs are anywhere from $20 to $40 per month for 15 to 30 megabytes of space on the most expensive Web portfolio sites. Yearly costs are in the hundreds. I have found that most portfolios for pay Web sites that are expensive provide a wide range of administrative, maintenance, and template tools. Basically, you are paying for more than just Web space when you use Web portfolio sites such as www.portfolio.com and www.bigblackbag.com. With these pay sites, you are paying for value-added services that you may or may not need. One potential disadvantage to these sites, besides the cost, is that some require you to work within their shell when creating a Web portfolio. This may also be seen as an advantage due to the fact that less development has to be done and artifacts can be simply uploaded for presentation. I think these sites take some of the learning value out of the Web portfolio process. Unfortunately, because they are so proprietary, they do not emulate real-world Web development environments that someone may use on a professional level in a work for hire situation. By creating a Web portfolio from scratch, you learn how to develop a Web site. The process of learning how to develop a Web site can be carried over to any Web site project.

A lower-cost, flexible solution such as my brain child, www.portfoliovillage.com. This site may suit you if you have a small, limited budget and you are willing to create your Web portfolio without templates. Focusing on helping faculty and students secure affordable Web portfolio space, this site provides 25 megabytes of space for $12 per year. The site provides limited tools and a relatively easy to remember subdirectory address standard (www.portfoliovillage/johndimarco), or a subdomain (jdimarco.portfoliovillage.com) for an extra charge.

When making a decision on Web portfolio; look at your personal budget and assess how important having a professional address on your résumé. If you do not feel that the address is important or the megabyte size provided by the host is adequate, by all means try to secure free Web portfolio space. But beware; free sites such as GeoCities had been known to have slow connections as well as a large number of annoying pop-up windows and ads. Now let's look further at the components you'll need to understand to begin to upload your Web portfolio and get it on the Internet for all to see.

File Transfer Protocol (FTP)

Once you have a domain name, server space and have the ability to get on to the Web, you can begin to upload your files to the server using **File Transfer Protocol (FTP)**. FTP allows a client to post files to a host computer or for a client to get files from a host computer. Accessing ftp requires software or FTP access from your host. All Web development software has FTP capabilities built in. These capabilities allow you to set up a local site on your personal computer as well as see the host computer from a file transfer interface. The concept here is as you work locally you can edit your Web pages and publish them on-the-fly. This allows you to make changes quickly and easily to Web pages after a site is uploaded and posted to the host server. File transfer interfaces within Web development software allow drag-and-drop uploading and downloading of files to and from a Web server. Setting up local Web files within your Web development file transfer interface is a good way to manage all the files used in a Web site during development and editing. What's great about managing the files within the Web development application file window is that if you move files around within the window the application will ask you if you would like it to update any links affected by the file movement. If you move files around within the root folder on your desktop or hard drive you risk breaking links and image locations. This will show up on the final site as an image with a gray box and a red X and pop up error messages stating file not found. We absolutely do not want either of those items to be in our Web portfolio. So be sure to move files only within the transfer area of your Web development application. If you move files outside of the application, you may have to replace broken images with the same images from the new location. If you move Web pages that are linked, you'll have to update the links.

Since we've been using professional tools throughout this text, we will continue to do so in explaining in detail how to use the file transfer interface within Macromedia Dreamweaver. Within Dreamweaver, the file transfer interface is called the **Site Panel.**

Dreamweaver provides FTP support and an easy to use interface to upload files. The **Site panel** allows you to manage all the Dreamweaver sites on your hard drive. Also of great value, Dreamweaver automatically updates moved files in the site panel so that links and image locations are kept operational. In a site panel you'll be able to view any files within the site folder you select.

To Create a New Site in Dreamweaver

Go to **Site>Manage Sites.** This will open up the Manage Sites window and allow you to set up the ftp information for your host and the local site that resides on your hard drive. For the local site choose your site folder which contains all of your site files including you are raw assets or choose only your root directory which is your first initial and last name. If you choose only your root directory you will not have access to any of the folders above it. You will have access to all the HTML files and the image files that reside in the images folder within the root directory. What's nice about having access to the files above the root directory is that you can see the names and then double-click to open the files within Adobe Photoshop or Macromedia fireworks. Once opened in the image-editing applications you can change the files and then re-export them. Once re-exported, the files will update any associated graphics within the Web pages. Again, all you really need to do in the site panel is focus on the root directory so that you can have access to the site files that will be uploaded. To set up a local site all you need to do is select the folder where the site resides on your hard drive. To get files up on the Internet you'll have to add host information to the site management section of the site files. The host information gets supplied by the host upon purchase of Web space. The host information is needed to set up FTP access and upload site files. The host information supplied will have:

- Host
- Directory
- Login
- Password

Managing Sites

The information provided is filled into the fields in the Manage Sites window in Dreamweaver and then you can connect to the server from your desktop computer. This log on brings you into the host computer and lets you put or get files just as if you were working on your own hard drive. You need to upload all the files for your Web portfolio into the server. Once files are uploaded, the site should be live and up on the Web.

Figure 9.1.   Dreamweaver site panel window (The site panel within Macromedia Dreamweaver provides an exploded view of the local files on your computer (right side) and the uploaded files residing on the server (left side). Dragging and dropping files between the local and remote sites allows easy uploading and downloading of Web files.)

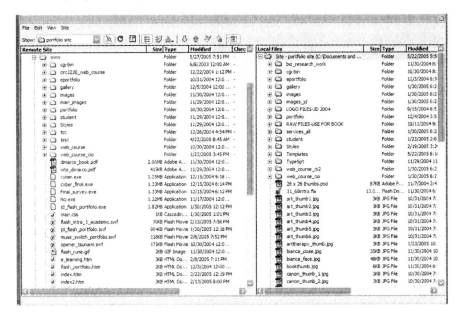

Files can be updated locally on your hard drive and then re-uploaded. Once the files are up, you can go to an Internet connected browser to check the changes. Remember to press the refresh button on the browser bar. The Web page needs to update the cache so that you will see the most recent version.

Dreamweaver uses the terms **get and put** when referring to file uploads (put) and file downloads (get) to and from a host server.

Uploading Files

One important note to remember: the folder structure of your hard drive site should be the same as the one the host provides. After your site is complete you can drag all the files into the root folder on the server. If you drag the entire root folder (first initial last name) to the root folder of the server, you will have a sub-directory. For example: siteurl/jdimarco. To fix this, in Dreamweaver's site panel, with all pages closed, rename the root directory to whatever the root directory name is on the host (e.g., public_html), and simply drag up all the files from your public folder to the hosts public folder.

Another way to upload to upload is to select the files you want to upload and then click on to **Site>Put.** This will put the files up to the server. When putting files to the host you will get a dialog box asking you if you want to include dependent files. The dependent files include images, sound files, SWF files and CSS files. When uploading you should include the dependent files if they have changed. This means that if you edited in image on a Web page and you really upload that page you should include the dependent files so that the changed image will be uploaded. If you are only uploading a Web page that has changed in text content or another way such as a background color change, you do not need to put up dependent files because there is nothing to be updated.

Moving Site Files

If you decide that you need to move files around with in your root directory, it is important that you do it inside the site panel of Macromedia Dreamweaver. If you move files around on the desktop or on your hard drive, you risk breaking image links and page links because file locations have changed. When you use the site panel in Dreamweaver to move files around, Dreamweaver provides a dialogue box that shows any affected image or page links. You have the option to update these links to the new file locations. When you let Dreamweaver update these links, the entire site gets updated and you do not have to worry about breaking connections.

Another great feature about the site panel is that it allows you to double-click on any of the files inside of it and it will launch a proprietary application that created the file and allow on-the-fly editing.

Deleting files from the site:

Select the files from the server (host side) and press delete. That will delete the files remotely from the server. The files will remain locally on your hard drive.

Testing and Usability

Now that the Web portfolio site is up, it is time to insure usability by performing testing. Usability testing is a very hot topic in human computer interaction and e-commerce. The ability for the user to get information easily and quickly is cornerstone to the scientific principles and theories surrounding the area.

One pioneer in the area of usability is Jakob Nielson. Nielson's work deals with research and testing on usability and interface design, particularly on the World Wide Web.

Nielson reports on his usability Web site useit.com that the study of heuristics is on the rise. He cites over 14,000 hits on Google pointing to heuristic evaluation. If you are wondering, heuristic evaluation is defined by Jakob Nielson on his Web site, http://www.useit.com, as:

> *"Heuristic evaluation is the most popular of the usability inspection methods. Heuristic evaluation is done as a systematic inspection of a user interface design for usability. The goal of heuristic evaluation is to find the usability problems in the design so that they can be attended to as part of an iterative design process. Heuristic evaluation involves having a small set of evaluators examine the interface and judge its compliance with recognized usability principles (the 'heuristics')."*

The work presented in the following by Nielsen and Molich has value on the system level as well as on designer and developer levels. The designer lacks usability foresight in many cases and needs to go back to grass roots usability design on paper. Creating flowcharts and storyboards, the designer fights their way back to usability standards and the brink of digital design insanity. If the designer had only followed the heuristic scale, the workload would be shortened immensely.

The heuristics that Nielson refers to on his useit.com site are explained in this list of ten heuristics for heuristic evaluation developed by Nielsen and Molich:

- **Visibility of system status**

  The system should always keep users informed about what is going on, through appropriate feedback within reasonable time.

- **Match between system and the real world**

  The system should speak the users' language, with words, phrases and concepts familiar to the user, rather than system-oriented terms. Follow real-world conventions, making information appear in a natural and logical order.

- **User control and freedom**

  Users often choose system functions by mistake and will need a clearly marked "emergency exit" to leave the unwanted state without having to go through an extended dialogue. Support undo and redo.

- **Consistency and standards**

  Users should not have to wonder whether different words, situations, or actions mean the same thing. Follow platform conventions.

- **Error prevention**

  Even better than good error messages is a careful design which prevents **a problem from occurring in the first place.**

- **Recognition rather than recall**

  Make objects, actions, and options visible. The user should not have to remember information from one part of the dialogue to another. Instructions for use of the system should be visible or easily retrievable whenever appropriate.

- **Flexibility and efficiency of use**

  Accelerators — unseen by the novice user — may often speed up the interaction for the expert user such that the system can cater to both inexperienced and experienced users. Allow users to tailor frequent actions.

- **Aesthetic and minimalist design**

  Dialogues should not contain information which is irrelevant or rarely needed. Every extra unit of information in a dialogue competes with the relevant units of information and diminishes their relative visibility.

- **Help users recognize, diagnose, and recover from errors**

  Error messages should be expressed in plain language (no codes), precisely indicate the problem, and constructively suggest a solution.

- **Help and documentation**

  Even though it is better if the system can be used without documentation, it may be necessary to provide help and documentation. Any such information should be easy to search, focused on the user's task, list concrete steps to be carried out, and not be too large (Molich & Nielsen, 1990, p. 1).

By applying Nielsen and Molich's usability heuristics in a customized fashion to test Web portfolio usability, we enable a path to further research which can focus on the specific information product structure we see in the Web portfolio.

Each of the heuristics listed earlier has a direct influence on the outcome of the user. In Web portfolio design, it is important to employ a heuristic evaluation as well. A good usage of the rules devised by Nielsen and Molich would be to adapt them to evaluate the usability of the Web portfolio. Many of the rules were addressed in the initial design of our Web portfolio. However we can learn by application of this usability theory to our own human computer interaction vehicle, the Web portfolio. Most people, after posting the Web portfolio, ask their friends and colleagues to "check out the Web site". That approach is great when you know that the Web portfolio site going to be successful. We can't be assured of that unless we ask some critical evaluation questions before releasing the site to the mass public. We can use a sample set of users, maybe friends, maybe colleagues, maybe strangers (most honest and valuable subjects), to explore the site, to test its usability from the real world view of the unassuming user.

With this in mind, I propose adaptation to the Nielsen and Molich work for the purpose of establishing usability evaluation questions for the usability of the Web portfolio. These questions can be administered to a group of subjects in order to test usability. This process can be low tech, or as Nielson describes, low fidelity paper prototype — a fancy term for a sketched paper prototype (your completed story boards qualify). Another usability testing media that can be used is a high fidelity paper prototype. These are screens that are printed out and administered to users for evaluation of usability. You can print and use screens designed in Fireworks or Photoshop for this type of usability test. If you have extensive text, you can print out the actual Web portfolio pages from a Web browser. Or simply pencil in text on pages that have only amounts of text. You can also place the text in the page in the screen design in an image editing application (Fireworks or Photoshop). Make the text portions separate slices so that you can delete them and replace the holes with editable HTML text. By using text in the image editing application, you are simply using the text for position only. You should however use the HTML font that you plan to use when and if you replace the text in Macromedia Dreamweaver later on. A quick review on Web text fonts — as mentioned before, we should only use Times or Times New Roman; or Helvetica or Arial for all HTML, Web based text. I am partial to the clean look of Arial. Use whichever font appeals to you, but keep it consistent throughout (hint: use cascading style sheets). Enough review, lets discuss Web portfolio usability standards some more.

Ask the user the following questions of the Web portfolio design and usability:

- In this Web portfolio, is there a visible, clear navigation path to the body of work?
- Was the navigation presented in easy, understandable terms?
- Did you feel you had control of the interface and portfolio content?
- Would you call the site the Web portfolio site consistent in its visual appearance?
- Did you encounter errors when using the Web portfolio site?
- Was it easy to quit out of the Web portfolio pop up windows?
- Was the design cluttered or confusing?
- Did you require help at any time while using the Web portfolio site?
- Did the music in parts of the portfolio make the experience better or worse?
- Were you able to control the multimedia (sound and animation) to you liking?
- How would you rate the Web portfolio experience you just discovered?

With the user giving honest answers, a scale of values would be developed to determine levels of user satisfaction, access attitudes, and usability ratings. A pilot study of usability in Web portfolios may be an interesting research topic not only from an academic standpoint but also from a communication perspective. The variable of persuasion can begin to be measured to determine the effectiveness of the portfolio and its work on user attitudes about the candidate or company. This is a broad topic that deserves more research. This will most likely occur due to the growth of Web portfolio popularity and governance.

On a simple level, testing the Web portfolio means going through it page by page, asset by asset, link by link to determine what is not working and what does not look good.

Towards Redesign

Every day you have your Web portfolio posted, you are one day closer to redesign. Inevitably your work and your identity will outgrow your design in some manner. Changes might be needed to be made structurally in the way you have classified your assets. It may be that changes must be made visually in the themes or colors that are used in the site. Or, there might be technical issues that you have to address which require you to go back and re-slice or export graphics or pages. Whatever the case is, you should plan to redesign your Web portfolio site many times over your careers lifespan. Other factors may cause you to redesign or re-create your Web site from scratch. A change in tools and technologies might cause you to redesign your Web portfolio simply to explore and learn. Redesign is part of lifelong learning. You'll realize how much you learned during the Web portfolio development process when you engage in redesign. The second time around developing a Web portfolio will be much easier and you will see that the process becomes part of you. You start to think about yourself and the identity that you present to your audiences. Redesign gives you an opportunity to reevaluate how you are communicating with your user and to assess the persuasion of your messages.

When redesign becomes your focus, it is important that you follow the same steps as when you initially created the Web portfolio. Don't try to skip over important steps such as creating a content outline just because you think that you already know what goes into the Web portfolio because of your past experience creating one. You should follow the process of conceptualization and content development when you begin to redesign. Then, you can focus on developing a new visual treatment for the portfolio. During a redesign, it is tempting to go directly to visual design and Web development simply because we are eager to use our new computer skills. But again I must stress that working on paper to develop your ideas and architecture is critical to success.

Conclusion

If you are at this point, you should have a good idea and hopefully a working prototype of a Web portfolio. Once the Web portfolio is created you have a product. The next step in this journey is to launch the product and then promote the product. We need to promote the product to the target audience. And as we have discussed throughout this text, our usual goal in promoting our Web portfolio is to gain work for hire. Work for hire situations can be considered employment, freelance work, a gallery venue, job promotion, and any other transaction between the Web portfolio author and the Web portfolio user. Now let's look at launching and promoting your Web portfolio to the world.

Chapter X

Launch and Promotion

Introduction

At this point you should be excited. You have created a Web portfolio and uploaded it to the Internet. You and your immediate circle of friends and colleagues may know about the site by now. Potential employers, potential clients, and other important contacts may not be aware that you have posted a Web portfolio. During the launch and promotion stage you will reach out to your audience with marketing communications that launch and promote your new Web portfolio. In this chapter we will discuss the launch and outline vehicles and methods that you can use to promote your Web portfolio.

We mentioned previously that the Web portfolio is a product. The Web portfolio truly embodies the meaning of a product. Pride and Ferrell (1987, p. 12) defined a product as a good, service, or idea. As a good, the Web portfolio represents you and to work as physical entities that can be bought. As a service, the Web portfolio can promote you as a freelancer who provides specific services. As an idea, the Web portfolio contains your philosophies, your images, your concepts, and your themes. And with all products the Web portfolio needs launch and promotion. Marketing and communications activities and vehicles are what drive launch and promotion. So to begin, we will talk about marketing and communications and how they fit into your strategies for getting your Web portfolio seen by the right people.

Marketing

Marketing your Web portfolio and the Internet requires you to make contacts and relationships with others who promote people who do what you do. For example, www.aquent.com is a creative staffing firm specializing in finding freelance and permanent work for hire situations for designers, copywriters, marketing specialists, and others who provide creative services. At Aquent site, potential employers can type keywords related to their needs such as Web design or illustration and a database will provide a list of potential candidates and their Web portfolios. When the freelancers who work for Aquent create their Web portfolio, they make sure to organize each category of work explicitly so that clients can have quick, direct access to samples. This form of marketing is highly effective for specialized fields such as creative services. If you have other specializations that are technical or business centered you can seek out other Web services that market your Web portfolio of work to potential clients. GURU.com provides Web-based, portfolio marketing services similar to Aquent.com. However, GURU.com has a wider range of specialization areas. There are a few issues with the Web portfolio capabilities of the sites. Typically, they only allow the person posting the Web portfolio to use their templates and shell. This can be a bit limiting and does not lend to the idea that creating a Web portfolio helped to build valuable and reusable technology skills. So I recommend using these marketing sites in addition to other activities in which your entire Web portfolio is showcased.

To showcase the entire Web portfolio you need to have server space and a host as we discussed in Chapter IX. When you do have your server space and your unique URL you can begin to think about communicating the Web address to others. Your new Web portfolio address should be highly visible on all of your professional communications. These items include your cover letter, your résumé or CV, your business card, your letterhead, the brochures, and your promotional items. When you drive people to your Web site, you should be prepared for feedback and be ready to discuss business if the site compels them to contact you.

At the Interview or Client Meeting

Getting contacted through the Web portfolio may yield an interview or client meeting. In this case you should be prepared with a print portfolio which backs up the Web portfolio and exhibits the projects that are most appropriate. During an interview you can discuss how created your Web portfolio and described the skills that you gained from the process. It is important to discuss the skills used to create the Web portfolio because they translate into important knowledge organization and technical capabilities that can be utilized by clients and employers.

Teachers need to present their Web portfolios for assessment and in some cases for tenure. Presentation of a Web portfolio in a classroom can be performed using an LCD presentation panel to project the Web site on a screen for group viewing. In addition, print outs of the Web portfolio pages can be bound and submitted with promotion and tenure applications.

Search Engines

Another method for marketing your Web portfolio is to submit your Web address and keywords to various search engines such as Google or Yahoo. These companies provide paid placements which give you a higher ranking during Web searches. The searches were relying on keywords that are in your Meta tags and within text inside your Web pages. You may not need to spend extra money on search engine placements if you plan to use only a Web portfolio as a job tool and not as a business tool.

Link Swaps

Another method for getting your URL in front of others is to swap links with other people who have Web sites that are related to your specialization. Good places to swap links are with associations, consortiums, galleries, user groups, schools, and other for-profit and nonprofit organizations. You can contact the Web masters of these sites and ask if there is a location for placing portfolio links or business links. In return, link to the sponsor Web site from your own links were resources page.

Publicity

Getting publicity for your Web portfolio means free promotion. Publicity can be generated in a number of ways. Press releases sent to media outlets such as newspapers and radio stations can provide news of your Web portfolio if there is something newsworthy about it. Winning competitions, having innovative content that presents something unique, and having important writings that others quote and cite all make the Web portfolio have newsworthy qualities. For example, if you are an artist who is presenting work in a gallery you might send out a press release telling the public about the event and about the art. In addition, you add the Web portfolio address to the press release under the promise of more information. You direct readers to get more information about the exhibit and the artist by going to the Web portfolio address. If you are a scholar or a teacher with a unique research project, you might query out research proposals to journal editors. In doing so, you can direct the editors to the Web portfolio to let them explore more about you and your work.

Invitations

You can design invitations for your Web portfolio launch. Invitations can created and sent in print or online. Print invitations are obviously much more expensive and time-consuming to develop and mail. Using print invitations might be a good approach to promoting your Web portfolio if you are a freelancer or a business that has a small targeted population of clients. By focusing on a small group you can maximize your advertising budget by sending out a small highly targeted communication that asks the reader to visit your Web portfolio. In the communication you must persuade the user by telling them about the virtues of the site which should include project samples, processes and philosophies, and an engaging experience. Print invitations work well when announcing redesigns or even for letting clients and potential customers what is new and fresh in your skills and experience.

You can send out Web invitations in the form of e-mail blasts and individual e-mails. E-mail blasts can be effective when targeting larger audiences with general announcements. Be sure that you get permissions and send blasts to only people who want them. Do not send spam, it is illegal. If you want to reach the customer or potential client in a more personal way you can send an individual e-mail that suggests viewing the Web portfolio. You can add direct links to the e-mail that brings the reader directly to a specific project that you have highlighted in the e-mail communication. This is a great way to get the person to visit the site.

Preparing for the launch, you should create a list of contacts that you will send an e-mail or printed invitation. Once the site is tested and you have completely sure that it is in working order, launch the site to your audience and most importantly be certain that you place the Web address on any personal or professional marketing piece that you distribute.

Review and Conclusion

As we approach the end of the Web portfolio process you have come to a point where the site design has been conceptualized in the production has been done. Now that you have a working Web portfolio you can launch it and promote it. Hopefully it will pay dividends with exposure, credibility, positive response, and maybe work for hire a form of a gallery exhibition, freelance project, or job. After reading the last ten chapters and following a guided in text tutorials, you should have some good perspective on how you will approach and develop your Web portfolio and the skills to get the job done.

In the remaining chapters discussion focuses on the study of server side technologies, Web portfolio cases, and a theoretical examination of the future of the Web portfolio in the information society. The chapter content is not critical to the tangible output of the portfolio. The goals of the next chapters are to give you some further information on topics surrounding Web and electronic portfolios processes.

In the next chapter, server-side technologies, I provide exposure to areas that allow robust integration of data driven Web pages and the Web portfolio.

Chapter XII presents dissection Web portfolio cases and interviews. I spoke with many people during the research process while writing this book. I found many good cases which illustrate the problems and challenges that others faced in developing their Web portfolios. In Chapter XII, I share the interviews with you and try to frame their efforts in a way that exemplifies the processes in creating a Web portfolio. Lastly, Chapter XIII presents theoretical discussion in relationship with the electronic portfolio/Web portfolio as a tool for communication and a vehicle for identity within the information society and new millennium.

Now it's time to move on Chapter XI and server-side technologies.

Chapter XI

Server-Side
Technologies

David Power
Canon, USA

John DiMarco
St. John's University, USA, and
New York Institute of Technology, USA

Introduction

When this book went out for review, one of the reviewers was insightful enough to recommend that I include some information on server-side technologies. As I thought about the scholar's comments, I came to a few conclusions about the importance of server-side technologies and their use within the Web portfolio. For the most part, you can create a simple Web portfolio by using only client-side tools. Client-side tools and technologies include Macromedia Dreamweaver, Adobe audition, Macromedia Fireworks, HTML, and JavaScript. But the reviewer made a good point in stating that ignoring server-side technologies seemed inappropriate. With this in mind, and with the help and research and writing contributions of my colleague and friend David Power, we provide a basic overview of PHP, ASP, ASP.net, CGI & Perl, and ColdFusion. These backend technologies have database driven components which may or may not be needed in today's Web portfolio. But as content grows in quantity, quality, and resolution, they need for large-scale database management even on personal Web portfolio levels becomes more evident. In the future, the integration of server-side technologies will surely become a large part of personal Web portfolio activities.

PHP

PHP is an open source scripting language that allows development of dynamic content Web sites. PHP creates interactive Web sites that process user submitted information and then generates content (Whitehead & Desamero, 2001). One main feature of PHP is its ability to work with numerous databases including MySQL. Databases used with PHP will provide users and authors data manipulation features that are not enabled in purely HTML Web pages. In the Web portfolio scenario, large numbers of content such as photographs, paintings, or papers can be cataloged in databases and then records can be easily updated, added, and deleted. PHP works seamlessly with HTML. PHP can generate HTML code for a page, or PHP code can be inserted into HTML code. This ease of integration with HTML allows you to enhance existing Web pages by adding PHP code into the HTML page code. PHP requires no special development tools (just a text editor) and works well with Macromedia Dreamweaver (Whitehead & Desamero, 2001). PHP is most likely a good choice to explore if you want to integrate database driven and dynamic in serving and collecting content and data to the user.

Active Server Pages (ASP)

ASP is Microsoft's server-side technology for dynamically-generated Web pages that is marketed as an adjunct to Internet Information Server (IIS). ASP has gone through four major iterations, ASP 1.0 (distributed with IIS 3.0), ASP 2.0 (distributed with IIS 4.0), ASP 3.0 (distributed with IIS 5.0), and ASP.NET (part of the Microsoft .NET platform). The pre-.NET versions are currently referred to as "classic" ASP. In the latest classic ASP, ASP 3.0, there are six built-in objects that are available to the programmer, Application,

ASPError, Request, Response, Server and Session. Each object corresponds to a group of frequently-used functionality useful for creating dynamic Web pages (Parnell & Martinez, 2003).

Most ASP pages are written in VBScript. Other scripting languages can be selected by using the @Language directive. JScript (Microsoft's implementation of JavaScript) is the other language that is usually available. PerlScript (Perl) and others are available as third-party add-ons. Programming ASP Web sites is made easier by various built-in objects, such as a cookie-based session object that maintains variables from page to page. In 2002, classic ASP was replaced by ASP.NET, which among other things, allows the replacement of in-HTML scripting with full-fledged support for .NET languages such as Visual Basic .NET and C#. In-page scripting can still be used (and is fully supported), but now pages can use VS.NET and C# classes to generate pages instead of code in HTML pages. According to news reports in 2002, the market share of ASP is declining, with the free open source alternative PHP overtaking it in the server-side scripting market.

ASP.NET

ASP.NET allows you to write dynamic, high-performance Web-applications with an easy programming model and flexible language options. ASP.Net simplifies creation of Web applications by greatly reducing the amount of code that needs to be created compared to classic ASP. Displaying data and uploading files to the Web server have been made easier and one of the distinct advantages of ASP.NET also is that it works in all browsers providing great flexibility for programmers. ASP.NET supports more than 35 .NET languages. ASP.NET lets you serve more users with the same hardware. Some of the outstanding feature sets which we will discuss include increased speed in complied execution, rich output caching, and Web-Farm Session State. ASP.NET employs dynamic compilation to ensure your application is always up to date. Most applications that migrated from classic ASP noted an increase in speed of up to five times over ASP. In terms of output caching, ASP.Net dramatically increases the performance and scalability of an application by executing a page just once and saving the result in memory when caching is enabled on a page. In addition, it sends the result to the user. When another user requests the same page, ASP.Net serves the cached result from memory without re-executing the page. Output caching is configurable, and can be used to cache individual regions or an entire page. Output caching can also improve the performance of data-driven pages by eliminating the need to query the database upon every request. ASP.NET session state lets you share session data user-specific state values across all machines in your Web farm. Now a user can hit different servers in the Web farm over multiple requests and still have full access to his or her session.

Traditionally, deploying server applications were painful cumbersome processes. ASP.NET simplifies installation of the application. With ASP.NET, you can deploy an entire application as easily as an HTML page by simply copying it to the server. Another significant feature of ASP.NET is it has support for new application models. ASP.NET makes it easy to call XML Web services from your application. No knowledge of networking, XML, or SOAP is required. ASP.NET Mobile Controls let you easily target cell phones and PDAs using ASP.NET. You write the application just once and the mobile control automatically generates WAP/WML, HTML, or iMode as required by the requesting device. The current and future communications channels provided by mobile devices will undoubtedly utilize technologies such as ASP and ASP.net. The potential reason for this is that these server-side applications provide more robust options than plain old HTML pages and are extremely friendly working with mobile devices.

Let's review some of the primary differences between ASP and ASP.net. Even though ASP.NET takes its name from Microsoft's old Web development technology, ASP, it is very different from ASP. ASP.NET was rebuilt completely from scratch and is based on the CLR shared by all Microsoft .NET applications. ASP.NET code can be written using any of the different programming languages supported by the .NET framework. The most popular .NET languages are Visual Basic.NET and Visual C#.NET (Parnell & Martinez, 2003).

ASP.NET brings the concept of a "form", from the desktop development, to the Web. HTML has the FORM tag, but in ASP.NET, a Web page is a WebForm. Instead of just writing HTML code into the HTTP stream (like CGI, ASP, and PHP), using ASP.NET you can use and create controls like Labels, TextBoxes and ListView, and add event handlers ("postbacks") to them. And instead of rendering a window in a desktop, it will generate the HTML output which will be rendered by user's browser. In the case of the Web portfolio, the use of ASP.NET based forms can help the Web portfolio author collect and store user data as well as use it to create content based controls.

The ASP.NET architecture uses the .NET Framework as infrastructure. The .NET Framework is a managed runtime environment (like Java), providing a virtual machine with JIT and a class library. Using the numerous .NET classes, can cut down on development time.

There are several software packages available for developing ASP.NET applications:

- Visual Studio .NET
- Visual Web Developer 2005 Express Edition
- Macromedia Dreamweaver MX 2004
- ASP.NET Web Matrix

CGI

CGI is the technology that allows a Web page to run scripts or programs on a server. It is not a language in itself, rather it is a specification for allowing the Web page to communicate with a Web server to write CGI applications in just about any language. In simple terms, it is an attempt to allow a Web page to interface with a Web server. HTML is very static and unchanging while the CGI interface is dynamic and changing. Lets take a closer look and define exactly what CGI is, what dynamic content is, and exactly how this all interacts with both a Web server and a Web browser. CGI stands for "Common Gateway Interface" and its major function is to define how Web servers and Web browsers handle information from HTML forms on Web pages. Web servers certainly have the capability of loading HTML pages that the user requests and sending it to them. This is typically a static request. However, if the user is requesting something more dynamic such as displaying information that may change many times a day or asking the user for information and saving that information to a database. These are prime examples of when we need the Web server to run a program, perform a task, and then send a results page back to the user's browser. A sample results page might be a feedback form that is used by a viewer at a Web portfolio to comment on work or request more information on the author.

After the form is completed and submitted by the user within the HTML page, it is sent to the Web portfolio author. The results page may be different each time the program is run. A common example would be creating a Web page in your browser that has a form in the page content. The form may request the users e-mail address, and when the user submits their information the Web server stores this information in a file that be accessed later. On the Web server side there is action taking place. When the user hits the submit button the Web browser makes a connection to the server, and requests the URL in the action parameter and also sends all the form values that the user entered. The Web server looks at the URL and realizes that is a program rather than a static file and runs it. The program then grabs all the data sent to it, performs an operation, and then returns the HTML page back to the browser as a response. This is the typical process that almost all CGI scripts will go through.

Before all of this can happen, however, you need to make sure the Web server is properly set up to handle CGI-If you plan on running CGI programs one should check with their Web master or ISP to see if the server is setup correctly. When the browser requests a URL from a server, the server needs to check if the URL requested a static file to just load and send, or if it is an actual program. This is decided by which directory the file is in and the file extension. CGI scripts need to be in the "cgi-bin" directory. This is a server configuration issue. The server is set up to know that any file in the directory is a program to run, and not a static file to send to the browser. CGI-Bin is a directory where executable CGI programs sit on a Web server. The second factor that determines if a Web server runs a file or loads it as a static file is the file extension. The extension of a file on the server — HTML, CGI, PL, TXT, and so on — tells the server what kind of file it is and how to handle it. The CGI extension is an example of an extension that the Web server is configured to recognize as a program it should run. Once the Web server has decided to run the CGI program it makes the request to the operating system to execute the file. The result may be a return e-mail or an autoresponse.

After filling out a feedback form about the Web portfolio, a message comes back saying thank you for providing feedback on this site. Using CGI is another way to add dynamic, forms driven interactivity into the Web portfolio. Most hosts provide free CGI scripts with code that you can copy and paste into a Web page. These scripts need to be set to the path of the cgi-bin provided by your host within the host server space that your Web portfolio resides in. Experiment with CGI scripts on isolated pages at first to see the results of the code you insert. Once you are confident in how the script works and what it will do when activated by the user, then place the object into a live Web portfolio page. Now let us discuss Perl.

Perl

Perl stands for Practical Extraction and Report Language and is a programming language that borrows features from many other programming languages. Perl was designed to be a practical language to extract information from text files and generate reports from that information. One stated design goal is to make easy tasks easy and difficult tasks possible. Its versatility permits versions of many programming paradigms: procedural, functional, and object oriented. Perl has a powerful regular expression engine built directly into its syntax. Perl allows the creation components that may enhance the functionality of your Web portfolio such as guestbooks and hit counters (Castro, 1999). The use of Perl scripts in the Web portfolio can be beneficial to those who have the ability to integrate them. However, using CGI scripts may be a better starting path for those who are new to using interactive forms on a Web page.

Perl is often considered the archetypal scripting language, and has been called by many "the glue that holds the Web together", as it is one of the most popular CGI languages. Its function as a glue language can be described broadly as its ability to tie together different systems and interfaces that were not designed to interoperate. Perl is one of the programming language components of the popular LAMP free software program for Web development. Perl is free software, available under a combination of the Artistic License (software license used for certain free software packages) and the GPL (General Public License). It is available for most operating systems but is particularly prevalent on Unix and Unix-like systems (such as Linux and FreeBSD) and is growing in popularity on Microsoft Window systems.

Perl is regarded by both its proponents and detractors as something of a grab bag of features and syntax. A huge collection of freely usable Perl models, ranging from advanced mathematics to database connectivity, networking and more, can be downloaded from a network of sites called CPAN, an acronym for Comprehensive Perl Archive Network. Most or all of the software on CPAN is also available under the Artistic License, the GPL, or both.

ColdFusion

The ColdFusion Markup Language (CFML) is a complete fourth generation (4GL) for scripting Web applications. Based on tags, CFML provides a comprehensive server-side programming environment with an easy to use syntax that cleanly integrates with HTML. CFML accelerates development by encapsulating complex processes like connecting to databases or e-mail servers with straightforward tags. CFML provides the ultimate environment for leveraging the features of the ColdFusion Application Server to create sophisticated Web applications. ColdFusion is the rapid server scripting environments for creating Rich Internet applications. ColdFusion enables developers to easily build and deploy dynamic Web sites, content publishing systems, self-service applications and commerce sites as examples. ColdFusion is highly desirable due to its ability to combine built-in search and charting capabilities, dynamic scripting and effortless connectivity to enterprise data. ColdFusion is the tag-based server-scripting language for rapid Web development. Processed entirely on the server, FML is easy to learn, yet powerful enough to handle the most demanding Web-application logic. FML uses a syntax hat closely resembles HTML and XML, so it is ideally suited to programming applications that use these markup languages. For new developers, tag-based CFML syntax makes complex programs easy. Advanced developers can easily extend and customize CFML through custom tags, reusable components, and user-defined functions, as well as take advantage of structured exception handling and integration with Java, C, C++, COM, CORBA, and EJB. ColdFusion is designed primarily for developers building dynamic Web sites and Internet applications. Easy-to use visual tools and an intuitive server scripting environment dramatically shorten the learning curve for new developers. At the same time, advanced features such as ColdFusion components, internet debugging, XML handling, Java integration, Web services, and the extensible event gateway architecture make ColdFusion ideal for developers creating complex Web applications and applications that need to be accessible from mobile devices. The use of ColdFusion and server-side applications will increase as Web portfolio usage finds it way into mobile computing devices.

Macromedia Dreamweaver MX 2004 provides a compelling development environment for building and testing ColdFusion applications. ColdFusion MX 7 provides new extensions for Dreamweaver MX 2004 to facilitate ColdFusion Development including integrated data source management, CFFORM design support, ColdFusion component recordsets, and a powerful login wizard.

Used together, Dreamweaver and ColdFusion provide an efficient, rapid development environment for building powerful Web applications. In addition to the powerful Flash Remoting capabilities already available in ColdFusion MX, ColdFusion MX 7 adds the ability to create rich Flash complex, multi-step forms. HTML form maintenance is a time-consuming and tedious task, but creating Flash forms is fast and intuitive for a ColdFusion developer. New Flash forms controls such as data grids, tree controls, and calendars are also available in ColdFusion MX 7 and can be easily used within the CFFORM tag to add rich controls to your applications.

To summarize ColdFusion has been used to write millions of Webpages and is generally recognized to be the easiest dynamic Web page language for people coming from straight HTML to learn. This is partly because it is tag-based like HTML is, and also because of the strong user community around ColdFusion. This includes user groups, listservs, conferences, and the Fusebox methodology for organizing ColdFusion code. You may want to explore ColdFusion first if you begin to engage in using server-side technology applications in your Web portfolio development process. Out of the popular server-side applications, it has the easiest learning curve for people familiar with HTML.

Conclusion

The server-side technologies presented earlier vary in their technical difficulty levels, cost of use, learning curves, and capabilities. All server-side applications allow dynamic content to be exchanged by users and servers. This content may contain feedback or user data that will be beneficial to the Web portfolio author. Also enabled by server-side technology are database driven forms and functions and Web application tools such as guestbooks and hit counters. Server-side components are not needed to create a great Web portfolio experience for your user. However, as your technical abilities grow and your content increases, you may want to think about database-driven methods for managing data. You may also think about how to raise the level of interactivity and responsive communication with server-side technologies.

We move now from technical jargon to real life cases and interviews. The next chapter deeply explores the Web portfolio in action with hopes of providing creative inspiration to motivate and guide you as your involvement in electronic portfolios and Web portfolios increases.

Chapter XII

Cases and Interviews

Kimberly DiMarco
Baldwin School District, USA

John DiMarco
St. John's University, USA, and
New York Institute of Technology, USA

Introduction

As I examined hundreds of Web sites promising electronic or Web portfolio data for this text, and performed observations and interviews with dozens of students and colleagues, I discovered some exemplary cases of Web portfolio usage. The Web portfolio phenomena and the rise in electronic portfolio development within all disciplines have prompted academic institutions to develop Web portfolio programs and to push these programs towards faculty and students. My general observations are that the institutions that make serious efforts to develop and manage a sound electronic portfolio program are getting good results. Right now, it is not conceivable for an institution to be able to have 100 percent of their student and faculty populations to have Web portfolios. At Penn State University, in the Dutton E-Education Institute, they are trying by providing 500 MB of Web portfolio space to all undergraduate students while enrolled. The institute recently reported in December 2004 that one in three undergraduate students activate their Web portfolio and use it for academic reflection and professional purposes. The Dutton Institute and Penn State's e-portfolio initiative are highlighted further in this chapter.

During interviews with students and faculty members who have created Web portfolios, I discovered some interesting themes that included fear of copyright infringement, technical worries, and lack of process knowledge. These themes encompass problems and positive events that shaped each Web portfolio authors experiences and these are also discussed later in the chapter.

Also in this chapter, a Web-based e-portfolio program proposal sample is included to give you a head start on creating a proposal for your institution or program. The sample is based on criteria for new technology proposals distributed by an academic vice president at a four-year university. It is not meant to be a one-size-fits-all proposal. It is meant to give structure to developing an initial program concept. Proposal adaptation based on discipline, industry, and curriculum would certainly be needed.

Finally, electronic portfolios are widely seen in the discipline of education. This chapter provides observations of teacher Web portfolios which include all levels of educators from elementary through higher education. These cases seem to have exemplary qualities that fit the teacher Web portfolio and can be transcended into the creation of Web portfolios in any discipline. The goal of examining these cases is to identify important components in the Web portfolios of teachers that represent evidence of professional development, project and skill sets, and persuasion. These teacher Web portfolio cases are effective models for use in any discipline.

Web Portfolio Program Case

Penn State University provides an interesting case on Web portfolios. David DiBiase leads the E-education Institute in the College of Earth and Mineral Sciences. Professor DiBiase has initiated a policy for all of his students in the Earth and Mineral Sciences Program (EMS) to create a Web portfolio of assignments in his geographic information sciences undergraduate course. Dibiase (2003, p. 1) requires students in the course to "publish" assignments in e-portfolios because he believes that "the information technology skills and reflective attitudes they develop in the process are both valuable learning gains". Dibiase has taken his e-portfolio rationale and fosters it through the E-Education Institute which performs research on student Web portfolio usage throughout Penn State University. Because of the large number of Earth and Mineral Sciences (EMS) Student Web portfolios, the recently published quantitative research on undergraduate Web space usage published by the institute provided findings on EMS and non-EMS student within the Penn State undergraduate population.

In the 9th Survey of Undergraduate Student use of Penn State Web space accounts, the researchers created a survey instrument consisting of a content database which recorded the presence or absence of evidence of different Web site characteristics. The list of characteristics was updated from a 2000 survey to reflect a simpler, academic-focused Web portfolio content structure. The 2005 survey categories included academic content which provides the student a place to reflect on formal and tangible learning and project experiences. The academic content section included course projects and assignments completed by students in formal coursework. The following section in the survey was supporting content. This section contained work that was not specifically targeted solely to academic experience or work within a specific discipline. Supporting content subcategories included résumés, personal information, and co-curricular information. A third and final category within the 2005 Penn State Web usage survey was reflection. This third section was previously defined in the 2000 survey instrument as a list of portfolio assets. That changed in 2005 with the goal of providing a space for publishing reflective thoughts and commentary throughout the life of the portfolio. Reflections in the study were defined as "activity that occurs within a comprehensive approach" and considered reflections or reflective evidence as important when focusing on direction within specific course outcomes. An example of this might be a daily journal compiled by an elementary schoolteacher which could be included in a Web portfolio reflection category.

Survey data collection was carried out on both EMS and non-EMS students from the undergraduate population. Results were divided up to list survey data that showed a higher number of EMS students activating Web space and more importantly using it for academic content. The study explained that this is very possible due to the fact that many EM courses require students to publish work online. Of the non-EMS students, only half of the population activated Web space accounts and at the time of the 2005 survey, less than half had used the Webspace to publish some form of academic work online. However, the study did show that non-EMS students' content increased in the quantity of reflective writing, which is a process that the study declares as "central to most general definitions of what is included in an exemplary in the portfolio" (Johnson 2005, p. 6). This case vividly illustrates the trend in using Web publishing to support academic achievement. It is critical to explain that faculty involvement in facilitating student Web publishing of assignments has tremendous residual value to students and faculty. Students in the earth and mineral sciences program at Penn State had always been more likely to activate Web portfolio space because of the pedagogy employed by instructors like David DiBiase. Faculty in disciplines such as education and art require portfolios and use them in their pedagogy, but we expect that. Making Web portfolios a part of curriculum in the hard and soft sciences as well as other areas including humanities will help to bring the Web portfolio to a higher level and ultimately it make it a standard part of assessment and learning within all disciplines.

The Penn State case is a comprehensive view of a flourishing Web portfolio program. This is not just seen in the yearly increase of student Web usage for portfolio purposes. But more importantly the program is exemplary because it has tackled administrative and technical hurdles which cripple faculty involvement. As well, the processes defined in the Penn State Web portfolio Web site are clear and are not intimidating. The process does allow for autonomy in technical development and software application training. There is no stock Web portfolio building application as is seen at many other institutions who have established a Web portfolio program. The Web site for the Web portfolio does however provide a wealth of tutorials and resources to help students get up and running using Web development applications such as Microsoft FrontPage and Macromedia Dreamweaver. The Web portfolio development program at Penn State works to empower students to gain the technical skills needed. I think this is in incredibly important in the Web portfolio development process. Another important feature to be noted about the Penn State program the ease of use built-in to the interface of the Penn State e-portfolio Web site. There is a clear path towards publishing a Web portfolio for the student to follow. The site guides the student to collect first evidence, also known as content or assets, and then leads them towards "crafting their message". Crafting their message is a step in which students define their concept and audience for the Web portfolio. It is in the crafting a message section the site notes that there are no hard and fast rules to creating a vision for the Web portfolio. I feel this is really important because it is getting students in a mindset and arena for free flowing conceptualization and expression while integrating creative thoughts outside of someone else's perceived criteria. After ideas are brainstormed and assets are collected, then students are guided towards creating pages. Students get linked to a Web space application in which they acquire the server space needed to post the Web portfolio. As mentioned earlier, the site offers numerous resources and tutorials to help students create Web pages and post them using industry-standard software including Macromedia Dreamweaver. There is even a section on design of Web pages. This is coupled with numerous resources to help students create visually compelling, well designed Web portfolios. Web portfolio examples are provided, but no templates are available. I agree with this methodology. When templates are the exclusive method of design, all the Web portfolios look the same and lose their creative punch as well as the individuality of the author. Lastly, students are encouraged to reflect continually on the artifacts exhibited in the Web portfolio. Sharing the author's thoughts with the user/reader of the Web portfolio with regards to projects, processes, and positive attributes is highly recommended on the Penn State a portfolio Web site. I feel that making reflection a priority is important to any Web portfolio program. Reflection should be constant throughout the life of the portfolio. Students need to think critically about their work, academic discipline, and own success to be able to explain to others why and how it is important. The Web portfolio provides a great platform for a reflection and therefore is justified throughout the life span of any person's professional career.

Student Web portfolios do not have infinite life at Penn State. The university provides a disclaimer in their technical section on the Web that informs students that their pages will only be up six months past graduation and they are warned to create a backup of the Web portfolio on CD-ROM or another removable media. Unfortunately, this is common at most institutions. To maintain a lifelong connection to the Web portfolio space needs to be provided after graduation. This is difficult due to cost and security concerns. Students need to be encouraged and guided towards Web portfolio space after graduation. Sites such as GeoCities and Yahoo provide free space. Low-cost space can be acquired at sites such as www.portfoliovillage.com and qfolio.com.

The Penn State e-portfolio program is exemplary in how it has evolved into a strong successful Web portfolio program model that has provided important resources to students in establishing content, developing a solid message, understanding technical and software issues, and reflecting on their own growth and learning.

Sample E-Portfolio Proposal

The development of an electronic portfolio initiative project requires you to develop a proposal and submit it for approval. There are many facets to an effective proposal. Concerns surrounding the development of electronic portfolio and Web portfolio program may include server space questions, level of student involvement, portfolio design concerns, access questions, actual level faculty involvement, and other issues involving security and plagiarism. These concerns are extremely important to address with context of each individual institutions staff and resources. It may be difficult to address all issues within a proposal due to the fact that problems are emergent and we can never really anticipate what may or may not happen next. This is especially true in the case of technology and learning. So I have attempted to create a foundation proposal that may be altered and submitted to an academic affairs officer to begin to explain the value of a Web portfolio program and importance of instituting university wide electronic portfolio initiatives. In the proposal, I do not attempt to outline extensive budgets and resources needed for hosting student and faculty Web portfolios. I omit this information because in most situations the university will turn to the IT department for guidance, clearance, and support of such initiatives. Instead, the proposal outlines some general curriculum scenarios that can be used as suggestions that are intended to focus on user needs and not on technical infrastructure. Technical infrastructure issues will be handled by IT and final usage by users will probably end up somewhere in between what you wanted and what the IT department wanted in the way of access and space. Most importantly, in the proposal sample I focused on rationale, objectives, and initial staff concerns. These items can be understood by an academic officer without being overly technical and should ultimately provide a clear picture of how and why an electronic and Web portfolio initiative project will benefit faculty, students, and the institution. Use this proposal as a basis for your own proposal focusing on how the program can be part of technological curriculum integration across disciplines.

The proposal is one part of creating the Web portfolio program and an electronic portfolio initiative. Getting support is another part of the process which requires you to seek out faculty who are interested in getting involved in the initiative and those who want to take the time to learn how to develop Web portfolios so that they can teach and mentor students in their disciplines. The interweaving of faculty and student activities in building a successful Web portfolio program is crucial to getting support from academic affairs for the initiative. The proposal must ultimately show how faculty will become facilitators of Web portfolio development within their own disciplines. To get faculty involved, Web-based tutorial and instructor led training must be discussed in any long-range plan with your faculty technology resource center. Faculty will not be 100 percent involved overnight. However, with a methodical, sensitive, informative, and structured approach, faculty in all disciplines can be taught how to mentor and teach students how to publish their coursework and other assets in an electronic portfolio. It is critical that the Web portfolio program stress faculty involvement and provide an indication of how faculty will learn and build Web portfolio components into their own pedagogy. I will try to describe the reasoning behind each section so that you can begin to formulate your own ideas specific to your particular institutional scenario.

Title Page:

The GENERIC University E-Portfolio Project

A Plan for Growth in Campus Wide Technology Skills and Student Achievement across Disciplines

Respectfully submitted by:

John DiMarco

Instructor, GENERIC University

Contact: jdimarco@.edu

Proposal Beginning:

Project Description

(Keep this short and to the point. Be sure to outline a universal goal for the program.)

This project aims to provide the coursework, advisement, and technology resources for teaching all faculty and students how to conceptualize, design, and develop an e-portfolio (an electronic portfolio delivered from the Internet or through CD-Rom/DVD). The goal is to facilitate student and faculty creation and publishing of e-portfolios across curriculums.

Rationale

(The rationale should position the initiative and program in the direction of campus wide improvement.)

Student portfolios are an important part of academic achievement and professional growth. The skills and capabilities to present accomplishments, knowledge, project samples, resumes, and professional identity on the Internet is priceless to graduates searching for career opportunities. In the digital age, the e-portfolio (DVD portfolio or Web portfolio) has become an important tool in helping people succeed in a wide range of disciplines. CUNY Institutions, New York University, and others in higher education nationwide are embracing the e-portfolio. E-portfolios serve as self-selected, self developed multimedia presentations of student work that offer deep and textured views of a student's learning and development. Driven by creative expression and college learning experiences, e-portfolios provide tangible evidence of growth and accomplishment. E-portfolios allow students to present research papers, essays, and academic projects that incorporate text, images, audio, and video. The e-portfolio can be delivered via the Internet or distributed on DVD or CD-ROM. The disciplines of computer science, art, and education have embraced e-portfolio development most frequently. However, students in all disciplines need an e-portfolio when they leave the university. The majority of all graduating students outside of technically savvy programs do not enter into their career search and first job interview with a Web portfolio or DVD portfolio. This proposal outlines project objectives, curriculum strategy, technology resources, and proposed outcomes for building an exemplary e- portfolio program across all disciplines at GENERIC University. This project will contribute to the rich tradition of innovative teaching that takes place at GENERIC University.

Project Objectives

(The objectives are critical to communicating a clear value to the institution, its faculty, and students. Numbered or bullet points should be blatant and complement the existing narrative.)

To attain a 100 percent success rate for e-portfolio development from graduating students in undergraduate and graduate programs across all disciplines.

To provide measurable, highly valuable Web design technology skills to students in all disciplines. ("Technology Across the Curriculum.")

To further validate the academic excellence provided by Long Island University by using Web portfolios to provide complementing existing outcomes assessment data with a richer, more individualized portrait of student learning.

To help the world better understand GENERIC University students, their professors and their combined vast academic accomplishments by incorporating many disciplines to support the growth of the "one college" philosophy.

To further explore the meaning of diversity at GENERIC University by considering the relationship of education to social and individual identity.

To provide a platform for faculty growth and interdisciplinary faculty development, linking curriculum, pedagogy, assessment and the integration of new technologies into teaching and learning.

To develop a student and faculty Web portfolio portal hosted by the GENERIC University Information Technology Department which will showcase exciting student work, providing opportunities for improved recruitment, fund raising, and advancing the mission of the University. The portal will serve as a global village of student and faculty scholarship.

To publish an account of this project as an effective model of innovation to the academic community.

Curriculum Integration

(Describe how the e-portfolio initiative will fit adapt an existing course description providing a vision of a credited course. Credit courses in Web portfolio development already exist in some disciplines at some institutions so make sure that you have researched existing programs at your school to see if what you are proposing can be is unique and can be implemented campus-wide.)

Coursework in e-portfolio design and development can be offered across disciplines to students who want to create an e-portfolio before they graduate.

Proposed Course Description (Sample Syllabus attached)

(No existing Web portfolio course description)

As part of the GENERIC COLLEGE School

> LIS 000 - E-Portfolio Design and Development
>
> This course provides the student with a creative opportunity to develop an electronic portfolio that is posted to the GENERIC U E-Portfolio Portal and the World Wide Web. Instruction includes conceptualization and categorization of assets and artifacts for portfolio development and technology lab tutorials in the use of digital imaging, MS Office output to Web pages, and tutorials in industry standard Web development software applications. Emphasis and final grading is based upon completion of an effective e-portfolio (Required for all majors) 3 credits.

Class Sizes and Locations

(Anticipate what resources you and other faculty members may need in developing a program that needs classroom and computer laboratory space.)

> Class size for the *E-Portfolio Design and Development* should be limited to 25 students.
>
> Courses can be taught in any Windows computer lab on the GENERIC University campus that accommodates 25 computer users.

Here is a possible scenario for implementation of this program:

(Cater this to what you know about your school and its current curricular guidelines.)

> Upon entering their last semester junior year, all students will be encouraged and possibly required to complete and post a e- portfolio to the E-Portfolio Portal on the World Wide Web. Upon completion of the e-portfolio, the student's final project advisor or thesis advisor will evaluate the e-portfolio and provide a pass/fail grade. The student will have several options to complete the e-portfolio requirement:
>
> *Attend a 3 credit course — E-Portfolio Design and Development,* in which students conceptualize, design, and post their Web portfolio. This course could be cross listed in all disciplines.

Create the Web-based e-portfolio on his or her own within a course provided by their department curriculum (e.g., education students who take a portfolio class).

Create the Web-based portfolio as an independent study with a faculty member in their department.

NOTE: One goal of the program is to empower faculty members to create their own e-portfolio. To do this, faculty can participate in training on how to teach and mentor students in the creation of an e-portfolio within their own disciplines. (This can be part of the Teaching and Learning Initiative for Faculty Members-In connection with the faculty resource center) Classroom training and online learning simulations will be available to assist faculty in developing the skills and confidence needed to develop and advise students on e-portfolio development.

Technology Issues

(Work with the IT department, technology savvy faculty, and your faculty technology resource center to develop a plan to pilot a Web portfolio project.)

Sever space for the pilot project is available on the GENERIC University server managed by

GENERIC School Assistant Professor XXXX. Professor XXXX, Professor YYYY, and myself will work with the faculty technology resource center to administer the Web server space and be involved in the development of the e-portfolio portal.

Security Precautions:

(Consult your IT department and other faculty for suggestions on securing appropriate content within student-created Web portfolios.)

Students will be monitored by a faculty member throughout the e-portfolio process to insure that content is regulated.

Student Updates and Lifetime Portfolios:

(This is a tough sell to administrators so tread lightly and do not expect an incredibly long life span for graduated students' Web portfolios. As well, do not expect universal open access for students to their Web portfolios. Next, I provide a suggestion, but this is not a tested idea yet, only a possible scenario which would need to be set in a pilot situation and monitored for issues, problems and success.)

The goal is to provide lifetime portfolios to every student and alum. Initially, during the pilot period, students will not have direct access to update their e-portfolio after their e-portfolio course is completed. After the pilot period, a system for updates can be developed and implemented. One possible method may be to have students who want to update complete an online form describing their updates. That form will be e-mailed to the e-portfolio program coordinator for review. If the content is acceptable, the changes are approved and the alum can then update to the site. Each update will require an electronic signature by the student indicating that the content uploaded does not contain illegal material not related to the purpose of the Web.

Timeline

(This is a loose timeline that can show expected progress in developing a program. Individual institutional challenges and learning curves will get in the way of progress. The focus is to show administration that there is a timeline for success and tentative milestones that if met will enable the program to flourish.)

The GENERIC University E-Portfolio Project can be piloted over Summer 05. Evaluation and assessment of classroom and overall summer program results will be recorded and distributed to the faculty consortium for review during September 2005.

May '05	Development of e-portfolio portal site
	Development of online tutorials for faculty
Summer '05	E-portfolio design and development is offered in the GENERIC school
	Extensive student evaluation of the course is recorded
	Faculty Workshops are provided
Fall '05	Faculty consortium and GENERIC school evaluate effectiveness of summer program

A Viable Research Front

(It is critical to communicate to the institution administrators that the e-portfolio initiative and a Web portfolio program will be a boost to the school, college, or university in the way of generating publicity on the Internet and beyond, as well as providing a highly marketable competitive advantage to their offerings in the educational marketplace. Obviously, there are great benefits to students. Web portfolio projects generate research questions and problems that can be investigated through quantitative and qualitative methods. The growth of electronic and Web portfolio research will indeed increase as the importance of having a Web portfolio increases over time. There are great opportunities for extensive ethnographic research within selected academic disciplines and social groups on Web portfolio development and publishing activities.)

> During my research on this project, I looked at the use of e-portfolios in academia and found that faculty and students were not public exhibiting a large number of e-portfolios on the GENERIC University Web site. It is true that, some departments use e-portfolios and even require them, however, they are in many cases poorly designed or do not work properly. A small portion of Faculty member have e-portfolios posted to the Web, but ultimately, the majority of the Long Island University community (students and faculty) do not have an e-portfolio posted on the Internet. I want to work with the GENERIC School faculty and students to help improve this situation.
>
> There are many obstacles to creating an e-portfolio. For students as well as faculty, the process can be daunting, often resulting in weak results and failure. I understand these obstacles and have developed strategies to help control them. I feel this proposal addresses a great opportunity for Long Island University and the GENERIC University Campus to build an effective e-portfolio program and eventually integrate it into the entire GENERIC Campus population.
>
> Based on the success of other institutions funding their e-portfolio projects (e.g., LaGuardia Community College), the GENERIC University E-Portfolio project has exceptional potential to gain grant support. Support of fund raising activities for the program will be a key objective in the overall program development.

Staff and Faculty Support

(Identify a coordinator and other key faculty and staff who will want to dedicate time and effort to launching the e portfolio initiative.)

John DiMarco — Faculty Member

E-Portfolio Program Coordinator (this is a proposed position, possibly a stipend position)

Roles:

Develop and implement a strategic plan involving all departments' campus wide to communicate the importance and value of e-portfolios in the academic community and job market.

Work closely with the GENERIC School, the E-portfolio Faculty Consortium, and the GENERIC University Information Technology Department to develop a stunning portfolio portal showcasing the e-portfolios of GENERIC University students across all disciplines.

Teach graduate and undergraduate courses in *E-Portfolio Design and Development* in the GENERIC School labs.

Seek out grant and research opportunities in e-portfolio development.

Coordinate with all departments and the Faculty Technology Resource Center to recruit and train faculty on how to integrate e-portfolio design and development into their pedagogy and how to teach the dedicated course in *E-Portfolio Design and Development*.

Manage e-portfolio activities for the Teaching and Learning Initiative at GENERIC University.

Work on development of online tutorials demonstrating software techniques and e-portfolio concepts.

Faculty Consortium

(The faculty consortium will act as a steering committee and a workforce for launching the e portfolio program. Faculty involvement is *the* key to getting institutional support.)

Professor XXXXXXX — Director, Media Arts Department

> **Role:** Provide support, advisement, and technical expertise on multimedia design and presentation. Eventually, Professor XXXXX has expressed interest in teaching the E-portfolio Design and Development course.

Professor XXXX — Education Department

> **Role:** Provide support, advisement, and assessment expertise.

Professor XXXXX — Information Science/Computer Science

> **Role:** Provide support, advisement, and technical expertise on Web architecture. Will serve as the Web Portfolio administrator providing support and management of the GENERIC server. Professor XXXXX will also work with the Faculty Technology Resource Center to provide Web portfolio services to all campus faculty members.

Director XXXXX — GENERIC Faculty Technology Resource Center

> **Role:** Liaison between IT and faculty. Will provide support for campus wide technology initiatives with faculty workshops on Web portfolio development.

Sample Syllabus

(Lastly, provide a sample syllabus if possible to bring the coursework to life. Integrate Web portfolios into an existing course which might require students to post a Web portfolio of class assignments. Or develop an exclusive e-portfolio course which can be used across disciplines to help students get a live Web portfolio. An exclusive technology course on Web portfolio development can be written to fit the specific curriculum offerings of academic areas such as Information science, computer science, or digital arts. Or the Web portfolio course can be added as a campus-wide, free elective. The curriculum processes and requirements of your particular institution will dictate placement of a developed course.)

Information Science Department

Generic University

Syllabus

LIS 000: E-Portfolio Design and Development

CONSULTATION

Instructor:	XXXXX
Campus Office:	Room xxx, Library Computer Lab
Office Hours:	
Office Phone:	xxx-xxx-xxxx
E-mail address:	
Web portfolio:	http://myWebportfolioXXXXXX

COURSE DESCRIPTION

Title: LIS 000: *E-Portfolio Design and Development*

Description: This course provides the student with a creative oppor
   tunity to develop an electronic portfolio that is posted to the GENERIC
   U E-Portfolio Portal and the World Wide Web. Instruction includes
   conceptualization and categorization of assets and artifacts for portfolio
   development and technology lab tutorials in the use of digital imaging,
   MS Office output to Web pages, and tutorials in industry standard Web
   development software applications. Emphasis and final grading is based
   upon completion of an effective e-portfolio

Credit hours: 3

PURPOSE

This course is designed to give students a working knowledge of principles
of electronic portfolio planning and design, Web development, multimedia
skills, and new media writing. Students should gain an in depth understanding of the role of the electronic portfolio in the context of their
discipline, career, and lifelong learning.

LEARNING OBJECTIVES

Upon successful completion of this course, students will be able to:

- Understand why the Web portfolio is an important tool for lifelong
  learning and communication
- Conceptualize and plan a Web portfolio

- Evaluate and execute artifact content collection decisions and processes
- Develop assets and messages
- Use industry standard software packages for design, content development, and Web authoring
- Critically review and evaluate Web portfolios to insure they meet specific disciplinary criteria
- Perform reflective writing for the Web portfolio

TEXTS AND READINGS

Electronic Reserve:

Greenberg, G. (2004). The digital convergence: Extending the portfolio mode [Electronic version]. *Educase, 39* (4).

Books:

Horton, S., & Lynch, P. (1999). *Web style guide: Basic design principles for creating Web sites.* New Haven, CT: Yale University.

Kimball, M. (2003). *The Web portfolio guide, creating electronic portfolios for the Web.* New York: Longman.

Kristof, R., & Satran, A. (1995). *Interactivity by design: Creating and communicating with new media.* Mountain View, CA: Adobe Press.

Visual Quickstart Guide for Dreamweaver MX 2004, Peachpit Press.

Visual Quickstart guide for Macromedia Flash MX 2004, Peachpit Press.

INSTRUCTIONAL ACTIVITIES

- Lecture and discussion
- In and out of class writing assignments
- Required textbook reading to prepare for class discussion and assignments
- Software technique demonstrations
- Technical lab time
- Reflective journal
- Group critiques
- Written exam

COURSE REQUIREMENTS AND GRADING

30%   Class exercises, assignments, reflective journal

10%   Class participation (Class attendance is expected and recommended)

50%   Final Web portfolio evaluation

10%   Final exam

Meeting only once per week, your attendance at all classes is expected.

Late assignments will be penalized one grade per class meeting.

COURSE OUTLINE AND SCHEDULE

Readings will be assigned in class

Week 1

Topic:

- Electronic portfolio definitions
- Web portfolio definitions
- Defining the Web portfolio within your discipline and context

Assignment 1:

- Based on class discussion, in a one page paper, describe how the electronic portfolio fits into your academic discipline and career goals.
- Find three URL's of Web portfolios from your discipline
- Assigned reading
- Start your journal

Week 2

Topic:

- Conceptualize/Brainstorm the Web portfolio
- Defining the audience
- Explain how the Web portfolio will be used to persuade the audience

Assignment 2:

- Prepare a written concept statement that defines the concept, images, messages, and themes that may be part of the Web portfolio
- Write a journal entry on your experiences

Week 3

Topic:

- Web portfolio content
- Content evaluation methods
- Writing the content list
- Writing project/work/artifact descriptions

Assignment 3:

- Research Web portfolios within your discipline and others to determine possible categories of artifacts and visual themes.
- Create your written content list
- Create your content outline
- Write two project descriptions using the format presented in class

Week 4

Topic:

- Information design
- Navigation issues
- Developing a flowchart
- Page counts and scope
- Combining the scope documents (concept statement, content list, content outline, and flowchart)

Assignment 4:

- Develop a flowchart of your Web portfolio site
- Submit complete scope report
- Write a journal entry on your experiences

Week 5

Topic:

- Visual design
- Developing storyboards
- Content development and digital capture techniques

- Screen resolution and graphical sizing issues
- Web resumes
- HTML and graphical text issues

Assignment 5:

- Develop your Web portfolio site storyboards

Week 6

Topic:

- Web page and graphic design
- Developing Web graphics
- Developing Web screens
- Developing navigation
- Digital Artifact Production (MS Office)
- Using Adobe Photoshop

Assignment 6:

- Develop your Web portfolio site screens and navigation using Adobe Photoshop
- Write a journal entry on your experiences

Week 7

Topic:

- Web screen slicing and exporting
- Using Macromedia Fireworks
- Exporting issues (GIF or JPG?)
- Setting up the folder structure properly
- Understanding the root directory of the Web portfolio

Assignment 7:

- Set up the folder structure on your USB drive
- Slice and export your Web pages

Week 8

Topic:

- Web authoring
- Using Macromedia Dreamweaver with Fireworks
- Web page functionality issues
- Web page development demonstrations and tutorials

Assignment 8:

- Add links, page properties, and other functionality to the Web pages
- Write a journal entry on your experiences

Week 9

Topic:

- Web authoring (continued)
- Using Dreamweaver to create Web pages
- Creating rollovers
- Creating pop-up windows

Assignment 9:

- Add rollovers, pop-up windows, and other Web functionality
- Create a Web resume
- Place artifacts and descriptions in pages and pop-up windows

Week 10

Topic:

- Work week/Catch up/One-on-one meetings

Assignment 10:

- Complete Web authoring

Week 11

Topic:

- Multimedia authoring
- Using Macromedia Flash

- Motion graphics
- Animation
- Text effects

Assignment 11:

- Create a Flash based text animation using fades
- Complete Web content of HTML pages

Week 12

Topic:

- Using bitmaps in Macromedia Flash
- Adding audio
- Adding Macromedia Flash multimedia files to a Web page
- Publishing a Flash movie
- Adding Macromedia Flash multimedia files to a Web page

Assignment 12:

- Create an introduction animation for the Web portfolio
- Add audio to the Web portfolio using Macromedia Flash
- Write a journal entry on your experiences
- Create a Web page(s) for the reflective journal describing your Web portfolio development learning experience

Week 13

Topic:

- Uploading the Web portfolio using Macromedia Dreamweaver and FTP
- Testing the Web portfolio
- Checking download time
- Checking links and pop-ups
- Testing usability
- Final exam review

Assignment 13:

- Test your Web portfolio for technical functionality

- Test your Web portfolio for usability
- Create a test report on usability and functionality
- Write a journal entry on your experiences and post it to the
- Journal Web page

Week 14

Topic:

- Uploading fixes
- Final exam
- Lab catch-up and one-on-one

Week 15

Topic:

Final critique

Interviews

The next section of this chapter provides interviews with educators who have created Web portfolios. These brief interviews provide some insight into the thoughts of teachers in the fields of art and education as they created their Web portfolios.

Kimberly DiMarco K-12 elementary teacher
Created First Web Portfolio 2000

Web portfolio address: http://www.portfoliovillage.com/kimlawrence

Q: *What is your current position or student status? How long have you been in you current industry or field?*

A: My current teaching position is as a special education kindergarten and first grade teacher. I also tutor in the areas of reading, writing and mathematics. I am a student at the University of Albany, earning my Master's Degree in Literacy. This is my fourth year as a special education teacher.

Q: *What does your Web portfolio content consist of? Please describe and list assets or artifacts presented on the Web portfolio:*

A: My Web portfolio content consists of my biography and credentials, contact information, my teaching philosophy and pedagogy, evidence of professional development and student work, curriculum, management and assessment measures, and a consistent visual layout. However, I did not include links to resources for my audience groups or integrate interactive features.

Q: *What made you decide to move forward and create a Web portfolio?*

A: Initially, the purpose for my Web portfolio was to advertise for hire. After doing some research on what other teachers had done, I created my Web portfolio as a marketing tool after my student teaching was complete. However, my current intent to redesign my Web portfolio is for employment purposes, assessment, and professional development.

Q: *What fears or doubts did you have before starting the Web portfolio?*

A: When beginning the Web portfolio, I doubted my ability to actually construct a Web portfolio, so I enlisted the help of an expert, my husband. From there, I doubted that I had enough of an impressive array of evidence to prove I was a strong teacher, and that was crucial since the primary reason for the portfolio was to obtain a teaching position.

Being fresh out of college, I was hesitant because I was not sure I had enough substance for the portfolio, such as student work and teaching experience. After I began to outline the portfolio and decide what pieces to include, I found that it was the quality of the work, not the quantity, that mattered.

Q: *What were the most difficult challenges you faced when creating the Web portfolio?*

A: Knowing that the construction of the Web portfolio, uploading, and so on was taken care of, the most difficult challenge I faced when creating the Web portfolio was deciding what to include in the Web portfolio. I had pictures, student work, teacher-created materials, lessons and projects but they were scattered samples from various student teaching and practicum experiences involving differing grade levels in both the general education and special education environments. I wanted the portfolio to display every aspect of my teaching abilities while maintaining a sense of structure and continuity. I did not want the content of the portfolio to be confusing or appear "piece-mealed" together.

Q: *Do you plan to redesign the Web portfolio eventually? If so, what might you do differently?*

A: I plan on redesigning my Web portfolio within the next three months. I have grown extensively as a teacher and as a student since the creation of my first Web portfolio. I have new experiences and information to share with colleagues, peers, parents, students and district supervisors and administrators. Although my portfolio will target each of these audience groups, the primary reason for redesign is to utilize the portfolio as an assessment measure to evaluate myself as a teacher and student.

When thinking of what I would do differently, I will keep the initial homepage but add a picture of myself so my audience groups can immediately recognize me as a person and teacher, not simply just as Kimberly DiMarco — Teacher. I want them to "bond" with me and a picture provides a face with the name. I will add more crayon colors, which act as buttons to link to areas of my portfolio, to provide new links. I will update my biography and credentials, define a purpose for my audience(s), and provide additional evidence of professional development, student work, teaching of the curriculum, management skills and assessment measures. I will include links to resources for my audience groups and integrate interactive features for easier user navigation and interest.

I will use a rubric, or set of criteria specifically for teacher Web portfolios, to choose the content and outline the portfolio. I want the portfolio to be simple, easy to navigate, informative and creative. After all, I am advertising myself and I want to convince my audience groups that I am an excellent teacher.

I will follow the stages of the writing process (brainstorm, write, revise, edit, and publish), along side of the 10 criteria for teacher Web portfolios, when developing the portfolio. This will give the portfolio structure and will help to organize my planning and publishing.

John Fekner, Educator

Created First Web Portfolio 1999

Web portfolio address: http://myWeb.cwpost.liu.edu/jfekner

Q: *What is your current position or student status? How long have you been in your current industry or field?*

A: Professor of art and director of the digital arts and design program at Long Island University since 1990 and a practicing artist for over 30 years.

Q: *What does your Web portfolio content consist of? Please describe and list assets or artifacts presented on the Web portfolio.*

A: Forty-four photographic documentations of temporary outdoor and indoor installations; four video documentation projects created as new unique works for Web (excerpts); 10 sound recordings (excerpts) QuickTime; four poems. Resume and other additional ephemera.

Q: *What made you decide to move forward and create a Web portfolio?*

A: As a professional artist, worldwide visibility and networking are major factors in outreaching to other artists, scholars, critics and researchers. Without a Web, an artist remains within a much smaller and narrower community of acquaintances, art dealers, critics, painstakingly created on an individual's typical personal snail mail list.

Q: *What fears or doubts did you have before starting the Web portfolio?*

A: At first, I had some reservations about allowing others the opportunity to disseminate and reconfigure my work, by changing and altering the original intention of the work. Then, due to the ephemeral nature of my work itself, I decided that this would a rather unique setting for the work to be presented to a much wider and newer audience, who were not aware of my creative work in art, computer graphics, video, and sound recordings.

Q: *What were the most difficult challenges you faced when creating the Web portfolio? Which steps in the process were most difficult? Was it conceptualization, content gathering, design, development, up-loading, or promotion?*

A: As a working artist in the field for over 30 years, a major hurtle was deciding what specific content would be the most vital and substantially interesting for viewers on net. Gathering an exhaustive body of work and then sorting through to reveal the most precious and important contributions was difficult. Now that I have tackled that hurdle, I can work "day forward" to add the latest accomplishments to my electronic narrative.

Q: *Do you plan to redesign the Web portfolio eventually? If so, what might you do differently?*

A: Yes. Although I would not completely rebuild the site, I intend on delivering more finished projects. Instead of providing only extracts and partial segments of my video and sound works, I will have the complete works in their entirety available for viewing and listening.

Richard Kirk Mills, Artist

Created First Web Portfolio 2005

Web portfolio address: http://www.richardkirkmills.com

Q: *What is your current position or student status? How long have you been in your current industry or field?*

A: I am a professional artist, art professor at LIU, principal of Return of The Bald Eagle Press and artist-in-residence at the Teaneck Creek Conservancy in Teaneck, NJ. I also have been an artist for 35 years, but with a substantial shift in direction over the past 10.

Q: *What does your Web portfolio content consist of? Please describe and list assets or artifacts presented on the Web portfolio.*

A: The categories are; contact info; professional history and artists statement; professional highlights (brief resume); projects (Broad Street Stories, Greenway, Hackensack River Stories, Proposals, R.O.B.E. Press, Teaneck Creek Conservancy, X Garden); resources (links and bibliography). I tried to limit each page to between two and six images. There is a brief sound track on opening.

Q: *What made you decide to move forward and create a Web portfolio?*

A: My perception of the necessity and importance of establishing a public, accessible, online identity (especially with the new direction in my work). Wasn't it the famous philosopher Rene Descartes that said "I Google, therefore I am"?

Q: *What fears or doubts did you have before starting the Web portfolio?*

A: I was afraid of the potential technical hurdles and knowing what to put in and what to leave out. I was afraid that the site would not represent my work and philosophy in the manner I expected.

Q: *What were the most difficult challenges you faced when creating the Web portfolio?*

A: Challenging aspects included finding the time, settling upon the right look, and simplifying everything. One challenge was to highlight important content by not putting it all in. In addition, finding the right mix of outside technical help and learning enough on my own to be able to intelligently discuss and maintain the site. Collaboration works!

Q: *Which steps in the process were most difficult?*

A: Conceptualization design came easily and I decided to employ first rate help in the development area mastering enough technical knowledge to proceed. I came to understand and accept that this will be a less than perfect, but ongoing process of learning.

Q: *Do you plan to redesign the Web portfolio eventually? If so, what might you do differently?*

A: Yes. There is no way I can ever just let things remain the same. I will add information as that accrues and will no doubt adjust design elements as my thinking changes over time.

Interview Conclusion

Getting insight into thoughts and challenges of creating a Web portfolio from others is a great way to build a frame of reference and a starting point for creating your own portfolio. Each person interviewed earlier was chosen because they had no experience in Web design before they created their Web portfolios. One common theme that arises from the interviews is that all the participants realize that they will need to redesign the Web portfolio and look at the process as a evolution of their own learning and growth.

Case Study of Teacher Web Portfolios

10 Criteria for Teacher Web Portfolios

Before assembling a Web portfolio, a teacher or any author, must have a goal(s) with objectives in mind. Just as an author brainstorms before beginning to write, a Web portfolio author must identify several key components, which will be used as a possible content guideline for portfolio development. These components are identifiable and often guide the reader through the Web portfolio. This is an important concept in Web portfolios and not just critical to those teacher Web portfolios in education.

The criteria offered in this section is not based on one rubric but is an assessment tool that can help guide you towards building an impressive and persuasive Web portfolio in any discipline. These criteria will change over time as the Web portfolio changes. What is important here is that there is no one right way to create a Web portfolio because it is such a personalized information instrument. Each person's goals are different, so the content, context, and visual nature of the Web portfolio should be different in each person's individual case. You should use this section as a basis to develop your own personal rubric that focuses on your specific goals and the protocol of your discipline and industry.

The following criteria have been developed and adapted to fit the needs of teachers and students in any discipline. Kimberly DiMarco heavily contributed to this section as a researcher and writer. As an unobtrusive observer, she based the established criteria on the theories and evidence provided in this text.

These teacher or student portfolio criteria include:

1. Audience/purpose/persuasion
2. Contact information
3. Biography/credentials
4. Educational philosophy/pedagogy
5. Evidence of professional development
6. Evidence of student work
7. Educational curriculum, management and assessment measures
8. Links for educators, parents and students
9. Interactive features
10. Visual layout

Now let's try to operationalize these criteria and measure them against randomly selected Web portfolios found in the field of education.

Audience/Purpose/Persuasion

Audience:

Before writing, an author must identify his/her audience. The author writes with an intended audience in mind, and often times, the content of the text is written for a specific target audience.

In a teacher Web portfolio, the teacher has an audience in mind when he/she writes the content or narrative for the portfolio. One such target audience is the employer. Colleagues and peers are another audience group. Parents are an intended audience, and students are a possible audience as well. A teacher's Web portfolio might target one or multiple audience groups.

Purpose:

An author writes with purpose. The writing is intentional, and the author has a reason(s) why he/she is writing. A teacher also has a purpose for creating a Web portfolio. Purposes vary and often times overlap. In addition for the reason(s) why a teaching Web portfolio is created, the teacher needs to also decide what to include and how to convey his/her message.

If advertising for hire, a teacher should state this on a homepage, so a potential employer will quickly identify the teacher's intent to be hired. A teacher may intend to distinguish him/herself among colleagues for peer or professional recognition. A teacher may intend for parents and students to familiarize themselves with his/her background, credentials, educational philosophy or professional development. The purpose may be to inform the public about a specific teaching method or program or to describe positive teaching and learning experiences as a means to generate public awareness and support. Whatever the reason(s) a teacher chooses to create a Web portfolio, there is always a purpose, or several purposes, in mind.

Persuasion:

Many times within the author's purpose is the intent to persuade the reader. Persuasion techniques may be obvious and blatant to the reader or subtle and less apparent. A Web portfolio offers the teacher an arena to present his/her purpose while persuading the intend audience.

If a teacher's purpose for creating a Web portfolio is to gain employment, the content will attempt to persuade the potential employer to hire him or her. If the teacher's intent is to show qualification for tenure or promotion, achievements and accomplishments may be a primary focus of the portfolio. When a teacher intends for parents or students to become familiar with him or her, the Web portfolio will display persuasive content, narrative, information, images etc. to motivate students and gain parent trust and support. If the intent is to distinguish him/herself among colleagues and peers, there will be strong evidence of professional development and accomplishments. When trying to gain public awareness or support, a teacher's Web portfolio may include descriptions, benefits, instructions, statistics, a history, progress and results.

Contact Information

Portfolios have contact information so the viewer can communicate with the author. A teacher's Web portfolio is no different. Contact information can vary and may include, an e-mail, school, university or personal Web address, office hours, and/or telephone number.

Biography/Credentials

In order to show credibility, a teacher will include a biography and/or credentials in his/her Web portfolio. This information can vary in description and quantity. Examples may include an educational history, a resume, vita, a timeline of instructional experiences, skills, transcripts, grade point averages, alumni, associations, affiliations, awards, honors, certifications, degrees and professional titles.

Educational Philosophy/Pedagogy

A teacher typically develops an educational philosophy describing their pedagogy. A mission statement, goals and objectives, philosophy statement, reflective accounts, journal entries, personal experiences, and reasons for becoming a teacher are often shared in a teacher Web portfolio.

Evidence of Professional Development

Be it to gain employment, earn tenure or prove credibility, a teacher Web portfolio includes evidence of professional development. Some examples of this may include: published work, research, case studies, conference speaking, past or current work, committee work, or conferences and workshops attended. There are various forms of professional development and multiple methods to highlight this in a Web portfolio.

Evidence of Student Work

Teacher Web portfolios include evidence of student work to demonstrate their teaching abilities. By showcasing student work, a teacher is "showing off" his/ her teaching talents and results. Teachers often include a narrative, describing the student work as well as describing the teacher-created unit, lesson, materials, and activities. Student work is one of the best and most effective pieces of evidence to "advertise" the teacher as well as the student.

Educational Curriculum, Management and Assessment Measures

Curriculum, management and assessment measures provide the reader with a sense of how the teacher teaches. They help to define the teacher and offer insight into the teacher's classroom.

Curriculum and Management

Curriculum and management examples are lesson plans, units, courses, syllabi, behavioral plans and management strategies. Teachers often demonstrate how they align curriculum with learning standards or implement current research-based teaching methods. Teachers may include management techniques and strategies as well.

Assessment Measures

Assessment measures help to indicate how students learn and progress. By including rubrics, a teacher demonstrates expectations for student learning as well as how he/she evaluates students. Student portfolios, anecdotal observations, teacher-created evaluations, informal and formal assessments, test scores, statistics and progress reports can be included as well.

Links for Educators, Parents and Students

Since a primary purpose for the teacher Web portfolio is to disseminate information to a mass audience, a teacher will often include links for educators, parents and students. These links may connect to professional Web sites, articles and other resources to which the intended audience may find useful.

Interactive Features and Visual Layouts

Interactive features and visual layout provides the teacher with avenues and opportunities to capture and maintain the viewer's interest and attention while helping to persuade the intended audience group(s).

Interactive Features

To "jazz up" a Web portfolio or to make the content easily comprehensible, a teacher may incorporate interactive features. Such interactive features can include: video clips, interactive lessons and activities, or printable materials.

Visual Layout

Visual layout is the design or look of the Web portfolio. It is the package of how the portfolio is presented to the viewer. Visual layout creates the appearance and presents the information in a variety of modalities, which include: color, font, typeface, pictures, images, flash animation, and audio.

Utilization of Criterion

For the following six case studies, I utilized this set of criterion to assess randomly selected teacher Web portfolios, found through Web searches on the Internet.

Case Study #1 — Elementary School Teacher

This is a case study of a randomly selected elementary school teacher's Web portfolio. This case study examines the teaching Web portfolio of K.F., an elementary school teacher (http://durak.org/K.F./portfolio/index.html), and uses the proposed 10 criteria for teacher Web portfolios as a rubric and assessment measure.

Audience/Purpose/Persuasion

Audience:

K.F.'s teacher Web portfolio appeals to two audience groups, employers and parents. On her homepage, K.F.'s content is clearly intended for potential employers, however this page could also appeal to parents. The remainder of her portfolio continues to target employers and parents.

Purpose:

K.F.'s primary purpose is to advertise herself. On her homepage, K.F. states:

> *Welcome to my hypermedia portfolio, which demonstrates some of my abilities and experiences arranged according to the Commission on Teacher Credentialing Standards. On May 23, 1997 I completed my Multiple Subject +CLAD Teaching Credential at San Diego State University. I am actively seeking employment as an elementary school teacher in Southern California. Please check out my résumé and feel free to contact me with comments, questions, and job offers!*

She clearly makes herself available for interviews and prospective employment. K.F. includes evidence of professional development, curriculum, credentials, and contact information on her homepage, which are four of the 10 criteria.

Persuasion:

K.F. is attempting to persuade potential employers to hire her. The buttons on her homepage link to other persuasive content, which include the following categories:

- Home
- Environment
- Instruction
- Teaching
- Motivation
- Cognitive
- Presentation
- Assessment
- Affective
- Cross-Cultural
- Professional

Each button takes the user to a visually consistent formatted page, filled with narrative and photographs displaying evidence of student work or professional development.

Although the visual layout features are the same, the content changes on each Web page. Nevertheless, the content continues to highlight K.F.'s teaching abilities, experience and credentials, which are aimed at earning her a job. Statements such as this one found on her cross-cultural page (http://durak.org/ kathy/portfolio/cross-cultural.html), "My classroom will be set up to facilitate second language acquisition through the use of many CLAD strategies including: visuals, role playing, realia, and hands-on activities" lead the reader to believe that K.F. intends to create this type of classroom environment when she has a classroom of her own. Otherwise, K.F. might have stated, "My classroom is set up..." rather than her actual quote. K.F. is "selling herself" to the reader.

Contact Information

K.F. places her contact information in the middle of her homepage, but she also places her contact information on the bottom of every Web page, under buttons that lead to other Web pages in her portfolio.

Biography/Credentials

K.F.'s credentials are displayed on her homepage as well as on a separate Web page linked to her "Professional" page (http://durak.org/kathy/portfolio/ professional.html). On this page, K.F. lists her resume, which reveals her degrees and student teaching experiences, certificates and conference attendance.

Educational Philosophy/Pedagogy

Although K.F.'s Web portfolio lacks a page or a narrative dedicated to describing her teaching philosophies or beliefs, K.F. includes pedagogical declarations as headings atop each Web page. Atop K.F.'s "Environment" page (http://durak.org/kathy/portfolio/environment.html), she writes:

> *Establishes and sustains a level of student rapport and a classroom environment that promotes learning, multicultural understanding and equity, fosters mutual respect among class members, and respect for linguistic differences...*

Evidence of Professional Development

Both K.F.'s home page and "Professional" Web page link to or list examples of K.F.'s professional development. K.F. even includes a picture of her nametag from a recent educational conference she attended on this page.

Evidence of Student Work

With the exception of her home and "Professional" pages, the remaining Web pages in her portfolio include evidence of student work. Pictures and scanned images of student worksheets are included as visual features. This is an example of how K.F. uses evidence of student work to display her ability to create teacher-made materials and assessments as well as advertises how she motivate students. K.F. writes (http://durak.org/kathy/portfolio/affective.html), "I created this word-seek game with each student's name to motivate and involve. Students seemed to really enjoy hearing their name and seeing themselves 'in-print.'"

Curriculum, Management, and Assessment Measures

K.F. refers to her experience teaching the curriculum on her "Instruction" Web page (http://durak.org/kathy/portfolio/instruction.html). She writes, "Vionie identifies and draws shapes seen around the classroom. Although handouts and district-endorsed worksheets have a role in my curriculum, it's great seeing what students can create on their own when presented with a new concept or challenge, such as my activity for kindergarten students to identify and draw found shapes".

K.F. also presents examples of her management skills and teaching approaches on her "Presentation" Web page (http://durak.org/kathy/portfolio/presentation.html). Here, K.F. describes her ability to provide instruction for individual students and create instructional centers.

To demonstrate her assessment measures, K.F. created an "Assessment" Web page (http://durak.org/kathy/portfolio/assessment.html). This includes the following statement:

> *Assessment of my students must include a variety of methods in order to measure their range of capabilities. Objective records balance subjective compilations of growth and exemplary works.*

Links for Educators, Parents and Students

K.F. includes a link for potential employers or parents to view her resume and education at San Diego State University; however, she does not include links to resources for educators, parents or students.

Interactive Features

K.F. includes interactive features in her Web portfolio. For example, on her "Instruction" Web page (http://durak.org/kathy/portfolio/instruction.html), K.F. states, "You can grab a complete copy of the unit plan and view it using free Adobe Acrobat 3 software" and creates a link to her unit plan on the water cycle.

lp-water-cycle-revised.pdf [63Kb]

Visual Layout

K.F. lays out her Web portfolio with a consistent format on each Web page. She uses the same colors, fonts, typefaces and pictures to present her information. K.F.'s pages all link directly to each other, making it easy for the user to navigate.

Case Study #2: Secondary Teacher

This is a case study of a randomly selected secondary school teacher's Web portfolio. This case study examines the teaching Web portfolio of K.M., a secondary school teacher, (http://www.mandia.com/kelly/) and uses the proposed 10 criteria for teacher Web portfolios as a rubric and assessment measure.

Audience/Purpose/Persuasion

Audience:

K.M.'s teacher Web portfolio appeals to multiple audience groups, including employers, parents, students and colleagues. On her homepage, K.M.'s content describes herself as a teacher and is intended for all audience groups.

The links below will demonstrate my teaching abilities. You will see that I am a highly motivated and organized instructor, I possess high academic standards, encourage students to perform with excellence, and I strive to make the learning experience enjoyable. Please view all the materials below to get the fullest picture of my abilities and examples of my work. (http://www.mandia.com/kelly/)

Purpose:

K.M.'s purpose is to describe herself as a highly trained, professional teacher. K.M. places her teaching philosophy on her homepage, directly under her initial description of herself as a teacher. Here is a sample from her philosophy:

My training and experience have shown me that students learn best when they are active participants in the learning process. Therefore, my approach promotes active student participation in academics. I utilize content to develop skills and challenge students through practices such as cooperative learning and authentic assessment.

Persuasion:

K.M. is attempting to persuade her audiences into believing that she is a superior teacher. The buttons on her homepage link to other persuasive content, which include the following categories:

- Examples of My Projects
- Examples of Cooperative Project Assignments
- Examples of Other Lesson Plans
- Examples of a Unit Plan

These categories link to other sections, where the content includes:

- Evidence of Professional Development
- Curriculum

- Assessment Measures
- Evidence of Student Work

Each button takes the user to a visually different-looking page; however, each page is filled with narrative and images displaying evidence of student work or teacher-created materials, lessons, projects, and unit plans.

Contact Information

K.M. does not place any contact information on her teaching portfolio Web page. Contact information is found on her Web homepage, and although there is a link from the Web to the teacher Web portfolio, there is no direct link from the teacher portfolio back to the Web.

Biography/Credentials

Again, this information is found on the Web homepage but not on the teacher Web portfolio itself. When looking at K.M.'s teacher Web portfolio, there is no evidence of her biography or credentials.

Educational Philosophy/Pedagogy

As previously mentioned, K.M.'s teaching philosophy is located on the homepage of her teacher portfolio.

Evidence of Professional Development

K.M. does not offer the reader any information about how she continues to develop as a professional educator; however, it is obvious to the user that K.M. continues to educate herself considering her portfolio demonstrates her knowledge and application of Internet technology and Web site development. There are several links, such as the link to "Design Your Own Web Page", her online guide to create a Web-based research project found on her homepage, which indicate that K.M. understands and can teach current technology.

Evidence of Student Work

K.M.'s teacher portfolio homepage links to several examples of student work. Two examples are:

- *Lock-n-Rock:* "Example of a student invention. This student constructed a miniature house with wires connecting to a stereo set to her favorite radio station. When the front door was opened, the music began to play!"

- *Student Designed Web Projects:* "Examples of Web-based research projects."

Curriculum, Management, and Assessment Measures

K.M.'s lesson and unit plans demonstrate how she teaches the curriculum. To demonstrate her assessment measures, K.M. created links to three of her grading rubrics for three different student projects.

Links for Educators, Parents and Students

K.M. includes a button to an "Educational-Related Sites" Web page that links to several resource Web sites.

Interactive Features

Although K.M. does not include any interactive features on her teacher Web portfolio, she includes a button that links to a series of interactive lessons on her "Design Your Own Web Page" Web page.

Visual Layout

K.M. lays out her Web portfolio on one entire Web page. Although she provides links to multiple lessons and teacher-created projects, there is no consistent criteria or structure to follow.

Case Study #3: Ed.D. Professor Web Portfolio

This is a case study of a randomly selected Ed.D. Professor's Web portfolio. This case study examines the teaching Web portfolio of J.B., a professor, (http://www.coe.ilstu.edu/jabraun/braun/professional.html) and uses the proposed 10 criteria for teacher Web portfolios as a rubric and assessment measure.

Audience/Purpose/Persuasion

Audience:

J.B.'s teacher Web portfolio appeals to multiple audience groups, including employers, parents, students and colleagues. On his homepage, J.B.'s content describes his biography and credentials and is intended for all audience groups.

> *Welcome to an electronic teaching portfolio where aspects of my professional work are organized as links in the tables below. Currently, I am Professor of Curriculum and Instruction in the College of Education at Illinois State University. My area of expertise is elementary-middle school social studies. Particular scholarly interests include the use of technology as an instructional tool and the social-emotional and moral development of students. If you are wondering where to begin your exploration of this electronic portfolio, I suggest the Narrative About Teaching from the Current Teaching links section. (http:// www.coe.ilstu.edu/jabraun/braun/professional.html)*

Purpose:

J.B.'s purpose is to describe himself as a highly trained, professional teacher and scholar. He includes categories that link to more specific information regarding:

- Education and Employment
- Current Teaching
- Scholarly Productivity and Service
- Contact information

These categories link to areas that highlight his teaching abilities and experiences.

Persuasion

J.B. is attempting to demonstrate that he is a highly qualified teacher. The earlier-mentioned categories, on his homepage, link to additional persuasive content, information and images.

Contact Information

J.B. places contact information at the bottom of every Web page.

Biography/Credentials

Although J.B. discusses his biography and credentials on his homepage, he provides specific information under the category "Education and Employment", which links to his:

- Educational history
- Employment
- Professional organizations
- Consulting experience

Educational Philosophy/Pedagogy

J.B. supplies two links to his educational philosophy. Found on his homepage, J.B. encourages readers to navigate his portfolio by beginning with his teaching philosophy (http://www.coe.ilstu.edu/jabraun/braun/professional/narrat.html). He also includes a separate category entitled "Current Teaching" which links to "An Electronic Teaching Narrative" Web page. Here the reader finds the link, "What is my philosophy of teaching" (http://www.coe.ilstu.edu/jabraun/braun/professional/philo).

Evidence of Professional Development

On his homepage, J.B. places evidence of professional development under the category "Scholarly Productivity and Service". He provides links to the following areas as a means which continue to depict his professional development:

- Conference papers
- Publications
- Grants
- Service
- Sabbatical study 1997

J.B. also provides two supplementary links, found on the "Narrative of Teaching Experiences" Web page, which further demonstrate evidence of professional development. They are:

- What are my efforts to improve teaching (http://www.coe.ilstu.edu/ jabraun/braun/professional/narrat.html#improv)
- What are my future teaching goals (http://www.coe.ilstu.edu/jabraun/ braun/professional/narrat.html#goals)

Evidence of Student Work

J.B. provides evidence of student work under the category "Current Teaching". He provides links to:

- Student feedback
- Student Web pages

On his "Narrative of Teaching Experiences" Web page, J.B. presents another link to student assignment and projects titled, "What are the student assignment/projects" (http://www.coe.ilstu.edu/jabraun/braun/professional/ narrat.html#assign).

Curriculum, Management, and Assessment Measures

J.B. offers a substantial amount of information regarding how he teaches curriculum, manages students and assesses student work. Also located under the category "Current Teaching" are links to:

- Assessment rubrics
- Walkabout tasks (Instructional methods, strategies and management skills)

Also, on the "Narrative of Teaching Experiences" Web page are the links:

- What are my current teaching responsibilities
- What instructional strategies do I employ

- How do I assess student work

Links for Educators, Parents and Students

Found under the category "Current Teaching", is an informational link for social studies resources. On the "Narrative of Teaching Experiences" Web page, a link provides the reader with more information labeled, "Where can additional data about my teaching be located" (http://www.coe.ilstu.edu/jabraun/braun/professional/narrat.html#append).

Interactive Features

J.B. includes several video clips that demonstrate his teaching abilities. They are located under the "Current Teaching" category on his homepage and link to a Web page entitled "Video Clips of Teaching" (http://coe.ilstu.edu/jabraun/braun/professional/video.html).

Visual Layout

The layout of J.B.'s teacher Web portfolio is highly structured and organized. Although similar information overlaps numerous Web pages, J.B. provides multiple links for easy navigation.

Case Study #4: Educational Consultant (Retired School Teacher) Portfolio

This is a case study of a randomly selected educational consultant's Web portfolio. This case study examines the teaching Web portfolio of S.S., a retired schoolteacher turned educational consultant (http://kids-learn.org/), and uses the proposed 10 criteria for teacher Web portfolios as a rubric and assessment measure.

Audience/Purpose/Persuasion

Audience:

S.S.'s teacher Web portfolio appeals to multiple audience groups, including employers, parents, students and colleagues. On her homepage, S.S.'s pictures and button-links portray her as a diverse educator. Her homepage is segmented into 6 buttons: biography, resources, journal, consulting, Webfolio, and e-mail (http://kids-learn.org/susansilverman/).

Purpose:

S.S.'s purpose is to represent herself as a qualified instructional technology consultant.

Persuasion:

Each button located on S.S.'s homepage links to diverse information, which matches the proposed criteria. For example, on her Webfolio homepage (http://kids-learn.org/), S.S. provides links to the following information:

- Examples of lessons and units of study
- Class Web sites
- Projects
- Assessments
- Student work
- Links for educators, parents and students

These links demonstrate S.S.'s ability to provide successful technology instruction, and influence the reader.

On her Instructional Technology Consultant: Presentations and Workshops Web page (http://kids-learn.org/susansilverman/consulting.htm), S.S. advertises her upcoming speaking engagements at educational conferences and conventions. She is attempting to persuade the reader to attend her speaking engagements or hire her consultation services.

> *The U.S. Department of Education recommends that school districts allocate 30% of their technology budgets for staff development. Below is a list of workshops and presentations I have and will be giving at conferences and schools. I am available to provide customized staff development at any location. (http://kids-learn.org/susansilverman/consulting.htm)*

However the Web homepage (http://kids-learn.org/susansilverman/) also links to her biography, reflective journal, resources for educators, parents and students, and e-mail address, which further indicate credibility.

Contact Information

S.S. makes contact information available on her homepage, consulting and Web folio pages.

Biography/Credentials

Buttons from the homepage and consulting page link to S.S.'s biography and/ or credentials.

> *Currently working as an adjunct professor at New York Institute of Technology, Touro College, and as an educational consultant, I mentor teachers, coordinate online collaborative projects, maintain the Web site for Comsewogue School District, conduct workshops throughout the United States for Tom Synder and present at technology conferences. My staff development workshops focus on integrating technology to meet state and national standards. (http://kids-learn.org/susansilverman/biography.htm)*

Educational Philosophy/Pedagogy

S.S. does not include an educational philosophy or pedagogy; however, she does include a button to her online journal reflections and narratives.

Evidence of Professional Development

S.S. supplies evidence of professional development on her biography and consulting pages.

Evidence of Student Work

S.S.'s Web folio Web page links to multiple examples of student work.

Curriculum, Management, and Assessment Measures

S.S.'s Web folio Web page links to multiple examples of curriculum, materials, and assessment measures.

Links for Educators, Parents and Students

S.S. dedicates an entire Web page linked to resources and Web sites categorized for educator, parents, and students. There are additional resource links on her Web folio page as well.

Interactive Features

S.S. utilizes pictures, video clips, online activities, printable materials, and images to advertise her portfolio.

Visual Layout

Each Web page has a different layout, design and content. Although S.S. provides multiple links, there are no consistent criteria or structure for the user to navigate or follow.

Case Study #5: Teacher Web Portfolio of Participatory Action Research

This is a case study of a randomly selected teacher Web portfolio about a teaching methodology called Participatory Action Research or P.A.R. According to the authors and creators of the Web portfolio, P.A.R. is

> ...an alternative research methodology that combines research, educational work, and social action. This type of research is viewed as a form of social action because community members identify the issues and these are used as the basis for increasing literacy skills. The issue or problem that is identified by the group is studied in a collaborative manner. Therefore, the project serves many purposes. The participants acquire literacy skills while they take action in critiquing and resolving relevant issues. (http://www.goingpublicwithteaching.org/ewolk/wolk_docs/what_is_par.htm).

This case study examines the teaching Web portfolio of P.A.R, created by an elementary school teacher, her students and members of the Carnegie Foundation, and uses the proposed 10 criteria for teacher Web portfolios as a rubric and assessment measure.

Audience/Purpose/Persuasion

Audience:

This educational Web portfolio appeals to anyone interested in P.A.R. On her homepage, E.W.'s pictures and buttons link to information about P.A.R.

Purpose:

E.W.'s purpose is to inform the public about P.A.R., and her intent is to gain public awareness and support. This is identifiable because the entire portfolio's content discusses and describes P.A.R. and not the individual teacher's accomplishments, credentials, philosophies, and so on.

Persuasion:

E.W. attempts to convince her audience that P.A.R. is a beneficial teaching method. Buttons link to components of P.A.R. and its benefits to students.

Contact Information

E.W. does not provide contact information on this teacher Web portfolio.

Biography/Credentials

There are brief biographical accounts in E.W.'s narrative found on the homepage, however, there is no information regarding her credentials as a teacher. Again, this appears to indicate that the purpose of this portfolio is to promote P.A.R. and not the teacher.

Educational Philosophy/Pedagogy

E.W. discusses her educational philosophies and pedagogy about P.A.R. in her descriptive narrative, found on the home page.

I want my students to learn basic skills. That is, I want them to learn the basic skills necessary to transform their world. I want my students to have opportunities to develop voice, engage in dialogue, take action and learn to reflect on their actions. And, because I want my students to engage themselves in their world differently, I know that teaching and learning has to look different too.

She also includes a teacher reflection about student P.A.R. learning at the bottom of her homepage.

Evidence of Professional Development

E.W. does not include any indications of personal professional development other than her own growth employing P.A.R. teaching techniques.

Evidence of Student Work

Although there are video interviews with students who participated in P.A.R., here is a student quote located on the homepage:

I joined this group because I wanted to have a better and safer community than it is. I like to come to our meetings, because the more time I have to work on this, the better my community will be. . . I have changed a lot because I was very shy and now I'm really loud. I've done presentations in San Diego in front of 300 people. I've also talked to reporters from newspapers and television. I've talked to dignitaries from the city. I think I've changed because of my friends because they're really loud too. And, I'm getting a lot of friends and my voice is getting louder.
Esme, PAR Researcher

Student narratives, reflections, evidence of work and classroom lessons and discussions are also included (http://www.goingpublicwithteaching.org/ewolk/wolk_docs/timeline.htm).

Curriculum, Management, and Assessment Measures

Students comment on the P.A.R. curriculum and a time line is presented. A teacher reflection, which discusses curriculum, management and assessment, is provided on the "Theoretical Thoughts" Web page. (http://www.goingpublicwithteaching.org/ewolk/getting_greenlight.pdf).

Links for Educators, Parents and Students

Although there are no links, for educators, parents and students, to other Web resources, the authors provide a link to "3 Steps to Start Your Own P.A.R" (http://www.goingpublicwithteaching.org/ewolk/wolk_docs/steps_to_begin_par.htm).

Interactive Features

E.W. utilizes pictures, video clips and interviews to feature P.A.R.

Visual Layout

Each Web page has a different layout, design and content. The pages are simple and easy to navigate.

Case Study #6: John DiMarco Teacher Web Portfolio

This is a case study of a specifically selected teacher Web portfolio. This case study examines the teaching Web portfolio of John DiMarco, the author of this book, (http://www.portfolio.cc/main.htm) and uses the proposed 10 criteria for teacher Web portfolios as a rubric and assessment measure.

Audience/Purpose/Persuasion

Audience:

John DiMarco's Web portfolio appeals to multiple audience groups, including employers, students and colleagues. On his portfolio homepage, John utilizes images, pictures, text, and categorized buttons to link to additional information. Although this portfolio appeals to various audience groups, the homepage indicates that John specifically targets employers since evidence of his current professional development, descriptions of his two authored books, are highlighted.

Purpose:

John's intent is to demonstrate his professional knowledge, teaching abilities, skills and experience. When the user clicks onto the photos and images button, a quote intended for all audience groups appears: "Helping people and organizations with communication design" (http://www.portfolio.cc/index2.htm).

Although John may specifically be targeting employers on his homepage, his message informs all audience groups that he is a teacher who wants to help with communication design. John's principal purpose is to communicate his ability to help people.

Persuasion:

John attempts to persuade his audiences to hire him in either an academic or professional capacity. He makes an effort to convey his expertise through various interactive features and visually appealing layouts.

Contact Information

John places a contact link on his homepage, contact information on his curriculum vitae, and his telephone number is displayed above the toolbar on every Web page.

Biography/Credentials

John's biography and credentials reside under the "About" category and link to his curriculum vitae. An extensive resume lists his credentials, education, course work, consultation, technology skills, and so on.

Educational Philosophy/Pedagogy

John's educational philosophy and pedagogy is simple. The photo images button, located on his homepage, links to a separate Web page where John states he wants to help people and organizations communicate design.

Evidence of Professional Development

Under the category titled "Portfolio" are links to galleries of John's work in print and Web , motion graphics, e-learning design, and digital art. Under the category "Design Lab" are links to John's professional publications and research, such as his authored books and interactive audio radio clip (http://www.campus-technology.com/radio/index.asp?id=7131) from an educational conference where he was a guest speaker.

Evidence of Student Work

John provides evidence of student work under the "Design Lab" category. Here, there are links to student galleries (http://www.portfolio.cc/student/index.htm) that display examples of student work in various computer and multimedia courses. This demonstrates the products of John's teaching capabilities as well as how he has helped his students.

Curriculum, Management, and Assessment Measures

At this time, John does not provide evidence of syllabi or course descriptions describing curriculum, personal reflections or statements regarding management skills, or project rubrics to indicate assessment measures.

Links for Educators, Parents and Students

Under the "Digital Lab" category, John includes a button which links to various publications, Webs, resources, museums, tutorials etc. for all intended audience groups (http://www.portfolio.cc/main.htm#).

Interactive Features

John incorporates an extensive array of interactive features, including music, flash animation, an audio clip, photos and images.

Visual Layout

Using a consistent color palette, typeface, and font, John DiMarco's teacher Web portfolio offers a variety of impressive features for the user to navigate the site. For example, the user is able to skip the introduction, turn musical accompaniments on or off, and preview photos, pictures, and images, of both professional and student work, in a series of thumbnail pictures which link to a larger view.

Review and Conclusion

This chapter provided a wide range of cases, interviews and ideas for you to explore within your own Web portfolio contexts. Examining specific cases in a range of disciplines will be valuable in the development of an e-portfolio initiative and Web portfolio program within your own organization. Whether campus wide, within your own department, or for purely individual reasons, integrating a program requires you to perform research on existing activities, develop a sound proposal, sell the superiors on the benefits, develop the technology relationships needed, create the coursework and support training for faculty, and launch the program. After launching the program, be prepared to be involved in action research that helps build on the effectiveness and illustrates that the e portfolio initiative is results driven-and you have the data to back the claim.

The Web portfolio cases and interviews provided in this chapter give you as a Web portfolio author a chance to read about some problems and challenges faced by others. This section also provided a list of criteria that may serve as a potential basis for developing Web portfolio components that adhere to a loosely prescribed, universal standard. Unobtrusive observation of Web sites was performed and data was funneled into the criteria to display matching themes and to illustrate how approaches to Web portfolios differ on different levels within the same discipline. In the study of a successful program, the Penn State University e-portfolio initiative and Web portfolio program provides an effective model that has strong program components in autonomous technology direction, technical support, curriculum standardization of Web portfolio usage outside of traditional portfolio disciplines, and faculty involvement. The Penn State E-Education Institute has quantitatively shown that mandatory Web portfolio assignments in coursework yields more student usage of Web space for academic and professional purposes. This chapter also holds some basis for further research in Web portfolio rubrics and e portfolio program initiatives on all levels of education.

In Chapter XIII, I provide theories of information scientists and other scholars to align them with my own theories on the future penetration of electronic portfolios and Web portfolios in the new millennium and within information societies.

Chapter XIII

Web Portfolios in the Information Society and Future

Introduction

This chapter offers theories behind why the networked e-portfolio (Web portfolio) will evolve into the post modern identity vehicle for the knowledge worker of the new millennium. Ideas behind how Web portfolios are narratives and can change society are established based on writings from information science theorists and scientists including Jean Francois Lyotard, Dr. Amy Spaulding, Professor Nicolas Negroponte, Alan Kay, and Frank Webster. Additionally, the effects of the e-portfolio as a media and information management tool in postmodern society are approached with reference to the writings of Marshall McLuhan, Margot Lovejoy, and Dr. Stephen Covey.

I wrote this chapter to focus on my specialization and fascination with information studies. However, the thoughts and predictions I offer will be driven by disciplines such as education, humanities, and natural sciences. These disciplines involvement in Web portfolio initiatives within curriculum are a factor in the Web portfolio evolving in professional and academic settings.

The Web Portfolio's Place in the Information Society

Frank Webster describes the scholarly debate that surrounds the notion of an information society. He explains that information society theorists contend that "technological innovation produces social change" (Webster, 2002, p. 264). On the other side of the debate, of which Webster is a staunch proponent, scholars charge that no information society exists and that information and technology are simply following a path of continuity with historical change. Webster states this point as: "scholars who, while happy to concede that information has taken on a special significance in the modern era insists that the central feature of the present in its continuities with the past" (2002, p. 6).

More importantly, Webster (2002, p. 6) makes the distinction that many scholars occupy various points along the continuum of both constructs. Webster explains that there exist five definitions of an information society. The definitions are driven by the thought that quantitative changes in information are evoking qualitative changes in society, thus contributing the notion of an information society: technological, economic, occupational, spatial, and cultural (Webster, 2002, p.9). I believe that Web portfolios fit into these information society definitions as an instrument that will specifically change occupational information activity. I feel the increasing trend towards Web portfolios have societal implications that will impact the technology applications, economic distribution, occupational scenarios, spatial arrangements, and cultural manifestations that represent acknowledgments that things are changing historically, but at the same time, society is building exclusive relationships that are going beyond technological advances and post industrialist contributions. The information society is a place that people want to be. They want be "in" on technologies adaptation of their lives. It may not be simply an upper income person getting the latest cell phone, PDA, or laptop computer to use in their $50,000 Jaguar; maybe it's a lower income person getting the latest DVD player and navigation system for their $2,000 Chevy Geo. Or, a young person who makes poverty level wages buying a $400 iPod. These examples are not to be misunderstood; having the right technology will be an important part of being part of groups, whether they are social or occupational. Personal perception of what is needed technologically will drive knowledge workers in the new millennium to embrace Web portfolios. Eventually, everyone who is "in" will have one. Without one, it will be difficult to secure work for hire and therefore one may be cut off from the opportunities that the information society deems as most attractive.

The Web Portfolio as Personal, On-Demand, Mass Media and Advertising

Media makes portrays life as more difficult without having the "technological norms" of your culture and environment. Media shapes perception by creating an environment that presents advertising as a primary news gathering process. As McLuhan (1964, p.227) states, "Ads pushed the principle of noise all the way to the plateau of persuasion. They are quite in accord with the procedures of brainwashing". McLuhan also extends that "ads are news", especially in the electronic age. I feel the Web portfolio is considered an ad or advertisement. It is an ad for someone or an organization. The Web portfolio fits McLuhan's theory that advertisements are news in several aspects. The goal of the Web portfolio is to persuade the user to act favorably, as with ads. The Web portfolio creates an ongoing narrative that provides news of accomplishment and presents a story of perceived importance merely for the fact that it is being delivered in the Web portfolio, as the "user"/reader of a magazine might believe. The Web portfolio is dynamic, such as news. And as with news and the Web portfolio, content becomes the true selling vehicle.

The Web portfolio also puts our identity and our public appearance in the social and cyber world at risk. The risk is exposure that is not favorable or that inflates truths about capabilities, history, and accomplishments. Any vehicle of credibility can work conversely to discredit the author. The extent of truth to the personal narrative presented in a Web portfolio is dependent on the morality and perceptions of the creator, as is in the case of any communication whether it is a resume or a corporate financial report. The truth lies in the personal moral compliance of the individual(s) whom created the communication. The Web portfolio will open people up to intrusion, but at the same time will generate opportunity. This is the pattern seen with all emerging technology.

The Web Portfolio
in the "Knowledge Worker Age"

As a product, tool, learning agent, and appearance of the information society, I feel Web portfolios are becoming an important technological instrument for social change in a person's capacity to gain work for hire in the information driven society.

When we speak of electronic portfolios and specifically of Web portfolios we are really focusing on information. Gathering information, massaging information, organizing information, classifying information, correcting information, and presenting information in an electronic form is really the guts of the Web portfolio, or any portfolio. The narrative that evolves out of the information and the visual and textual components that illuminate that narrative allow an unlimited venue for publishing creative thoughts. This is a powerful concept that will become a standard feature of the information society. What will the role of the electronic portfolio be as the evolution of the information society continues? The prospects of Web portfolios becoming an important agent for social change are possible. A universal e-portfolio trend will guide people into joining the information society and increase knowledge management in everyday life. Think about it, having an identity on the Web will be critical to financial prosperity and to electronic and public appearance. The Web portfolio will allow people to tell their own stories through dynamic mini narratives that will interweave their personal and professional lives into a global medium that can enable unlimited opportunity. Their stories, presented electronically, will become part of their public appearance, appeal and ultimate success. The narratives that engage the world from the Web portfolio platform will not only be based on facts and exclusive perspectives, but will be driven emotions as well as data. The Web portfolio spike of the future will be a direct result of the emergence of what Dr. Stephen Covey describes as the "knowledge worker age" (2004, p. 5). In the knowledge worker age, Covey states that their will be a movement towards creating human capital, both social and intellectual, that will supersede the wealth creation movement by focusing on people rather than money (Covey, 2004). A major communication vehicle and personal marketing tool that will tell peoples personal career stories will be the Web portfolio.

Ultimately, knowledge work enables innovation which translates into money. Money can be acquired through persuasive communication through multiple media. Telling people about skills can yield work for hire opportunities to use those skills. The knowledge worker is characterized by a high degree of information centered skills that reinforce their abilities to live and thrive in what Dr. Covey calls a "permanent whitewater, a constant state of change and in a rapidly evolving electronic environment" (Covey, 2004, pp. 104-105). Based on literature review of postmodern information society theories, I believe the personal identity, communication vehicle that will emerge in the turbulent electronic networked environment will be the Web portfolio.

The Web Portfolio
as the Postmodern Appearance

In the historical shadow of McLuhan's notion of electronic media being an extension of the central nervous system, I feel the Web portfolio will, in time, become the appearance and identity of the knowledge worker in postmodern global societies. The Web portfolio in its development stages and existence can be described as new media art. As art and art making, and as a communication medium, the Web portfolio is not a private experience, it is a public experience, as demonstrated by the notion of an appearance. The Web portfolio is a public experience which opens up new opportunities for communication and public discourse. In her book *Postmodern currents: Art and artists in the age of electronic media*, Margot Lovejoy (1992) quotes Anna Couey on the radical new options provided by new media in the postmodern world:

> *Postmodern art is characterized by its involvement with new media which cross traditional boundaries between art and life. This is manifested in such trends as crossover, populism, and performance. The significance of postmodern art is in its move away from private aesthetics, and personal expression and representation, toward an actively communicating public aesthetic.* (p. 243)

The appearance of Web portfolios will metaphor the appearance of people in everyday life. Some people are polished and some are sloppy. Many people tend to be organized, many are not. Some people have sense of style, other do have one or don't care. Those personal attitudes and behaviors will be evident in the Web portfolio. Overdoing it also will be evident in the bad Web portfolio world. Inside these bad Web portfolios, content will be overwhelmed by wasted and distracting interface components. Overzealous creators with little or no design background will provide a mess of blinking, lime green, midi playing, grammatically horrific, and unsuccessful Web portfolios. But, it is a start. Revisions of the Web portfolio is common, so redesign is inevitable, hopefully improving during each cycle and through the evolution of technologies that help take the design knowledge out of the looking good equation. Things like templates and customizable applications will allow people to create wonderful Web portfolios simply by uploading content.

The Web portfolio will be completely in the future, meaning that handheld, mobile devices will deliver Web portfolios to people on their PDAs, cell phones, laptops, and iPods. People will promote themselves and tell their story electronically. Interpersonal communication transactions will be complemented by visits to a person's Web portfolio during the interaction. This ability to promote and persuade by telling your story digitally will be critical in work for hire situations. Hiring people will want to see and hear the narrative of the knowledge worker. This narrative, and its delivery success, will be important to the outcomes of interpersonal activities.

The Web portfolio will extend into social realms as well. The everyday acceptability of online dating and meeting people through the Internet has shown that social communication is going to change with the growth of Web portfolios. An online dating service is basically providing a digital narrative of each client. In this realm, each client is equal in stature and is presented by his or her own perception of themselves, thus presented categorically, based on gender and preferences. Online dating gives a person an appearance within the digital medium. Online dating provides a social communication that uses a Web portfolio system. The user's goal while using the online dating service is to persuade someone into initiating contact which may lead to a fruitful relationship. The Web portfolio has the same goals. The Web portfolio is consistent with the online dating concept in that it is conceptualized, built, and delivered to persuade someone to act. The fact that the truth may or may not be present does not matter. Ultimately, the medium becomes the message and credibility may be assumed because of the virtues of the visual elements and the electronic delivery system.

The Web Portfolio
as Postmodern Narrative Connection

In the book, *A Postmodern Condition: A Report on Knowledge,* Lyotard (1999) argues that all aspects of modern societies, including science as the primary form of knowledge, depend on narratives to exploit and represent knowledge. On the macro scale, "grand narratives", stories a culture tells itself about its practices and beliefs (Lyotard, 1999, pp.18-20), are rejected by postmodernists as failures. These failures include examples such as Marxism, communism, and fascism and are prime cases of socialist approaches to defining a grand narrative which ultimately resulted in failure. The postmodern viewpoint as expressed by Lyotard and expanded on by Webster is that historical change and its "pretension to discern the truth has lost its credibility", meaning that what we are not destined to believe a truth as it is told to us by society in what Lyotard's grand narrative scheme. More importantly, to the case of the Web portfolio and its inevitable place in postmodern society as an agent of change for knowledge workers, "Totality", and the view that there is one evident and defined truth, is highly rejected by postmodernists such as Lyotard. The postmodernists believe that there can only be versions of the truth, represented by what Lyotard called "mini-narratives", stories that explain small practices, local events, personal accomplishments, rather than large-scale universal or global concepts (Lyotard, 1999). These mini-narratives are being delivered through Web portfolios. People will want to be defined in the postmodern age by creating their own identities rather than masking their skills, abilities, talents, and creativity behind the identity of a company or organization.

Web portfolios are becoming required for educators in K-12 higher education. And due to state education department requirements, Web portfolios can be associated with the concept of the e-portfolio becoming a grand narrative of the information society. As well, mini-narratives will serve as the content base for the grand narrative evolved out of e-portfolios. People will update their Web portfolios as their lives change and their accomplishments and identity grow. Content on the Web portfolio will mirror the appearance that the knowledge worker wants to display to the world.

When people started willingly working for others, the personal visit and conversation were the first communication methods and strategies used in work for hire situations. Meeting the business owner on personal recommendation, briefly speaking with him about capabilities, discussing wages/arrangements, and shaking hands constituted the job seeking and job securing processes. The proximity of jobs was limited to the local town borders. Then, industrialism changed all that. Too many people, too many companies, how will they connect? The answer was mass media and the power of communication technology in the forms of radio, television, and print, and, the development of mass transportation with the steam engine. With media and technology, there always is a market that results due to involvement of a public also known as an audience. Mass media helped to create the "job market" and the way people connected with jobs and companies changed. In the industrial age, jobs were posted in mass media and applicants needed to visit, but only to fill out an application. Securing employment using the application stayed, but only in lower level scenarios or in bureaucratic situations which control needed to be enforced. The application does not lend itself to creative thinking or narrative. It lists items using chronological order, true, but the application merely uses this as order, not necessarily as narrative. The resume emerged as the instrument of the professional job seeker as technology gained momentum and modernism came through for the job seeker with the typewriter and the ability to type a resume and have it copied or printed at a print shop. The resume allowed expansion of the personal narrative to more than the application. The resume explained someone's history in print. The resume is a mini-narrative, but is still lacking unique personal expression. Along comes the electronic era and new media is born. The Internet becomes the newest media of choice for the new age worker, also known as the knowledge worker. The Web portfolio trumps the resume. The Web portfolio will ultimately evolve into a staple instrument for work for hire communication transactions in the knowledge age.

The Web portfolio evolution is emerging now and will continue to be fostered by third party conduits that connect people with other people to transact work for hire. These third parties are in the form of employment agencies and online job search databases such as Monster.com. The Web portfolio is expanded by creative talent agencies such as Aquent.com, who carry the Web portfolios of their work for hire artists, designers, and copywriters. Another site that posts Web portfolios of knowledge workers is Guru.com, the name says it all.

This brings up another case for describing the Web portfolio and all electronic portfolios as knowledge age narrative that is built for telling the story of the knowledge worker to the work for hire audience and public, whoever they may be. In her 2004 book, *The Wisdom of Storytelling in an Information Age*, Dr. Amy Spaulding's thoughts on the importance of story and narrative thinking present a clear path to the use of the Web portfolio as a new media narrative with persuasive power. Dr. Spaulding (2004) makes reference to the importance of imaginative creativity on the outcome of wisdom. She explains:

> *This kind of creative thinking is fostered by narrative, which encourages story listeners to consider several of the very different possible outcomes that might proceed from particular circumstances. Narrative develops sequential thinking and promotes the idea that someone can choose how to react to circumstances — and that different responses produce different outcomes that are worth thinking about beforehand — either as goals worth being pursued or as fates best avoided.* (2004, p.11).

I think that the Web portfolio qualifies for a good example of portraying wisdom through the use of narrative based on the description put forth by Dr. Spaulding. The Web portfolio is a vehicle that is interactive and nonlinear in design, but can be developed to be intuitive in guiding the user down a sequential path towards information that yields reaction. In the case of the Web portfolio, the reaction can be a successful work for hire connection, showing that the Web portfolio is a medium that connects people through narrative. The development of the Web portfolio will therefore build imaginative thinking, demonstrating the power of skill building and learning that comes with the Web portfolio process.

A Web Portfolio Makes You Digital in a Wired World

Ann Leer's *Masters of the Wired World* (1999) is a blockbuster compilation chronicling the global information society as exalted by today's most compelling information science gurus. In his chapter, Being Digital in the Wired World, MIT Media Lab Director, Nicholas Negroponte wrote that:

> *Being digital has three physiological effects on the shape of our world. It decentralizes, flattens, and makes things bigger and smaller at the same time. Because bits have no size, shape, or*

*color, we tend not to consider them in any morphical sense.
However, just as lifts have changed the shape of buildings, and
cars have changed the shape of cities, bits will change the shape
of organizations-be they companies, nations, or social structures.* (Leer, 1999, p. 386)

As medium, tool, and skill that "makes you digital", Web portfolios exemplify
Professor Negroponte's statement on the three physiological effects being
digital has on our world. Web portfolios and their integration into the appearance and voice of the new millennium knowledge worker are decentralizing the
structure of organizations that have had traditional roots based on prescribed,
time honored standards, untarnished by the evil pitfalls and obstacles of
technology and new media. One such institution is the K-12 education system.
This system now institutes a teacher portfolio requirement. That portfolio
requirement was previously built on using traditional media to create a two
dimensional portfolio book. Now, the movement in education is to document
learning and illustrate vocational expertise by having teachers create Web
portfolios, rather than print portfolios that are used for assessment, reflection,
and validation. Teachers now have to become digital. How will they do it? Web
portfolios are the answer. For the teacher, the Web portfolio will as Negroponte
says decentralize, flatten, and make things bigger and smaller at the same time.
One of the things he is referring to is reach and proximity for effective
communication. This is seen in the ability of teachers to communicate with
potential schools anywhere in the world and show off their talents, a viable
reach to a big community. At the same time, locally, the Web portfolio will be
used a barometer for the value of some ones abilities as a teacher who has
progressed with professional development and is actively pursuing lifelong
learning. As well, on the local or small scale, the Web portfolio is also a student
portfolio that will provide a communication platform for others, eventually;
students will spawn their own Web portfolio and begin to continue progression
into a mature knowledge worker in the global information society. It may be true
that a visually strong, content rich Web portfolio may help increase perceived
knowledge worker value, thus building the competitive edge of someone in the
information society. The overall appearance presented by the Web portfolio
may persuade a user and viewer over someone with more experience and a less
than attractive or grounded Web portfolio. This may become an important
factor in computer mediated human communication processes invoked by Web
portfolios. Just as nonverbal communication factors such as appearance play

a part in roles and behaviors portrayed by people in societal scenarios — symbolic interaction, human computer interaction with regard to Web portfolios may be seen as an important factor in the communication interaction between the user and the Web portfolio author. This connection occurs through the content, structure, and usability of the Web portfolio.

The Web portfolios out in the global information society will find a new frontier of communities to gather in and then disperse. Communities will be physical and digital, but will have common connection and common platform through the use of the Web portfolio. Yahoo Groups are an example of a community based portfolio system. People join groups that share common interests, fetishes, ideas, or things. Each member of the group creates an identity and then shares limited content which is posted to a template design within a controlled environment that creates a mini-narrative about each member's feelings on the group's masthead topic. Web portfolios at grand scale will have similar induction into major Internet group depositories, except for the limited content and template design. The loss of appearance is very evident in Yahoo Groups and other similar environments. The creativity factor is low due to the limits and therefore the group environment is starving for content. Chatting and photo exchange may be the most popular activities, but the real reflections and persuasive style that is shown in the unfiltered Web portfolio cannot be matched be online communities, they can only coexist, as the digital communities do with the physical communities. Again, Nicolas Negroponte (1999) describes the transformation this way: "It is hard to imagine that our highly structured and centralist world will morph into a planet full of loosely connected physical and digital communities, but it will" (Leer, 1999, p. 390).

One of the most important evolutions of on line groups that will emerge will be the central use Web portfolios to communicate, appear, and persuade other group members and people outside of the small group that makes up a niche Web portfolio community. The communities will not discriminate. Everyone in the knowledge worker realm will have a Web portfolio. Eventually anyone who works will have a Web portfolio. Mechanics, doctors, lawyers, retail salespeople, and CEOs will all have Web portfolios in the future. And they will all congregate in communities that will loosely fit together to make a global information society. This statement is based upon Negroponte's ideas that "in the digital world, neighborhoods cease to be places, and become groups that evolve from shared interests" (Leer, 1999, p. 390). What this means is that this new form of localism found in the digital world will be shared and enhanced by the Web portfolio due to the abilities of the knowledge worker to get a portfolio up on the Web quickly and easily. Templates and Web portfolio space are available for free, but the persuasion factors that are negatively affected are too vital to allow the appearance of the author to tolerate it — maybe. Who wants pop up windows jumping out every few minutes on their Web portfolio — and have no control over it? This type of annoying feature found on free or very cheap commercial Web portfolio sites does not persuade the user that a connection should be made in a work for hire situation or any situation. The speed and efficiency that one can develop and publish a Web portfolio becomes a critical skill in the knowledge age. So as the knowledge worker evolves and his or her skills flourish, so will the Web portfolio and the communities that will evolve based on shared interests. In the future, groups of Web portfolios will be seen within varying contexts. But just the fact that you became digital by creating a Web portfolio to initiate work for hire or social identity communications, means that you become part of the group that looks at Web portfolios as highly important — the global information society. In which, you will establish an identity and maintain an appearance using a Web portfolio as you morph into digital existence and prominence in the wired world.

The Web Portfolio
as a Personal Knowledge Portal

The Web portfolio will serve as a personal, narrative knowledge portal for individuals. It is contextual and humanist, open to interpretation, and vigorously unyielding to a defined truth that is universally defended. This is not to say that scientific knowledge may not be part of the Web portfolio content. The Web portfolio will also serve as a personal portal of scientific knowledge in some cases. Scientific knowledge being defined by Lyotard as validated and proven, not open to interpretation.

The e-portfolio fits comfortably in the realm of new media and contributes to the concept of how the increase of quantifiable information creates a qualitative change in society and social arrangements — thus supporting the idea that an information society exists. As the mass media commercial, business card, promotional brochure, press kit, and identity all rolled into one, the Web portfolio becomes as a strong media-based informational space for visitors of all categories. This audience will cause content to be driven in a certain way, which will cause changes. Some of the changes that will be seen with the mass utilization of the Web portfolio are an increase in the knowledge worker to act as a freelancer or independent contractor. The knowledge worker will be competing with the old school worker left over from the industrial and post industrial era where status quo was enough to maintain employment. This new era of knowledge will be a time where knowledge workers gain opportunities through traditional networking, but maintain fruitful relationships and add new ones through the use of Web portfolios which serve as knowledge portals. Web portfolios will become more and more vital to the bottom line of everyone and therefore the content and design parameters will increase dramatically. Knowledge workers will provide valuable information (training, specifications, and samples) on their Web portfolios in order to have a value added experience for the user and to enhance their respective credibility to the work for hire and social publics.

To extend the notion of a value added Web portfolio, Alan Kay contributed to the 2002 edited book by Packer and Jordan titled *Multimedia, from Wagner to virtual reality*. Kay wrote an essay in 1989 titled "User Interface, A Personal View" and in the text he affirms McLuhan's notion that the computer is a medium and not simply a tool. The networked computer as a medium acts as a communication platform via e-mail, Web sites of all types, and of course, Web portfolios from people of all types. Kay goes on to synthesize the "computer as something to communicate with our selves, our tools, our colleagues and others, and our agents" (Packer & Jordan, 2002, p.130). Kay, when writing the piece in 1989, saw the computer as a communication medium that concentrated most frequently on communicating with our tools and ourselves. What I believe he means is that we spend time using computers for purposes that do not communicate to the public in a valuable way. Examples such as over chatting and downloading music come to mind. Kay contends that society, academic or others need to "extend everything we do as a grand collaboration — with one's self, ones tools, other humans, and, increasingly, with agents: computer processes that act as guide, coach, and amanuensis" (Packer & Jordan, 2002, p. 130). Kay reminds us that the translation of personal visions and knowledge as represented by tangible evidence of experiences in the Web portfolio will be useful only if the author pays attention to interface design. The key to having communication succeed is to eliminate and overcome barriers. The Web portfolio interface design needs to address those problems that might exist in communicating the messages delivered by the Web portfolio.

The Web Portfolio as a Responsive Environment

The postmodern technologies have shown us Web capabilities that go beyond simple search and retrieve. The Web has become a responsive environment which enables real time interaction. Filling out forms, sending immediate dynamically generated e-mails, and responding and posting to chat rooms all provide a responsive environment. The key to responsive environments is an interaction. The interaction must be provoked by communication.

The Wiki may become part of the Web portfolio as a responsive environment. Wiki.org defines the Wiki as:

> *a piece of server software that allows users to freely create and edit Web page content using any Web browser. Wiki supports hyperlinks and has simple text syntax for creating new pages and crosslinks between internal pages on the fly.* (http://wiki.org/wiki.cgi?WhatIsWiki, 2002)

Wiki is unusual among group communication mechanisms in that it allows the organization of contributions to be edited in addition to the content itself. There may be Wiki sections in the Web portfolios of the future. Like many simple concepts, "open editing" has some profound and subtle effects on Wiki usage. The ability for a Web portfolio to allowing everyday users to create and edit any page in a Web site is exciting in that it encourages democratic use of the Web and promotes content composition by non technical users (wiki.org, 2002). This may contribute to Web portfolios becoming places where collaboration occurs. Various collaborations will happen on home site, a possible expression for your Web portfolio or mine.

The possibilities are endless when it comes to creative expression and collaboration and Web technology as a whole. Web portfolios may also use computer mediated technologies to provide real time communications. Such environments include the Macromedia Breeze platform and the Webex collaborative Web solution.

Chat rooms and bulletin boards have been used for electronic communication since networked computing began. These responsive environments will be embedded into the Web portfolios of the future, as well as they will dedicate content sessions to discussing their Web portfolios and how the Web portfolio is affecting their lives and success in finding work for hire.

Blogs are personal Web sites that provide updated headlines and news articles of other sites that are of interest to the user, and also may include journal entries, commentaries and recommendations compiled by the user. Blogs act as personal diaries and can be considered a type of Web portfolio. They are also ads that engage curiosity about the author and the products they might be pitching. Keeping with the humanist, qualitative experience that the Web portfolio can deliver and combining it with the positivist reliability of seeing and understanding someone abilities and qualifications, the Web portfolio ultimately exists to communicate with the user to accomplish the goal of contact, and reciprocal communication that may lead to favorable outcomes, which translates into work for hire or sales of some kind. The Web portfolio will provide a responsive environment for the user to place an order for a relationship.

Conclusions

To conclude, I feel that it is important to discuss several items that were presented in this text. The first is an understanding that the Web portfolio has a place in the information society. That place is somewhere between the continuum of both constructs that surround the ideas that there is an information society, or that information follows a path of continuity with historical change. What this means is that the Web portfolio will be defined by certain groups who share the same goals and have a need to communicate. Having a portfolio in the future will help you get "in" and promote yourself for opportunities in the knowledge worker age, the conceptual age, and as Dr. Covey revels, the age of wisdom.

The Web portfolio will also emerge as personal mass media advertising. The Web portfolio will become a technological norm that will provide an outlet for culture and personal environment. Because the Web portfolio is a media it will shape perceptions. In fact, its goal will be to persuade a user to engage in communication and hopefully will cause a reaction that will be favorable and will result and work for hire. This process will be critical to the endeavors of the knowledge worker. The knowledge worker will have to add value to the Web portfolio by making it a value added proposition. This will be done by creating an online environment which benefits the user as well as sells the author. This environment will be an on going advertisement for the skills and abilities of the creator/subject. It will also constitute a postmodern appearance in the electronic media. The Web portfolio will serve as a new aesthetic for artists and technologists, but also for everyone who commits to success in the knowledge worker age.

The Web portfolio will make people digital in a wired world. As the world decentralizes and flattens, the playing field between people and opportunities will level due to the Web portfolio. The wired world will be full of skilled people who need to exist there simply to exist in their vocations. One such example is teachers.

The Web portfolio will serve as an individuals "personal knowledge portal" for everyone to explore. The value added portal will not only offer information but provide instruction to educate the user, thus exemplifying the expertise needed in the knowledge age to be truly "project effective". The Web portfolio will serve as a gateway of grand collaboration that will extend intelligent activities learned by the Web portfolio creator or the users who experience the Web portfolio.

Finally, the Web portfolio can evolve into a responsive environment that will serve creative curiosity with new media tools and technologies that make the user part of the Web portfolio. Maybe through open code Wikis, chatting, or blogs, the communication platforms available to Web portfolio creators and viewers will become integrated. Keeping up will be an everyday challenge of the knowledge worker as he or she attempts to survive and thrive in the knowledge age, the conceptual age, the information society, and the age of wisdom.

References

Abbot, P. H. (2002). *The Cambridge introduction to narrative*. UK: Cambridge University Press.

Arpajian, S. (1996). *How to use HTML 3*. Emeryville, CA: Ziff-Davis Press.

BambooWeb Dictionary: Open Content Encyclopedia. (2005). Retrieved February 4, 2005, from http://www.bambooweb.com/articles/A/c/Active_Server_Pages.html

Benedetti, P., & DeHart, N. (Eds.). (1997). *On McLuhan: Forward through the rearview mirror*. Ontario: Prentice-Hall Canada.

Bhangal, S. (2000). *Foundation ActionScript*. Birmingham, UK: Friends of ED.

Birmbaun, B., & Papoutis, K. (2004). Using electronic portfolios to assess children with special needs. *Center on Disabilities Technology and Persons With Disabilities Conference 2004*. Retrieved March 23, 2005, from http://www.csun.edu/cod/conf/2004/proceedings/12.htm.

Bloom, B. S. (Ed.). (1956). *Taxonomy of educational objectives: The classification of educational goals: Handbook I, cognitive domain*. New York: Longmans, Green. Retrieved May 31, 2005, from http://www.coun.uvic.ca/learn/program/hndouts/bloom

Braun, J. A., Jr. (1999). *Electronic teaching portfolio.* Retrieved May 28, 2005, from http://www.coe.ilstu.edu/jabraun/braun/professional.html

Campbell, D., Cignetti, P., Melenyzer, B., Nettles, D., & Wyman, R. (2001). *How to develop a professional portfolio: A manual for teachers.* Needham Heights, MA: Allyn and Bacon.

Carliner, S. (2005). E-Portfolios: The tool that can increase your marketability and refine your skill development efforts. *Training and Development,* 70-72.

Castro, E. (1998). *HTML: For the World Wide Web, Visual Quickstart Guide.* Berkeley, CA: Peachpit Press.

Castro, E. (1999). *Perl and CGI for the World Wide Web, Visual Quickstart Guide.* Berkeley, CA: Peachpit Press.

Chun, R. (2002). *Macromedia Flash Advanced for Windows and Macintosh, Visual Quickpro Guide.* Berkeley, CA: Peachpit Press.

Cold Fusion Markup Language. (2005). Retrieved May 11, 2005, from http:www.houseoffusion.com/cfdocs1/cf3/gettingstarted/gs030003.htm

Cole, D. J., & Ryan, C. W. (1998, February). *Documentation of teacher education field experiences of professional year interns via electronic portfolios.* Paper presented at the 78th annual meeting of Association of Teacher Education. Dallas, TX.

The Concise Tech Encyclopedia. (2005). Retrieved February 3, 2005, from http://www.tech-encyclopedia.com/term/application_server_provider_(asp)

Coupland, K. (2002). *Search: The graphics Web guide, interface, typography, illustration, photography, animation, film and video.* New York: Universe.

Covey, S. R. (2004). *The eighth habit.* New York: Free Press.

Curtis, H. (2000). *Flash Web design: The art of motion graphics.* Indianapolis, IN: New Riders.

Desamero, J., & Whitehead, P. (2001). *PHP, Your visual blueprint for creating open source, server-side content.* New York: Hungry Minds.

DiBiase, D. (2003). Retrieved April 22, 2005, from http://portfolio.psu.edu/about/e-PortfolioRationale.pdf(p1)

DiMarco, J. (2004). *Computer graphics and multimedia: Applications, problems, and solutions.* Hershey, PA: Idea Group Publishing.

DiMarco, J. (2005). *Electronic teaching portfolio*. Retrieved May 30, 2005, from http://www.portfolio.cc/index.htm

Fiore, Q., & McLuhan, M. (1967). *The medium is the message*. New York: Touchstone.

Fisher, K. (1997). *Kathleen Fisher's web Portfolio*. Retrieved May 28, 2005, from http://durak.org/K.F./portfolio/index.html

Greenberg, G. (2004). The digital convergence: Extending the portfolio mode [Electronic version]. *EDUCAUSE Review, 39*(4), 28-37.

Hatch, T., Liyoshi, T., Pointer, D., & Wolk, E. (2002). *Pio Pico student researchers participatory action research: From classroom to community, transforming teaching and learning*. Retrieved May 28, 2005, from http://gallery.carnegiefoundation.org/

Horton, S. (2000). *Web teaching guide: A practical approach to creating course Web sites*. New Haven, CT: Yale University Press.

Horton, S., & Lynch, P. (1999). *Web style guide: Basic design principles for creating Web sites*. New Haven, CT: Yale University.

Johnston, J. (1998). *Information multiplicity: American fiction in the age of media saturation*. Baltimore: The Johns Hopkins University Press.

Jordan, K., & Packer, R. (2001). *Multimedia, from Wagner to virtual reality*. New York: W.W. Norton & Company.

Kilbane, C., & Milman, N. (2003). *The digital teaching portfolio handbook: A how-to-guide for educators*. Boston: Ally and Bacon.

Kimball, M. (2003). *The Web portfolio guide, Creating electronic portfolios for the Web*. New York: Longman.

Kristof, R., & Satran, A. (1995). *Interactivity by design: Creating and communicating with new media*. Mountain View, CA: Adobe Press, 31.

Leer, A. C. (1999). *Masters of the wired world*. Wiltshire, UK: Redwood Books.

Lovejoy, M. (1992). *Post modern currents, art and artists in the age of electronic media*. New Jersey: Prentice Hall.

Lyotard, J. (1999). *The postmodern condition: A report of knowledge*. Minneapolis, MN: University of Minnesota Press.

Macromedia Inc. (2000). *Macromedia Flash MX: Action Script Reference Guide*. San Francisco: Macromedia.

Mandia, K. (2005). *Kelly Mandia's teaching portfolio.* Retrieved May, 29, 2005, from http://www.mandia.com/kelly/

Martinez, J., & Parnell, R. (2003). *ASP.NET, Development with Macromedia Dreamweaver MX: Visual Quickpro Guide.* Berkeley, CA: Peachpit Press.

McGloughlin, S. (2001). *Multimedia, concepts and practice.* Upper Saddle River, NJ: Prentice Hall.

McGraw-Hill. (2003). *Instructor's guide to FolioLive.* New York: McGraw-Hill.

McLuhan, M. (1964). *Understanding media: The extensions of man.* New York: McGraw-Hill.

Minaz, F., & Goldsby, D. (2001). Now that your students have created Web-based digital portfolios, how do you evaluate them? *Journal of Technology and Teacher Education, 9*(4), 607-616. Retrieved March 24, 2005, from http://www.aace.org/dl/files/JTATE/JTATE94607.pdf

Moonen, J., Tulner, H. (2003). *E-learning and electronic portfolio: Some new insights.* Universiteit van Twente, The Netherlands. Retrieved April 4, 2005, from http://www.connict.nl/pdf/moonentulner-portfolio.pdf

Negrino, T., & Smith, D. (2004). *Java Script: For the World Wide Web* (5th ed.). Berkeley, CA: Peachpit Press.

Penn State e-Portfolios. (2005). Retrieved April 22, 2005, from http://portfolio.psu.edu/about/index.html

Pride, W., & Ferrell, O. (1987). *Marketing, basic concepts and decisions.* Boston: Houghton Mifflin Company.

Sanders, M. (2000). Web-based portfolios for technology education: A personal case study. *The Journal of Technology, 11. Studies.* Retrieved February 27, 2005, from http://scholar.lib.vt.edu/ejournals/JOTS/Winter-Spring-2000/pdf/sanders.pdf

Sauer, G. (1998). *Using Web-based portfolios to assist technical; Communication program development.* Retrieved January 15, 2005, from http://www.cptsc.org/conferences/conference2000/Sauer.html

Siegel, D. (1997). *Secrets of successful Web sites: Project management on the World Wide Web.* Indianapolis, IN: New Riders.

Silverman, S. (2005). *Susan Silverman at kids-learn.org.* Retrieved May 28, 2005, from http://kids-learn.org/susansilverman/

Spalter, A. (1999). *The computer in the visual arts*. Reading, MA: Addison-Wesley.

Spaulding, A. (2004). *The wisdom of storytelling in an information age, A collection of talks*. Maryland: The Scarecrow Press.

Stewart, M. (2002). *Launching the imagination: A comprehensive guide to basic design*. New York: McGraw-Hill Higher Education.

Tabbi, J., & Wutz, M. (Eds.). (1997). *Reading matters: Narratives in the new media ecology*. Ithaca, NY: Cornell University Press.

Towers, J. (1999). *Dreamweaver 2 For Windows and Macintosh, Visual Quickstart Guide*. Berkeley, CA: Peachpit Press.

Tufte, E. (1990). *Envisioning information*. Chesire, CT: Graphics Press.

Tufte, E. (1997). *Visual explanations: Images and quantities, evidence and narrative*. Chesire, CT: Graphics Press.

Tufte, E. (2002). *The visual display of quantitative information*. Chesire, CT: Graphics Press.

Webster, F. (2002). *Theories of the information society* (2nd ed.). London: Routledge.

Wikipedia, The Free Encyclopedia. (2005). Retrieved February 4, 2005, from http://en.wikipedia.org/wiki/ASP.NET

Williams, R. (1994). *The non-designer's design book*. Berkeley, CA: Peachpit Press.

Web References

http://www.qfolio.com/sales/product_overview.shtml

http://www.wofford.edu/studentPortfolio/default.asp

http://www.csun.edu/cod/conf/2004/proceedings/12.htm

http://www.uwec.edu/AcadAff/policies/assessment/FAQ-students.htm

http://arch.ced.berkeley.edu/people/students/portfolio/syllabus.htm

http://arch.ced.berkeley.edu/people/students/portfolio/syllabus.htm

http://www.cptsc.org/conferences/conference2000/Sauer.html

http://www.azkenwebdesign.com/portfolios.htm

http://www.resumeresults.net/services/web-folios.phtml

http://www.blueskyportfolios.com

http://lrs.ed.uiuc.edu/students/mcreech/projectproposal.html

http://connecting.vccs.edu/feature-3.htm http://www.resumes4results.com/webportfolios.htm

http://srv5.fountainheadcollege.com/studentweb/

http://www.rileyguide.com/resprep.html(resumes)

http://www.cptsc.org/conferences/conference2000/Sauer.html

http://www.is.wayne.edu/fls/teachptf.htm

http://www.freelake.mec.edu/FLMS/seventhgradewebs/seventhgradepages.htm

http://portfolios.music.ufl.edu/requirements.html

http://directory.google.com/Top/Business/Employment/Resumes_and_Portfolios/

http://64.233.161.104/search?q=cache:wFYXAQZzWXUJ:darkwing.uoregon.edu/~arch/aia/aia01_cheng_webport.pdf+web+portfolios&hl=en

http://www.corporatewarriors.com/01-therealm/about.cfm

http://www.mcli.dist.maricopa.edu/dd/eportfolio02/examples.php

http://www.castleton.edu/pt3/resources.htm

http://www.portfoliovillage.com

About the Authors

John DiMarco has been helping people and organizations succeed with communication, technology, digital design, media, and marketing for more than 10 years. Professor DiMarco holds adjunct faculty positions at St. John's University, New York Institute of Technology, and Nassau Community College. He held the position of assistant professor of Long Island University, where he taught courses in digital art, multimedia, and communication design. He has trained hundreds of people in Web portfolio development on graduate, undergraduate, and professional development levels. He is the founder of www.portfoliovillage.com. John DiMarco has extensive academic and corporate experience and has worked with organizations including Canon, USA, Inc., SUNY Farmingdale, Long Island University, MTA, Garden City Public School District, Plainview-Old Bethpage School District, Flexographic Technical Association, and Teaneck Creek Conservancy. His first book, *Computer Graphics and Multimedia: Applications, Problems, and Solutions*, was published in 2004 by Idea Group Inc. (www.idea-group.com). He is pursuing a PhD from Long Island University, C.W. Post in information studies. His research focuses on information products for communication, technical communication, and information design. He holds an MA in communication design from Long Island University, a BA in communication from the University of Buffalo, and an AAS in business administration from SUNY Farmingdale. He can be reached at jdimarco@liu.edu.

* * * * *

Kimberly DiMarco is a special educator teaching kindergarten and first grade students. She has worked with students of all ages and disabilities. She specializes in early childhood and has extensive experience in creating and implementing authentic assessments. She currently teaches on Long Island, New York. She holds a Bachelor's of Science in special education and elementary education and is New York State certified in elementary education. She is completing a master's degree in literacy from the University of Albany.

David Power is a curriculum development specialist and instructional designer for Canon, USA, Inc. He has worked in the graphic arts and office technology fields for more than 10 years. He holds a BA in finance from St. John's University in New York City.

Index

V

visual design 63

W

Web authoring 122
Web color 94
Web page design 105
Web page size 96
Web portfolio 64, 193
Web resumes 102
Web text 110
Web type 81
Weight 77
WYSIWYG (what you see is what
      you get) software 123

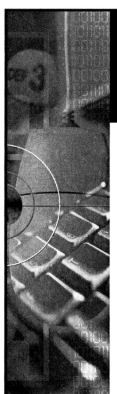

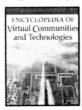